Locked In
Daring to Break Free

A Memoir

Katrin Den Elzen

Leschenault
PRESS
Great Stories from Great Writers

Image credits:
Cover Design by Brittany Wilson | Brittwilsonart.com - from original imagery provided by the author.
Front cover artwork: Maria Hiske
Photo of Mark Den Elzen: Grant Hobson
Author photo: Pille Repnau

To Mark,
Rahel and Joschka

Praise for Locked In – Daring to Break Free

Locked In – Daring to Break Free is unflinching, courageous, and compassionate. It is searing, heartbreaking, and also informative.

The language is well carved and keeps a fine pace, the sentences are well honed. It shows readers not only what it means to grieve openly but also how to grieve. And it will provide inspiration and guidance for all who face not only the vicissitudes of grief but must navigate the dehumanizing medical systems that give hope and then steal it away. Throughout the memoir, Katrin Den Elzen demonstrates the chronological dislocations of trauma; she also portrays the tender connection between her husband and her – evidence of the continuing bonds that mourners hold onto.

To be able to signify mourning and pain is a human feat; to write about it is an even greater feat, too.

Judith Harris, (PhD). Poet, Author of three books of poetry, including *The Bad Secret*, which was nominated for the Pulitzer Prize, and the highly acclaimed book *Signifying Pain: Constructing and Healing the Self Through Writing.*

How does one imagine the unimaginable: the loss of one's beloved young husband to a stroke that could have been prevented by competent medical treatment? In this harrowing story, Katrin Den Elzen succeeds in conveying her husband's locked-in syndrome and her own sense of being imprisoned by anguish and despair. Readers will be deeply moved and inspired by her experience of love, loss, recovery, and resilience. Perhaps most important, readers will discover how writing enables her to escape from her own locked-in existence.

Insights abound in this masterful memoir that chronicles her journey from being a student of grief to an expert on wellbeing.

Jeffrey Berman, Distinguished Teaching Professor, Department of English, Author of 22 books, including his grief memoir *Dying to Teach: A Memoir of Love, Loss, and Learning* and *Writing Widowhood: The Landscapes of Bereavement.*

Locked In – Daring to Break Free is a spellbinding memoir and an exquisitely expressed portrait of life, love, and traumatic bereavement. The story takes the reader through the natural stages of young love, marriage and family life, to the extreme hardship of sudden acute illness, and eventually to the choice that only the bereaved can make: will I allow myself to be happy again? Can I move forward without guilt and bitterness? I was moved to tears many times as I read this book and recommend it to anyone who has the secret hope that hardship – while ripping away our certainty – can also open our hearts if we are willing to be deeply honest with ourselves. What made this story unique and stand out from other widow memoirs is the author's incredible ability to reflect on her journey while staying close to her feelings. It also begins with the meeting and love story, instead of her spouse's death as many memoirs do. Katrin Den Elzen weaves perfectly paced vignettes of the love story to an unflinching account of her husband's illness. In this way, it represents the full context of the meaning and impact of the loss of a beloved spouse. This book is also a testament to the power of writing for wellbeing – it is superbly written and despite the grief, Katrin succeeds in sparking the reader to feel hope and move towards wellbeing.

Dr. Reinekke Lengelle, award-winning author of *Writing the Self in Bereavement: a story of love, spousal loss, and resilience*.

About the Author

Katrin Den Elzen holds a PhD and a Master's in Creative Writing. She is a grief counsellor, researcher and Writing for wellbeing facilitator, and is widely published in academic journals on grief, loss, and post-traumatic growth. She was special editor for the British Journal of Counselling and Guidance for the two special issues on *Living with Loss*. Katrin has published the book *Writing for Wellbeing: theory, research and practice* (2023) and teaches graduate counselling students in Writing for Wellbeing. She lives in Perth, Western Australia, her chosen, sunny home.

Foreword

Curiously, perhaps, I should preface my comments about Katrin Den Elzen's astonishing grief memoir, *Locked In – Daring to Break Free*, not with a remark about *her* personal disclosures, but rather with one of my own. In the course of my career, I have been requested to draft countless brief endorsements of books written by colleagues known and unknown, nearly all of them worthy and a handful positively inspired or inspirational. But if only because of the sheer number of such requests, I must confess that only in a few instances did I read every word of the book sent me; balancing the blurbs with the rest of my very full life commonly required me to skip and skim text, and concentrate on representative content that particularly called to me. This was typically enough to convey the style and substance of the work, and to position me to offer my recommendation honestly to potential readers. And of course, I am realistic enough to realize that a similarly selective scanning of my own books characterizes the great majority of the endorsements of them offered by others!

But with Den Elzen's book, this simply was not possible for me. From the opening vignette to the resonant reflections with which the book concluded, I was hooked, drawn into a deeply authentic account that time travelled between a magnetically captivating and evolving love story and a surreal and inexorable tale of tragedy, trauma and ultimately life transition. In limbic language that at times verged on the poetic without ever risking affectation, the author drew me into moments of almost indescribable beauty and horror in hospital rooms, hospice facilities, courtrooms, cafes and her own incandescently lit living room following the heartrending diagnosis of her husband's brain tumor and resulting hydrocephalus, which resulted in months of unrelieved physical anguish for him, and years of psychological torment for her. Ironically, the neurologically "locked-in" condition of her husband, unable to utter a single syllable, finds eloquent expression in Den Elzen's riveting account of his journey and her own through a world made alien by his injury and ultimate death. Grounding in the lucid details of settings, people and the crisply spoken dialogue between them, the author portrays her innermost emotions, intentions and ultimately discoveries, while situating them in the drably impersonal setting of a High Dependency Unit, the imposing context of a judicial proceeding, and the awe and majesty of a remote strip of coastline at which two oceans merge and meld. With equally acute attention to her inner landscape and that around her, Den Elzen takes us on a tour of liminal spaces, most of which the reader hopes never to occupy, as she also lays bare the incredible fragility of the human condition and the equally impressive quest for meaning and connection in the face of unutterable loss.

Having worked as therapist alongside countless clients struggling with shattering losses of their own, I am hard pressed to think of one who would not have benefitted from reading this memoir slowly, savoring its emotional truths as I did, and being instructed by the author's transparency and determination to reclaim life in abundance despite, or perhaps because of the enormity of her loss. Throughout, Den Elzen speaks with candor and artistry to the heart of our mortal existence, to our capacity for resilience, and to the hard but necessary choices that gradually return a sense of wholeness and growth to a world hollowed and shrunken by traumatic bereavement. It is a book for every heart that has been broken open by grief, and for every friend or professional who commits to stand and eventually walk beside a mourner toward a future that is deeply informed, but not dominated, by the past.

Robert A. Neimeyer, PhD
Director of the Portland Institute for Loss and Transition,
Professor Emeritus of the Department of Psychology, University of Memphis. Author of 35 books, including *Living Beyond Loss: Questions and Answers about Grief and Bereavement*, and over 600 journal articles and book chapters.

Author's Note

In writing this book, I drew upon my personal journals, my husband's medical notes, court transcripts and researched facts and called upon my own memory, in particular emotional memory, of these events. I have changed the names of medical staff and some individuals to protect their privacy. The GP and the lawyers involved in the medical negligence trial have been given pseudonyms.

A memoir forces me to stop and remember carefully. It is an exercise in truth. In a memoir, I look at myself, my life, and the people I love the most in the mirror of the blank screen. In a memoir, feelings are more important than facts, and to write honestly, I have to confront my demons.

Isabel Allende

1

Cairo, February 1984.

It is a sunny, wintry Friday morning. I am waiting for my train to arrive. A trace of cardamom lingers in the air. A singsong, disembodied voice bellowing a seemingly never-ending prayer through loudspeakers grates on my ears. Two women dressed in full-length, dark blue traditional robes with long veils walk past me. The heavy, textured material sways with each step. The eyes of a large throng of soldiers stare at me across the tracks like a crocodile surveying its prey. I pull down the long sleeves of my black T-shirt to my palms, wrapping my fingers around the material. Acutely aware that I'm on my own, and only nineteen, I clutch my train ticket, checking the carriage number again, making sure that I'm standing in the right spot. I pull my arms across my chest, hugging my torso. My gaze wanders up and down the platform and lingers on several small groups of backpackers further down, about a hundred metres away. I'm startled when a young Egyptian man wearing a crisp business shirt speaks to me.

"Excuse me, can I help you, Miss?" Noticing my look of surprise, he continues, "You seem a bit lost and I work for the railways."

My hand points towards the backpackers. "Yes, you can help me. See those European travellers over there? I'd really like to be seated on the same carriage as they are."

He nods. The train pulls into the station, screeching. We race along the platform. All the foreigners get on at the same carriage. I get on too. Inside, only one young man is on his own; the others are all seated in pairs. Animated voices infuse the compartment with excitement. I point to the empty seat, asking the young guy if it is free. He nods and breaks into a smile that lights up his face.

"Hello. How're you?" he asks, his head tilted lightly to the side.

I sit down and lean back into the seat to catch my breath, and, after a moment, respond with a hello.

"I'm Mark. What's your name?" His smile, wide and open, has settled in. A woollen, moss green sleeveless top shows off his muscular arms.

As we pull out of the station, the carriage is lit by brilliant sunshine.

"I'm Katrin," I reply. "Where're you from?"

"I'm from Australia, from Melbourne."

"Oh, I've never met anyone from Australia before." A sudden surge of heat sets my face on fire.

"And you?" He leans slightly towards me. "You're from Germany?" Transfixed by his jungle green eyes, I nod.

A few stations later a man carrying a chicken in a cage appears next to me, holding onto a ticket. I fumble through my bag, extricate my ticket and gesture that I have a numbered seat elsewhere that he could have. Without changing his impassive expression, he turns to leave.

"Phew!" I slump into the seat.

Mark stands up, and, with a cheeky smile, points his two index fingers first at me and then towards his seat. As I slide across to the window seat I brush past his chest. My heartbeat quickens. He breaks off a piece of his stale bread and offers it to me.

"So where've you just come from?" I enquire. I lean towards him to take the bread.

"For the past three months I've been on a kibbutz. My job was to carry bunches of bananas. Pretty hard work, but then I had a lot of fun. It was great actually, meeting so many people."

I smile and try to get a closer look at him. He is athletic, bronzed and radiant. His blonde curls are sun-bleached. I snuggle into my seat.

"Have you travelled much?" I ask.

"Well, I went to India for a month before Israel, but this is my first trip overseas," he replies.

My eyes widen in surprise. "Really, you've never been overseas before, never left Australia until now?"

"Yep, that's about right."

"And how long are you planning to travel this time?"

"About a year. After Egypt I'm off to Europe. I've got relatives in Holland … I look forward to meeting them, actually." He puts his bread in a crumpled paper bag.

"What sort of relatives?" I'm curious.

"Aunties, uncles and cousins," he explains. "Both my parents were born in Holland. Though they met in Melbourne."

For twelve hours we sit and talk – or rather, Mark chats and I soak up his stories: swimming in Wilsons Promontory, a comedy club called *The Last Laugh* in Melbourne. I have no inkling that his chattiness is unusual, that he does not normally talk this much. Engrossed, I stay awake.

Eventually the train pulls into Luxor. Both of us get up. Luxor is near the Valley of the Kings, a major tourist site. I'd thought that all the backpackers would get off here, but surprisingly Mark and I are the only travellers leaving. Here we are, walking through the village looking for accommodation. As darkness sets in, we come across a budget hotel that appears quite clean. A local man, wearing a dark blue suit, approaches us in the lobby. He speaks impeccable English.

"You two will follow each other around the world," he remarks.

Mark and I exchange a bemused look.

"We're not a couple, you know," Mark says. "We actually just met."

Undaunted, the man replies, "I'm telling you. You two will criss-cross the globe for each other, settle down and get married."

After a while, we find out that this man is a senior pilot for Egypt Air. The strange prophesies he has made clash with his distinguished appearance.

∼

Perth, Australia, February 2004.

"Your husband is on the brink of dying."

All the noise and sounds of the Emergency Department evaporate.

"The only thing that might save his life is emergency surgery at Sir Charles Gairdner Hospital," the doctor continues, clutching her clipboard. "Fremantle Hospital doesn't have a neurology department."

Four days later, the team of neurosurgeons turned and hurried out of the Intensive Care meeting room. The walls started to spin. *Mark, as you know him, is gone* echoed through my head. Ricocheting around, bouncing off the sides. Impossible to settle. Impossible even to slow down.

I was close to fainting. My legs buckled and gave out. Jonnine grabbed me and the two of us stumbled through the milky sliding doors of the ICU. Ina, one of my oldest and closest friends, rushed over to me and sat me down. The room continued to seesaw. I was barely keeping a grasp on reality. I no longer seemed to inhabit my body. Numbness blurred my vision. Ina got hold of a paper bag, held it around my face and told me to breathe into it.

She decided to take me to the Emergency Department, as the ICU staff was not allowed to supply medication to me. A male orderly turned up with a wheelchair and placed it alongside my chair. I felt two pairs of arms on either side of me raise me up like a rag doll.

As I was wheeled into the ED, we headed straight for the spot where Mark had been lying just four days earlier.

"No, no," I cried out. I raised my hands in front of my face. The image of Mark lying on a stretcher surrounded shoulder to shoulder by white coated medical staff haunted me.

Despite my palms covering my eyes, absorbing the neon lights into blackness, sharp memories in high definition from the previous Friday invaded my mind. Mark had kissed me goodbye as he left home for work. By mid-morning he rang me up. His barely audible voice whispered to pick him up, said that he felt too dizzy and nauseous to drive. After looking up the address he had given me in the street directory, I phoned Jonnine, who lived around the corner, and together we raced there with the children perched on the back seat, silent. Once I got him to the Emergency Department, Jonnine took the kids home.

Mark deteriorated at lightning speed, thrashing his body about in agony. I stared at him, shocked by the ear-splitting beeping the monitors spat into the room. Finally, the medical staff whisked him off for a CAT scan of his brain. It was then that the young doctor, her forehead creased, told me Mark was close to dying.

An ambulance raced Mark, with me in the front clinging to the handrail on the dashboard, to the other hospital, half-way across the city. And he ended up in the same area of the ED that I was in now. Frozen in time for an excruciating eternity, he had remained there before finally being taken to the theatre.

"Please get me away from here," I begged Ina.

It required all of her persuasive skills to get the orderly to wheel me around the corner, where I faced a different part of the ED. A nurse helped me into a bed. All I remember is her white short-sleeved top and a round silver stop watch dangling from a chain from the breast pocket that sported a small bright red stripe. She diagnosed shock. A doctor prescribed tablets.

Slowly, it came back to me what had happened. I had been in a meeting with Dr. Nemeth, Head of the Neurology department, in the ICU. As I had walked into the small, oppressive room he stood there, flanked by several male doctors, and came straight to the point. He saw no need for a greeting or introductions. His eyes looked straight past me, as though he was addressing the wall behind me.

Ina moved her chair close to my bed. I squeezed her hand. As I raised myself up on the pillow, she slid her arm around my shoulders, her head close to mine.

"Ina," I whispered, "the doctor said that Mark's got total brain damage." I paused, remembering Dr. Nemeth's impassive face, his rigid body. "He said that there's no hope of recovery. That Mark, as I know him, is gone."

Ina's head dropped onto my head. She squeezed my shoulder.

"He told me that Mark has a very rare brain tumour."

Ina lifted her head, still holding onto my shoulder.

"He said that the removal of the tumour isn't possible right now because of the swelling of Mark's brain," I whispered. "Then he talked about some other surgery that I didn't understand."

"And?" Ina asked, her voice barely audible.

"He said that the third option is aggressive treatment, and that's what he's recommending." My nails dug into Ina's hand. "I asked him what that is … and he replied it means no treatment at all … That's when everything went black."

Footsteps approached, rubber soles squealing on the linoleum floor. Dr. Steven Mayer, one of the registrars from neurology who'd been at the meeting, appeared next to my bed, his lips pursed.

"Are you all right, Katrin?"

"Oh, Dr. Mayer, it's you. No, I'm not. I can't withhold treatment from Mark. It's cruel, and it's too much responsibility."

"It's not a question of you assuming responsibility, but of us doctors suggesting what is in Mark's best interest and of you consenting to our advice."

"What if this isn't the right decision? Will I be living the rest of my life wondering whether I did the right thing? If something could've been done to help Mark?" I covered my face with my hands and then looked up at the doctor. "This is all so fast."

"Katrin, you will never be asked to live with that kind of responsibility; that would be inhumane. It's our responsibility. We would never suggest anything that wasn't in the patient's best interest."

What? This morning the doctors had stressed the importance of waiting for the intense swelling of the brain to go down before making a diagnosis. And now all of a sudden that's supposed to be irrelevant? No. Joschka and Rahel are too young to grow up without their dad. They're only eight and eleven.

I was sure of one thing though – I was the one who needed to sign the consent form and that it was therefore my responsibility to be certain that it would be the best course of action for Mark.

Jonnine came up to my bed. "The rest of the family needs to know what Dr. Nemeth said." I could make out her swollen, red eyes.

Just then I remembered that Mark's family, his mother and two sisters, as well as Mark's father and his wife, had flown in from Melbourne. All were staying at our place. Mark's parents had barely spoken to each other since their divorce twenty-five years earlier.

"They need to be told tonight," Ina agreed.

"I can't do it." I shook my head. "I can't even go home and see them."

"I'll do it," Jonnine volunteered.

~

The scraping of the curtain on the metal rail pierced into my consciousness. Jonnine went off to look for the nurse. Ina closed the curtain around my bed, the curtain rings clonking against one another. Was it light green or light blue? It swayed onto my bed every time someone walked past. The world was miniscule inside this cubicle.

"Ina, I need to tell my parents. Do you think you could call them at home in Germany?"

"Yes, of course."

"I'd really like them to book a flight to Australia as soon as possible."

Where will I sleep? I wondered. I can't handle going home with all of Mark's family there. I wish though I could curl up in my bed. I can't go to Jonnine's house either as both Rahel and Joschka are staying there. I don't want them to see me like this.

Sometime later Ina returned to my cubicle. My parents had said that they would come to Australia as soon as possible. Ina decided to stay with me during the night. We worked out a plan to sleep at my friends' place one street away from our home. Rahel and Joschka … My mind kept wandering to them.

We drove in silence through the night. Ina pulled her car into Pete's concrete driveway and jerked it to a halt in the dark carport. Pete hastened outside. He and Ina supported my arms and pulled me out of the car. I stumbled along the grey square pavers to the front door. A single bright floodlight blinded me. We turned sharply to the right through a pair of old sliding doors. The textured glass was cold against my hand. Two single mattresses covered the living room floor between the wall and the sofa. I was gently lowered to the ground. A beam of white light shone across the windowsill and onto the dark material of the sofa. Unfamiliar shadows moved across the wall. My gaze wandered to a scarlet vase on a single bookshelf high on the wall.

I heard Ina's short breaths. We were lying very close to one another, our shoulders and arms almost touching. The coughing of the aging air conditioner interrupted the silence. It blasted welcome cold air into the humid room. I placed two sleeping tablets in my mouth, their sugar coating smooth against my tongue. As I descended into a tablet-induced darkness, my mind drifted back to Egypt.

On the second last evening in Luxor we were walking back to our hotel along a dusty road.

I'm cradling a green scarab that I had bought just before in an overcrowded market stall at the side of the road among a cacophony of shrill voices and the sharp scent of cardamom and cumin. The sculpture sits flat and cool in my palm. Mark turns to me, his silhouette bathed in the orange hues of the setting sun. I look up at him and see the outline of the ancient temple against the glowing sky. The pale moon is beginning to show.

"Katreen, I was wondering, do you have any plans after Luxor?"

The exotic pronunciation of my name bathes me in its soft ring.

"Mmh, I want to see Mt. Sinai," I reply.

He hesitates, as if thinking something over. "Would you like to travel with me?"

I nod.

2

I woke up a few hours later, with the unfamiliar three-seater couch to my left and the wall shelf bathed in darkness. The old air conditioner rattled. The memories of the previous day forced themselves into my consciousness. I opened my eyes wider.

Within seconds my mind was alert and sharp. I knew what had to be done. Rahel and Joschka had not seen their dad yet. They had to visit him before they received the news that he had extensive brain damage. I wanted them to see him through their own eyes, not through the view coloured by the neurosurgeon's news. One look at me would have alerted them to the fact that something was seriously wrong. The best person to take them in would be Jonnine, as both kids were staying with her already.

My mind was working with the precision of a Swiss clock. As the first daylight eased through the window, I made out the dark green and blue chequered pattern of my bedding. Agitated magpies squawked through the window. I turned my head towards Ina. Only a few wisps of her fine blond hair poked out above the white sheet draped around her shoulders. The air conditioner blasted straight onto her neck.

I rang Jonnine around eight that morning. She agreed with my plan on the spot. Once Rahel and Joschka had visited their dad, they would be informed about the results of the MRI scan. I called the hospital to set up a meeting with the social worker and Melanie, the doctor from the ICU, so that we would talk to the kids about Mark's medical condition together.

As Ina and I pulled into the hospital grounds, we drove past Jonnine and the children on the footpath. The whites of my knuckles showed as I gripped the car seat. Rahel was walking along with the usual spring in her step like a gazelle. Her green and white checked school uniform glowed against the dirty cream-coloured hospital. The shiny white collar made her look even younger than her eleven years. Joschka was wearing his favourite red school T-shirt with the pale black motif of his faction on the front; his tanned arms swung with each step. Though Rahel was the shortest girl in her class, she towered over Joschka.

Ina and I went up to the ICU in the rattling elevator, our eyes downcast. Paint flakes had been chipped off the push button. Inside the ICU I peeked through the window into Mark's room. Rahel was at the end of her dad's bed, talking to him. Her head was tilted forward, her body relaxed. She gestured with her hands, underlining her words. Joschka sat next to Jonnine, unmoving. His hands were in his lap cupped in a tight fist. All the colour was drained from his ashen face, his lower lip pulled tight. His back was rigid and did not touch the upholstery of the chair. He glanced at the floor.

Rahel continued to chat to her dad, refusing to be fazed by the tubes and breathing apparatus. After one last glance at Joschka I pried myself away. I asked the receptionist when the doctor and the social worker would be available. Not for a while. I ached to hold Joschka and turned around to join the children. This was the first time that I visited Mark since Dr. Nemeth had announced that he had suffered complete brain damage. The doctor's frigid blue eyes flashed through my mind. I shivered.

As I walked into Mark's room, my hands trembled. I pushed open the door and felt an immediate sense of peace surrounding Mark. As if he were able to say, here I am, in the room with my children.

"Mama!" Rahel and Joschka exclaimed simultaneously.

My daughter threw herself into my arms. Whilst holding onto her with my left arm, I bent down on one knee and held Joschka tight with my other arm. Jonnine, drained and tired, returned home. Our eyes locked for a moment.

It was time for the meeting. We sat down in a narrow corner of the sombre ICU waiting room. I perched on the edge of the chair while Melanie, the doctor, addressed Rahel and Joschka.

"What do you think happened to your daddy?"

Rahel talked about how the brain fluid had been building up and that, in order to release the pressure, the doctors had to put a drain into Dad's head on the day he was rushed to hospital and that he had not woken up since then.

Melanie nodded. "Daddy may never be able to work again."

Joschka was stunned, his eyes wide open. He had not imagined that possibility. Melanie explained that the doctors had found a cyst in their dad's brain, and that this had caused the brain fluid to build up. She avoided using the term brain damage.

"Do you have any questions?" she inquired.

Rahel had questions about the cyst; Joschka said nothing. Melanie explained that the cyst was still blocking the brain fluid, and that this was why Dad still needed the drain to release it from inside his head.

"Daddy may never come home," Melanie said as the kids got up from their chairs.

They both froze, their movements suspended. Joschka slumped back down onto the edge of his seat. Rahel opened her mouth, but no words came out. She turned to face me. My composure was hanging by a thread. I needed to get out of that room, ached to be alone with the kids.

I stood up. My legs gave way but I was able to regain my balance. I took a step forward and slipped my hands into Rahel and Joschka's. We turned around, left the waiting room and headed for the relatives' room that had been made available to me the previous day so that I could be by myself.

The doctor had handled the situation well. She had also prepared for the meeting by researching whether or not Mark's cyst might be hereditary. It was not. She told Rahel and Joschka that the brain cyst wasn't cancer and that there was no chance that they would inherit it from their dad. Her voice quivered as she relayed this information.

In the relatives' room the children distracted themselves by playing with the two hospital beds. They tilted, raised and lowered the beds. Then they began to fight. I had not anticipated that the children might not understand what was happening straight away. Instead, I had expected an immediate response from them.

After a couple of hours in the room, Joschka walked over to me.

"Mama, what does it mean that Dad may never come home? Where will he be?" Then, after a brief pause, "Will he die, Mama?"

I gasped for air. Little streams of salty tears ran down my cheeks. My body began to shake. I could hardly see Joschka's scrunched-up face. I placed my hands onto his shoulders.

"Maybe, Joschka. I'm not sure."

Rahel walked over to us and started to shake Joschka's arm. I stroked his arm and ran my fingers through his hair. He climbed onto the bed and lay down, his knees pulled up into his chest. I offered to hold him, but he shook his head. Then the questions began.

"Will you be a single mother?"

"Will you have to go out to work?"

"I promise you that I won't work full-time. I'll always be there after school to pick you up."

"The pain is too big to fit into my head, Mama. I'd like to go and see Adrian now," Joschka said as he sat up.

I stroked his hair. "Yes, of course, mein Schatz. You can go and visit your friend."

Ina came in. She had invited Rahel to come over to her place, as Ina's daughter and Rahel were friends. Rahel left with Ina. She hadn't asked me anything. I was aware that she wasn't grasping the ramifications yet. I knew it would happen sooner or later.

"I want to say goodbye to Dad." Joschka put his hand into mine.

I looked down at him, touched by the steadfastness of his voice. Swallowing down the lump in my throat, I nodded. We made our way to Mark.

~

My parents arrived on the midnight flight. It was now six days since Mark fell into the coma. Jonnine had offered to drive me to the airport to pick them up. Rahel was eager to come. The three of us waited inside the international airport. My hands clutched the cold metal handrail in the arrivals lounge. Rahel swayed back and forth next to me, holding onto the rail, the tips and heels of her light green suede shoes alternately touching and lifting off the floor.

"Nana!" Rahel exclaimed, and swung herself under the rail to race towards her grandparents. They manoeuvred the trolley past the exit area. My mum hugged me tight, her head nestled into my chest, her tears moistening my T-shirt.

"I've been so worried about you." My dad embraced me for what seemed like minutes. His whole body quivered. We steadied each other under the bright neon lights. The last time I had seen my father cry was nineteen years beforehand, on the day I migrated to Australia.

At the hospital the next morning, the situation worsened. Dr. Nemeth had used the term "aggressive treatment". Now the details emerged of what this entailed. It meant no surgery, no drain. Nothing. What transpired during the course of the morning evoked such terror in me that I could not believe they were even suggesting this.

Through asking a multitude of questions I learned that, without treatment, the external drain in Mark's brain that had been inserted on the first day would become infected and then slowly block up. I was told that an external drain only has a life-span of a maximum of two weeks at best. Then surgery would be needed to keep him alive – the insertion of a shunt. I had never heard of it.

"A shunt is a device that is surgically inserted into the brain and then tubing goes all the way down along the neck to the abdominal cavity to release the brain fluid there and to divert it into the abdomen," Dr. Mayer explained to me.

"And the shunt just stays there?"

"Yes, it does. This is the most common treatment for patients with hydrocephalus. Some people live with shunts for many, many years, a decade or more."

"So at some point it will have to be replaced?" I clarified.

"Yes, if it stops working."

Once the external drain stopped functioning, I came to understand, the pressure in the brain would rise again, bit by bit. As it did when it caused Mark's strokes and resultant brain damage in the first place. The hydrocephalus, the medical term for the increasing and relentless pressure within his head, had been the reason for the worsening and severe headaches that he'd had for about ten days before he fell into the coma. The alternative to insertion of a shunt would be to turn off his life support. But if I gave permission for the breathing apparatus to be turned off, there was the possibility that Mark's death might take some time. Days even. If he started to breathe without the respirator, which was possible, even likely, according to the doctor, it was certain that he would not slip away immediately.

I ran into the toilet and bent over the sink. I retched and retched. When I caught a glimpse of myself in the mirror, I did not recognise the woman with the sunken eyes and ashen colour.

I could not knowingly let Mark's brain pressure build up, could not let him die over several days. How could they ask me to do that?

In the afternoon, I approached the ICU doctor and asked him about Mark's brain damage. The tall, skinny doctor directed me into a quiet corner. He had a sombre expression, which made the dark rings under his eyes appear even starker. I wanted to know how the doctors could be so sure that Mark's brain activity had stopped when I had been told in a previous meeting that a full diagnosis was not possible until the swelling of his brain had receded. I could feel Mark's presence when I was in the room with him. It was palpable.

"Katrin," he explained, addressing the issue of proceeding with treatment, "if you choose to have the shunt inserted, Mark will continue to live, albeit in a vegetative state. This means that if you decide later, after he had the shunt inserted, that you don't want him to live like that, you cannot go back in time to help him to die."

"Are you really sure that Mark is brain dead?"

The doctor's face scrunched up. He looked at my throat. "There is no hope of recovery. Though he could live for years with the shunt in place."

"Where would Mark be looked after?"

"You would need to find a place for him in an aged care facility."

"What do you mean?"

The doctor put a clenched fist in front of his mouth and cleared his throat.

"A nursing home. He would not be able to stay long-term in hospital once his treatment has stopped."

"How can you be so sure that there is no hope of recovery so soon?"

"The results from the MRI scan are definitive. They show the extent of Mark's brain damage."

Over the next few days, several doctors conjured up images of Mark slowly vegetating his life away, without change in his condition, his awareness.

I wanted to spare him the fate of withering away in a nursing home. I needed him to help me. Mark, where are you? What am I going to do? All I had to go by were my feelings which told me that Mark was still there inside his body.

I thought about how, a couple of days ago, he had opened his eyes, had looked at me and his mother. His eyes had not been glazed over or vacant. On the contrary, he had focused on us for a moment. Another time he had been startled by the sudden, screeching sound of a plastic bag being crunched up. He had actually jumped a bit in his bed. His presence was palpable.

I was profoundly confused. The doctors said there was no hope of recovery, but my perceptions told me that Mark's consciousness was still there. At the same time, I was indoctrinated to believe the specialists, who exuded an air of educated knowledge, underscored by their diagnostic test results. But I felt what I felt. My voice was silenced and I did not assert my perceptions in the face of specialist medical expertise, fervently expressed.

The nights stretched into eternity. Darkness behind me and darkness ahead of me. Sleep eluded me. What was I going to do? Over the next few days, I kept asking different medical staff about Mark, ICU doctors and specialists, always receiving the same answer – there was no hope of recovery.

~

I heard Rahel's footsteps on the wooden steps, coming upstairs, and I walked towards her. She was dressed ready for school. As she looked at me, something must have clicked inside. She frowned.

"Will Daddy never come home?"

We had our customary long good-morning hug. Then we went downstairs into her room so that we could talk undisturbed.

"Where will he live?" she wanted to know.

I sat on her bright red student chair and glimpsed the pain that flashed across her face. In that moment I witnessed her realisation that it was possible that her dad might die. Her face went white. Her body started to shake from her sobs.

"But I'm only eleven. I've only had my Daddy for eleven years, and Joschka's only had Dad for eight years."

I went over to her, kneeled down and wrapped my arms around her, holding her in a tight embrace. "I'm so sorry, sweetness." The moment the words tumbled out of my mouth I realised that *sweetness* was Mark's term of endearment for Rahel. I'd never called her that before.

She looked straight into my eyes. "Mama, you won't have a husband any more. You'll be a single mum."

The room began to spin. I hadn't thought about that yet, *not having a husband any more*. This is not supposed to happen. I'm only thirty-nine and my own dad is still alive.

"If only I could hug Daddy again," Rahel said, "but he has so many tubes and cables."

"We'll make it happen, Mäuschen, I promise you."

The following day, one week into Mark's coma, the two of us went to the hospital in the afternoon. A new nurse was on duty that day. I asked her if my daughter could hug her dad. The nurse turned around and, bending her petite body down slightly, looked straight at Rahel.

"Would you like to lie next to your dad in bed?" she asked in a husky voice.

Rahel's eyes lit up. "Yes!"

There was only one window in the room; it was in the internal wall that led to the main room of the ICU. The grey metal blind clonked as the nurse pulled it closed. Then she pumped the metal lever at the bottom of the bed with short, swift bursts to lower the bed. She grabbed a visitor's chair and placed it flush against Mark's bed next to his left shoulder. With a soft slow movement she lifted Mark's tubes with her left hand, straightening his arm and, raising it a few centimetres, she put it on a pillow on the chair. Once she had used another rectangular pillow to cover Mark's shoulder and arm, as well as his main intravenous line, the crook of his shoulder was neatly cushioned. Rahel and I observed her from the corner of the room, holding hands.

"Come on, you can lie down now," she said.

Rahel smiled, sat down on the edge of the bed and took off her sandals. Then she eased herself onto the bed.

"My head won't hurt Dad?"

"No, your dad is all right."

Rahel turned to the right and snuggled into her dad's body, her head resting on his cushioned shoulder. She gently placed her left hand onto his chest, avoiding his tubes. Though the room was windowless, her eyes glowed as if reflecting sunlight. Her cheeks had a light pink tinge as she started to talk to him.

Although Rahel had to get up a few times when Mark started to cough, she stayed there with him for a whole hour. At one point a male doctor, carrying a bunch of beige manila folders under his arm, opened the door. As his eyes focused on Rahel, he frowned and his mouth dropped open. He spun around on his heels and vacated the room.

It was getting late, but Rahel said that she could not tear herself away. Before she moved, she gave her dad a "pinky-promise" that she would never forget this moment – when Rahel had her little finger wrapped around his, she said he pulled his little finger and pinky-promised back. I saw the movement in Mark's finger too.

3

On Thursday afternoon, six days into Mark's coma, Dr. Nemeth, the neurosurgeon who advocated withholding all treatment, had made an appointment with me for Monday morning. It was made clear that the purpose of the meeting was for me to give consent to the withdrawal of treatment.

The weekend was one long nauseous blur. I kept thinking about Mark and the decision. My body responded with dry-retching and diarrhoea. I agonised with Mark's family over the issue. His parents and sisters wanted to heed the advice of the neurosurgeon to let him go.

On Saturday evening, I was alone in the room with Mark. At this time of day, it was getting quieter in the Intensive Care Unit. The pace was slowing down. Doctors had stopped coming in to check on Mark. I switched on the dim warm light on the wall behind his bed and walked over to the door to turn off the bright neon lights. Returning, I sat on the edge of his bed, bending down close to his face. My warm breath on his cheeks was in stark contrast to the freezing temperature in the room.

"Mark, you need to do what's best for you," I implored him. I wiped my tears with the back of my hands, not wanting to get up for a tissue. My little finger was covered in black eyeliner.

Then, all of a sudden, Mark moved his body. I stumbled over one of the wheels of the bed as I scrambled out of the room to get a doctor. Excitement and hope swelled up in my veins. The young ICU doctor who came took one look at Mark.

"These aren't movements, they're only reflexes." As if oblivious to the blow his words dealt me, his voice was toneless.

I gazed at my husband. Everything about him was familiar to me. His handsome face, high cheekbones, thin mouth, muscular arms, and freckled back. What would happen to Mark if the respirator was to be turned off? I could not "fit this thought into my head", as Joschka had put it.

~

Monday morning. I had tossed and turned in bed. The stillness of the night weighed down on me. My throat felt tight with the scream that never escaped.

I had to get up. I had to drive to hospital. I had to make my decision.

My father accompanied me to the hospital. The closer I got to the entrance, the wobblier my legs became. I could barely set one foot in front of the other.

We were asked into the meeting room of the ICU, my dad and I, Mark's mother, his sisters and his dad with his wife. We sat down along the sides of a grey laminated rectangular table. Dr. Nemeth strode into the room, to the head of the table. He stood next to the chair, his face blank, as though he was wearing a dried-up face mask that had not been peeled off.

"Things have changed over the weekend," he announced immediately. "Mark has begun to move over the weekend, so we want to operate now."

It took a moment for the information to sink in. It felt as if I had just lived through an earthquake; the ground had split open under my feet and swallowed me up. And now, the earth was willing to spit me back out.

"What does that mean, that he has moved?" my dad inquired.

"It means that everything is possible now, from Mark being able to walk on one end of the scale to the possibility of him dying on the other extreme." The specialist remained standing.

Silence ensued.

With tears running down his cheeks, my dad whispered, "We have to help Mark. We have to help him."

And with that, Dr. Nemeth's slim, wiry figure disappeared.

I did not know then that Dr. Nemeth's conduct was the first instance in a long string of injustices and betrayals, of professional transgressions, that were to occur in the space of just one year. That they would stretch beyond the medical institution into the financial and legal realms. And that each one would register its seismic tremors with forceful magnitude on my internal Richter scale.

A cocktail of emotions flooded my body. I was still suffering from the horror of the decision I had been asked to make, a decision that was non-existent now. This was entangled with relief and hope.

I rushed the few metres from the meeting room to see Mark for the first time that day. I had not had the heart to see him before the meeting. As I stood in the door to his room, catching my breath, I could hardly believe the picture that presented itself to me. My gaze fixed on Mark's body. Both his arms and legs were in motion – his arms moved in and out in swift jerks, his left leg dangled off the side of the bed and the right leg moved from left to right like a pendulum. Goosebumps ran down my arms, sensitising the fine hairs on my skin.

My father walked up to me. He placed both his hands on my shoulders, his body shaking. I felt his warm breath on my cheek as he too glanced at his son-in-law's limbs moving across the white sheet. I placed my hand on my dad's hand, squeezed it, and entered the room.

"Mark!" I leant over him, too scared to touch his body for fear of interrupting the flowing movements. I heard the thumping of swift footsteps coming closer. His family was also crossing the Intensive Care area towards us. Oblivious to the "only two people at a time" intensive care rule, all seven of us lined up around the bed, hypnotised by the change in his condition. His mother Rikie and I locked eyes.

In the afternoon, Dr. Mayer knocked on the door.

"Katrin, could I speak to you please?" He pointed to paperwork in his hand. "I need you to sign the consent form for Mark's surgery." He motioned with his head to step into the hallway.

"I need to let you know all of the possible risks."

I nodded.

"As you know, hydrocephalus is treated with a shunt to allow the brain fluid to bypass the obstruction." He gripped the folder with both hands. "Unfortunately, Mark's cyst is in such an awkward position in the third ventricle that we will need to insert two shunts, not just one. One on each side of the brain."

He paused to let this sink in. My brain did not react to this information.

"Every brain surgery bears some risks. With a shunt operation, the possible risk of infection is about one percent. There's also a minimal risk of meningitis and bleeding."

I swallowed. My brain tried to compute – one percent doesn't sound too bad. I'd expected the risk factor to be higher.

Dr. Mayer held a biro out to me and pointed to the signature line. I signed my name in large, free-flowing letters. This was to be the only time when it felt good to give permission for surgery. The ramifications of needing two shunts instead of one did not register in the face of my relief.

When I returned to the room Mark had been repositioned in bed by the orderlies. His hands were now loosely tied to prevent him from pulling at the respirator.

~

Looking back on that time, I don't know why I never confronted Dr. Nemeth over his repeated assertions that there was no hope for recovery. Why had he pushed me to make a decision only a week into Mark's coma? This is not so much an existential why, as a logical why. His own registrar, Dr. Mayer, had been the first to inform me of the results of the MRI, of the visible brain-damage on the scan. But the young specialist had stressed that a definitive diagnosis could not be made for about a fortnight until the swelling of Mark's brain from the hydrocephalus had lessened. Until the MRI results came in, nearly a week after Mark's arrival in the ED, nobody had known the cause of his hydrocephalus. The doctors had different theories. The same day that Dr. Mayer said we needed to wait for the swelling to go down, his boss, Dr. Nemeth, had told me that Mark had total brain damage and urged me to withhold treatment in the same breath.

It was not in my nature to remain silent. But the senseless horror of having to make the decision to withhold treatment had rendered me mute. I could not find the words to give shape to what had happened. The sense that Mark had been violated, his right to live infringed upon, had overwhelmed me. A murky, dark rage had built up. It was too explosive to be conveyed to the Head of Neurology in a civil conversation, in any conversation. In the days following the meeting my focus had been on Mark, on the upcoming surgery. Performed by Dr. Nemeth himself. And so the conversation never happened.

~

The next day Mark moved even more. He tried to pull off the breathing mask, shaking his head in short, uneven movements. The nurse explained to me that after a while the respirator dries out the mouth and starts to hurt. Mark had to be sedated to stop his agitation.

Salma, a young ICU doctor with olive skin and expressive, almost black eyes, informed me that, apart from the shunts, Mark also needed another operation: a tracheotomy, so that the respirator could be removed. She explained that an incision would be made in the front of the neck in order to create an alternative airway. A tube would be inserted into this hole, allowing Mark to breathe through it instead of his nose or mouth. I sighed and looked at his agitated face. It would be good to have the painful respirator removed. My eyes moved down and rested on the soft tanned skin of the hollow just above the collar bones.

The medical jargon and uncertainty fogged up my brain. Sleep-deprived, I operated on adrenaline. Perhaps it was a blessing that I did not know what lay ahead.

The surgery to insert the shunts took place thirteen days after Mark fell into the coma. The doctors suggested we should not come to the hospital until the surgery was over. When we received the call that Mark was out of recovery, I drove his mother and myself to hospital. The pungent smell of disinfectant hit me as we walked through the main entrance. We did not know what to expect, had no idea what Mark would look like after the surgery. Entering his room, I noticed that his head was partially shaven, that his soft golden curls were gone. To our surprise, he moved his arms and stirred his legs. I pulled the grey visitors' chairs right up to his bed and held his hand between mine. I took a deep breath. My muscles relaxed, releasing some of the tension.

This was the first time that I saw Mark without the respirator covering his mouth, cheeks and nose. Now I could look at his familiar face. My fingers traced his eyebrows and ran down his cheeks. I circled the top of his cheek bones, thinking how I loved their distinct roundness, the unique mixture of cheekiness and kindness they conveyed. I looked up and noticed that the external drain was gone. In its place was a wound held together by silver staples; the metal stood out against freshly shaven pink skin.

~

Nine days after flying home from Egypt, my phone rings in the evening.

"Isch bin in München." A cheerful voice echoes through the receiver, followed by expectant silence.

"Mark, is that you?" My heart thuds against my chest. I can feel the heat rising in my cheeks. "You're in Munich? Would you like to visit me?" The words tumble out of my mouth.

The next evening, Mark is dropped off at my doorstep by a colourful VW Kombi van. Two young guys who had picked him up hitchhiking diverted off the Autobahn to deliver him to my front door. Mark scrambles out of the side door, embraces me tightly and kisses me.

"What happened?" I eventually ask.

"Well." Mark blushes slightly. "After you left, I started to miss you." He looks down at his hands. Pauses. "I've never felt like this before, you know. I told you when we met that I've never been in love, that I thought it was all a bit of drivel, so I didn't know what was going on with me." As he looks down at me, his gaze unusually serious, warm ripples surge through my stomach. "I just had to come and see you."

My parents are away on holiday. So we have the apartment to ourselves for a week and spend most of the time in bed. The night before my parents are due back, Mark sits down next to me on the couch in our living room, holding my hand in his.

"Katreen," he says, his voice thick, "I love you with all my heart."

I hold my breath. My skin tingles all over.

"Could you imagine living in Australia?" he continues, his hands clammy.

I run my fingers through his curls. Is this fairytale for real?

"I want to be with you too, Mark." Tears warm my eyes and roll down my cheeks. "I'd have to see Australia first though, to see if I like it. But hearing all of your stories, I'd imagine I'll probably fall in love with the place."

Mark lets out a deep breath. His body relaxes. He stops squeezing my hand, turns to me and strokes my face. His smile lights up his face.

4

The day after his operation, Mark was shifted from Intensive Care to the High Dependency Unit, where care was less intense, but patients were still under observation at all times. Despite moving immediately following the surgery, the following week, Mark did not move. Not at all. Nothing. I could not stop crying.

"He's recovering from yet another brain trauma," my father tried to reassure me. "Once the swelling of the brain has gone down things will improve."

Mark's family returned to Melbourne. Now only my parents stayed with us. About a week after the surgery Mark was moved into a single room.

Finally, there was some good news. The young nurse who looked after Mark that day smiled at me. "Mark moved his leg a lot when I washed him this morning." The cheerful rhythm of her Irish accent made the news sound even happier.

The 19th of February, twenty days into the coma, marked an important event, something that nurtured real hope. As I arrived in Mark's room, the physiotherapist stood next to him, her hand on his shoulder. He was sitting in a wheelchair, his head propped up by a rectangular foam cushion.

"Mark did what we call a purposeful move." Her voice rose in excitement. "He deliberately moved toward the source of pain and grabbed the needle while he was given an injection. This isn't just a random move."

Later that day a neurosurgeon I hadn't met came to see me.

"This deliberate move requires quite some brain coordination. Much more than we thought Mark would be able to do." His almond-shaped eyes focused on me.

"So, this is a positive sign, right?"

"Yes," he replied, "but Mark still may never wake up."

Thinking back on that time, it infuriates me that the doctors painted the worst-case scenario, delivered in blunt terms, when they talked to me. Another time shortly after this incident I received more bleak news. The physiotherapist had assessed that Mark would be able to swallow on his own, which meant that the tracheotomy could be removed at some point. This was good news, as it visibly upset Mark. I had seen him coughing, gagging and struggling to breathe. But first he had to be weaned off the trache, a difficult process that could take some time.

A registrar came to talk to me about it. Perspiration marks had stained his mustard-coloured, long-sleeved shirt.

"Katrin. You need to know. The tracheotomy may never come out."

Bloody hell. Why this incredible negativity?

The following afternoon I was in the hospital when the physiotherapist worked with Mark, who was propped up in a wheelchair. I was relieved to see her. Therapists were always busy, and it was often unpredictable when they would come and therefore difficult for me to make sure that I was present.

"When Mark wakes up he'll progress well. He has very good muscle tone," the therapist said.

When, not if, he wakes up.

"I feel that Mark will definitely be capable of swallowing and handling his saliva and secretions. He's just not quite there yet."

"Does that mean the tracheotomy will come out?" My hands held onto each other in a tight fist.

"Yes. It'll happen. It's only a matter of time."

Later on, a nurse walked into the room. "We're starting to decuff Mark's tracheotomy now. We believe that he's ready. He's swallowing well. You can stay in the room."

This, a day after the doctor warned me that the tracheotomy may never come off. The process to get Mark to learn to breathe without it went so well that it was removed.

The bleak predictions left me demoralised and made the already heart-breaking situation so much more difficult to handle. Especially because they'd already made a major mistake, misdiagnosing Mark as being in a vegetative state. But then, mistakes are apparently not that uncommon. I remember the newspaper clippings that hung on the wall of Ward 52, the neurology ward, framed for posterity. The articles reported cases of brain tumours that had not been diagnosed by the medical establishment despite strong symptoms ranging from severe headaches to blackouts, but the patients were eventually saved through surgery in Sir Charles Gairdner hospital. This was obviously why they were so proudly displayed at the entrance right next to the nurses' station, heralded as success stories. How can this be perceived as a success story, I kept thinking every time I walked past the glory wall. The worst article still sticks in my mind. A fifty-year-old patient had visited her male GP repeatedly over a period of twelve months because of blackouts. She asked for a CAT scan but was told that she had symptoms of menopause and to go home and rest. Finally, she'd admitted herself to the Emergency Department. A fist-sized brain tumour was found and successfully removed.

I am in awe of the professional skill of the neurosurgeons, the incredible tasks they perform in surgery. The lives they save. Unfortunately, this is often in stark contrast to the poor interpersonal skills they offer patients and their relatives. It is this gap that made decision-making in hospital extremely challenging for me and that became an emotional roller-coaster.

~

The following day, I saw Mark practising his fine motor skills with his forefinger and thumb. They actually touched. Ina and I had come to visit Mark together. The physiotherapist faced him as we walked in.

"Mark. Lift your right hand." Her voice was steady, but had a slight tremble of insistence.

About twenty seconds later he responded and did indeed lift his right hand. My eyes widened, awash with anticipation. The nurse turned to look at us.

"This is a delayed reaction and therefore inconclusive."

Nevertheless, I felt excited. He did it. He actually raised his right hand. He can hear. He understands!

Mark tried so hard to work with the therapist. I could tell from his demeanour, the tension in his body, how much effort he was putting into this, how much energy it required.

"Lift your right hand, Mark."

About twenty seconds later he moved his right hand. Another delayed reaction.

"Lift your left foot."

Mark's left foot responded straight away. A slight but distinct movement. This time there was no doubt.

"Mark has definitely moved on command. This is significant."

As I looked at Mark propped up in the wheelchair, his stiff body bent to one side, the neck twisted, I was at a loss as to what a coma actually meant. In the movies, patients are always portrayed as waking up all of a sudden, from lying motionless in bed, to having their eyes wide open and focused. This was far removed from reality. Mark, who was hanging in the wheelchair, had just moved his limbs when prompted. And yet, he was still classified as comatose.

~

In the afternoon, Mark was allowed to be wheeled into the courtyard for the first time. Rikie was there too. She had flown over from Melbourne again to visit her son. We were excited to take him outdoors. I hoped the wind brushing over his face and the sun kissing his arms would arouse his senses for a moment. We stopped the wheelchair in the middle of the square courtyard, pulled up two chairs and sat on either side of him, leaning forward towards his face. And then we chatted to him about the kids. I began to tell the story of how we'd met in Egypt, sitting next to each other on the train. Mark's eyes filled with tears until they slowly rolled down his cheeks, leaving a glistening path. I stopped in mid-sentence. Rikie and I stared at each other.

Although Mark's sadness was unbearable, it was clear that he understood what we said. Proof that he was intelligently present. And cognisant of being paralysed and locked into his body.

At home, especially in the quiet hours of the night, images kept flashing across my mind of Mark lying awake in the dark, with no means at his disposal to contact the outside world, and nothing to spark his hungry mind. He had spent almost all of his free time reading. Mark had always been more inclined to be a solitary thinker than to debate topics. He liked to go to bed late, around midnight, unless he had to get up early, and to sit outside in the garden, the paper splashed over the circular glass table, under a canopy of greenery, with a VB beer can, a remnant of growing up in Melbourne, with his navy-blue packet of Drum tobacco perched on the table. This space, his space, allowed him to satisfy his urge to read and to philosophise.

~

On the day after our courtyard outing, it was distressing to see Mark. He did not show any reaction. And yet a friend of ours went to see him in the evening and read a Roald Dahl story to him.

"He smiled about the story, he really did smile," she told me on the phone later on.

It was impossible to tell from one day to the next how Mark would be. Every morning at dawn, with the first rays of daylight seeping through a gap in the curtains, the same questions spun around my mind.

What will it be like today? Will he be awake? Will he respond?

Staff raised the issue of where Mark would go from the hospital. Perth only had one public rehabilitation centre, in Shenton Park. A doctor from that clinic visited the hospital on a weekly basis to assess a patient's suitability for rehabilitation.

Tuesday morning, I woke to clammy hands. The rehab doctor was scheduled to see Mark at 10 a.m. The nervous tension in my stomach refused the fruit I tried to eat. The stakes were high. Unbearably high. The only alternative to this public rehab facility was moving to a nursing home.

"It's too early to tell. I'll be back next Tuesday to see Mark." The slim figure of the rehab doctor, dressed in a pin-striped grey business skirt, was strangely at odds with the blue uniforms of the nurses.

Mark was in bed when I entered his room. Pearls of sweat collected on the creases furrowed into his forehead. He was making noises of discomfort.

"What's the matter with Mark? He looks distressed," I queried the nurse.

"Well, it could be a lot of things, such as muscles aching, because he hasn't exercised for so long, or pain. We'll do our best to make him comfortable."

Does this mean that he's coming out of his coma? I wondered. Why can't they give me any answers?

The early peaceful days when Mark looked angelic, when his body was relaxed, were gone. The contrast was hard to handle.

The emotional, physical and mental strain took its toll on me. Having spent many hours at the hospital, I barely managed to drive myself home, my eyelids heavy, my alertness wavering. Insomnia had become my bedfellow since Mark had been admitted to hospital. The never-ending hours of darkness morphed into a battle ground and wore down whatever resilience I was still able to muster. I did not take sleeping tablets. Perhaps it would have been wiser to relax my firm beliefs on taking medication – who's to know.

~

I went to Bonn University after high school, not really knowing what subject I was drawn to, but aware that I had a deep desire to study, to be immersed in meaningful learning, in different ways of thinking. I mistook my strong interest in social justice as an interest in politics and enrolled in the subject. Philosophy would have been a much better match for my desire to understand the meaning of life, including the existence of injustice. But it never came to mind at the time. Politics served as a gap filler. Because of my interest in languages, I also tried out German and then English Studies. When Mark visited me in Germany en route from Egypt, the semester had begun.

"Hey Mark." The words tumble out after I return home from university. "A fellow student just told me that there's a room for rent in the house she's living in." I'm still standing. "Apparently it's in an old manor."

Mark's eyes light up with distinct enthusiasm.

"Really? Sounds great. How old d'ya reckon this building is?"

"Well, I've no idea. If it's a manor in the old part of Bonn, then it'd have to be a few hundred years old."

"D'you wanna go and check it out?" Mark jumps up from the couch, dropping his usual laid-back demeanour.

The room turns out to be a shoe-box. The sloping ceiling makes the seven square metres shrink even more. But a cosy shoe-box, rich in history. Perfectly located in the heart of the old city. Much to Mark's delight, it is right around the corner from a castle.

We only need a place for about three months. Before I met Mark I'd already made plans to go on a holiday to Thailand and Malaysia with my friend Gesa from uni. The dates are set and the tickets bought.

We move in a week later, jubilant and carefree. A place of our own. On our first day, Mark lures me to Poppelsdorfer Schloss, the nearby golden yellow Baroque castle. I take a photo of him, both hands in his trouser pockets, beaming. That the castle now houses a department of the University of Bonn doesn't lessen the thrill of living within a stone's throw of a *real* castle.

5

Life was throwing up other challenges. Mark had been self-employed. He had worked mostly as a swimming-pool maintenance subcontractor for a large company that manufactured and sold swimming-pools to the public, but he also had some private clients, who had to be notified. I didn't know who they were and had to search for clues in his mobile phone and diary. When my dad helped me to clean the business van, he found a number of unmarked gate keys. I never did get to give them back.

It soon became clear that without Mark's consent, I was not in a position to deal with the administrative side of his business. What was I going to do with the van? After Mark had been driving the same old van for five years, we'd only just purchased a brand-new one a few months ago. There was the loan for the business, the van, and our mortgage.

I found myself in a precarious financial situation. There was no money coming in. We didn't have any money in the bank, as Mark's income only stretched far enough to cover our living expenses. We had been concerned about our lack of savings, so about six months before Mark fell ill, we had decided on making some extra money with an investment home that we would either rent or sell once finished. Ironically, the driving force behind this decision had been to build up a financial safety cushion in case Mark fell ill. The scenario that we had envisioned was the possibility of a broken leg as Mark climbed over people's roofs installing long rows of rubber solar heating for their swimming pools. Now the house was partly built, and I faced the additional task of having to oversee the building process on my own.

Mark did have some income protection insurance, but there was a waiting period of several weeks before we would become eligible for the payments. A lot of paperwork needed to be filled in. As the maximum rate of income protection is only a percentage of the income, the payments were not that much. More or less just enough to cover the mortgage, with no money left over for food and bills.

Three weeks before Mark fell ill, we had applied for a life and trauma insurance policy and signed and posted it at a time when Mark was a healthy man. The insurance company received the application while Mark was well. However, there is a period of about three weeks before they accept or reject an application, during which time they research the information provided on the application form. It was precisely during this period that Mark fell ill. We had taken out the policy with S., who is a relative of Mark's. As a close family member, S. was told straight away of Mark's illness. He immediately informed the insurance company of the changed circumstances and of Mark being in a coma. The insurance company subsequently rejected the application for Mark. In a macabre twist of bureaucracy, they accepted my application. This meant that Mark was the policyholder for *my* policy, whilst it had been denied to him.

The moderate trauma insurance would have taken a big financial load off my shoulders. Had we made the application just a little earlier, say a couple of weeks, I would have received the trauma payout, because even though there was a waiting period of two months for certain illnesses such as cancer, in Mark's case, this waiting period would not have applied because he did not have cancer. His cyst was "benign".

I could not have foreseen then what bizarre financial obstacles lay ahead of me, and the central role S. was to play in them.

~

As weeks turned into months and Mark's health did not improve, I had to make decisions in relation to the business. What was I going to do? Sell the business? And if so, how would I go about it? In the meantime, what would we live on?

The social worker at the hospital approached me to discuss how to deal with the administrative issues I faced. We sat down in a tiny, windowless room. Chipped metal chairs with old, stained upholstered seats that would have been beige in their heyday lined the two walls.

"Katrin, I know this must be really, really hard for you. But I'm going to tell you what you have to do in practical terms."

I bit my lower lip, nodding.

"You have to take out guardianship for your husband."

A groundswell of tears surged forward. "You mean I have to declare him incompetent?"

"Well, yes. This is the only way you can handle his affairs, sell the business, apply for the insurance payments and so on."

"I don't know if I can do that."

She leant closer in to me. "You need to apply to the guardianship board to be nominated as Mark's guardian. I have the application forms for you. I can help you with papers that you have to supply, such as doctors' reports."

My hands trembled as I took the paperwork. I left the room. Despite Mark being locked into his body, I never did look at him as being helpless. Does applying for guardianship equate to a loss of dignity, I wondered?

~

Mark had always sat down at every opportunity with a non-fiction book or the newspaper in his hand. He was reliant on that intellectual stimulation – where would he get it from now? He had a strong interest in philosophy, politics, history, the environment, nature and social issues. This passion led him to get a university degree in philosophy, politics and sociology. Mark's favourite TV programmes were historical documentaries, political reportages and foreign affairs such as *Four Corners* on the ABC. As well as Australian Rules football. Rarely, if ever, did he watch movies. This disinterest in movies was a source of disappointment to me. I like cuddling up on the sofa, watching a romantic comedy. I could have compromised and watched a drama. Mark, however, preferred to sit at the dining table, reading the newspaper. He savoured our companionship, being in the living room with me, sharing some remarks here and there. Mark encouraged me to go out and watch a movie with my girlfriends, but would not go out on a movie date night with me. On anniversaries and birthdays, it was me who initiated and planned a night out at a restaurant, and someone to look after the kids. Today I regret that we didn't get a babysitter for the kids and had regular evenings out together, just the two of us. I don't have many regrets, as I believe in accepting the choices I've made. But this is one of the rare occasions I do feel regret. In the throes of child rearing, I didn't know how important some couple time alone is.

~

Friendship played a crucial role at the time of Mark's illness. Ina's unwavering support, turning up at the hospital to be there with me at the drop of a hat, the offer to call her any time, day or night, gave me a much-needed anchor to hold onto.

In fact, in the years to come, her support would extend beyond dealing with the challenges of making the right decisions in hospital for Mark and comforting me, to backing me up at times of injustices and making herself available to discuss the legal implications that would arise after Mark's death. To be a shoulder to cry on. Not many people could handle seeing me extremely upset. Or perhaps that was just my own perception. Either way, I avoided sobbing in front of others. Crying, though, had become so much part of my life that tears softly rolled down my cheeks in front of others regularly. Ina was one person with whom I felt comfortable enough to allow all of my feelings to show, no matter how intense.

Because of the emotional involvement and caring that's the hallmark of friendship, at times of crises, situations can become tricky. One such issue was friends calling me to ask about Mark. Initially, they had held back from phoning me. A few weeks into Mark's illness, all of a sudden it seemed no one could wait any longer. The phone began to ring all the time, shattering my sanctuary, demanding an answer. Telling the story over and over drove me to the threshold of my endurance. I didn't know what to do. I was touched by their caring and their offers of support. But the constant repetition of detailing Mark's illness was grinding me down. I never did come up with a solution. I answered the phone when I could and didn't when I could not.

Friends asked to visit Mark. I was uncertain how he might react to them seeing him paralysed. He would have sensed the other's distress, which would have multiplied his own. If only I had a way of knowing who Mark would want to see, or rather, would be okay with seeing him like this. His work colleagues never asked to visit. That would have posed a real dilemma for me, as I didn't know how he would have felt about that. Young men embody strength, vitality and masculinity. Mark's locked-in syndrome was the exact opposite of these culturally celebrated characteristics.

A few friends visited Mark. Some never returned. A small number became regular visitors. Ina's husband, Michael, was one of them, giving Mark a massage on weekends. This was crucial, as immobile muscles deteriorate and perish. Also, it was important for Mark to have some male interaction.

Seeing Mark for the first time always evoked the same reaction. Utter terror in our friends' eyes, undisguisable. The colour seeped out of their faces, exposing a mask carved out of sheer disbelief. I could not bear seeing that expression, for it mirrored my own turmoil too closely.

Reactions occurred distinctly along gender lines. Men generally found it much more difficult to cope with the experience of seeing Mark. They could not bear to be in the room with him longer than about twenty minutes, including his male relatives. There were only a couple of exceptions, my dad being one of them.

Looking back, it strikes me what a source of comfort it was to me that, without exception, everyone who visited Mark felt his presence. His bright green eyes were the one part of him that resembled his former self. Focusing on this mesmerising feature, I could connect with him as a person, rather than staying caught up in the pain of seeing the locked-in Mark.

It became obvious that I wasn't alone in my perception of Mark's eyes. The eyes, always the eyes, touched people. Mark's window to his essence, filled with expression, substance and presence.

"Katrin, I'm sure he recognised me. Something in his eyes. A flicker. A subtle change of expression. I really felt it." This or a similar sentiment was expressed by visitors when they returned and overcame their initial shock at seeing him.

6

Over the three months that we live in the heart of Bonn, Mark continues to be fascinated by the old buildings that surround us. He strolls down his favourite street every day. Poppelsdorfer Allee is a tree-lined boulevard spanning all the way from the castle to the city centre. A natural clay footpath is nestled under a canopy of old, knotty trees. The cobblestone road borders countless old residential houses.

Shortly after moving into our room we stroll down the boulevard together. Mark walks up close to the buildings to study the details of the moulding above the arched windows and the old timber entrance doors. He stops in front of a majestic old house.

"Katreen, how old do you reckon this house is?" He pulls me to a stop and spins me around so that I face the building.

"Oh look, there's a plaque on this one." I step closer to read the sign. "It says 1574."

"Holy moley," he says with a radiant grin.

"Holy what?" I laugh.

"Hole moley. That's Aussie slang."

Mark's cheerfulness and his refreshing and uplifting, easy-going nature make me think that they might be characteristic of Australia, and the idea of moving there is very enticing. He embodies the sunshine that I crave to enliven the cloudy, bleak weather I grew up with and that has settled into my bones. As long as I can remember, I have yearned for sunshine. From November until April, when I opened my curtains in the morning, my eyes met an overcast sky heavy with a sense of gloom that I was unable to shake off. Mark's happy nature seems the perfect antidote to the heaviness I perceived all around me. His gentle and sunny nature expresses the warmth that I feel drawn to.

~

One weekend, friends and I visited Mark. The five of us took him to the courtyard. I held Mark's left hand and asked him to squeeze it. We could all see the muscles along his left arm twitch, from top to bottom. His brain was relaying the correct message to his arm. It just would not respond with a movement. I then asked him to move his right hand, left foot and right foot. The messages got visibly passed to the corresponding limbs.

Later on, after we'd been in the courtyard for two hours, I asked Mark if he wanted to go inside, as it was getting pretty windy. Spontaneously, he mouthed the word NO. My jaw dropped. I looked up and locked eyes with Rob, one of his oldest friends who'd come over from Melbourne. He nodded and placed a warm hand on my shoulder. He'd seen it as well. Despite being *awake* and responding to directives to move his limbs, and now, answering a question with his mouth, Mark was still classified as being comatose. How does that work? I didn't understand it.

Back in the room, Mark gagged on the mucus lodged in his trache. I stared at the white plastic contraption covering his throat. A reminder that he had not been able to taste anything, least of all a cold beer, for weeks.

An image of Mark flashed by, nestled in our ocean blue shell-back sofa, his head tilted backwards, resting on the padding of the settee, eyes intently fixed on the TV screen watching SBS news, absentmindedly crunching on Twisties, the yellow and red packet grasped in his left hand. Remote control perched on the seat beside him.

Mark loved his snacks. Twisties and Arnott's savoury shapes were his favourites, and he had a packet of one or the other every evening.

"Schatz, you know you shouldn't eat a whole packet in one go. They're not that good for you." I eyeballed him.

A glint of cheekiness lit up his eyes. "Ah, you see, I didn't eat a whole packet." He stretched his arm towards me, proudly waving the packet in front of my face.

I leaned forward and peeked inside. A lonely savoury shape huddled in the furthest corner of the bag. I chuckled. I couldn't help it. From then on, I kept finding packets with just one savoury shape or Twistie in the cupboard. It always made me giggle.

And yet here Mark was. Unable to move. Unable to read or watch TV. Unable to swallow. None of the spices dusted on the top of savoury shapes had caressed his taste buds since January. How did he live with this sensory deprivation? It is one of the questions that still conjures deep emotion in me today.

~

The doctors kept talking to me about the possibility of personality changes. I didn't know what that was supposed to entail. These were the same doctors who refused to acknowledge Mark as a mentally present person, often discussing him in the third person in his presence.

There was such a stark contrast in the approach to Mark between the doctors and the nursing staff, with exceptions to the rule on both sides. The nurses generally treated Mark with dignity and spoke to him directly, addressing him by name, and, most importantly, explaining things to him. I witnessed Dr. Nemeth repeatedly speaking about Mark in the third person, his head bent over his patient's head. I never observed him greeting Mark or addressing him directly.

One time I heard about a male nurse who came into Mark's room unannounced with the intention of taking blood. He proceeded to grab his arm and jammed a needle into it without explaining what he was about to do. Mark was completely startled and his arm pulled away in response to the unexpected pain. On the other hand, nurses told me that he was very cooperative when he was told slowly what was about to happen to him, such as being washed.

Being constantly on display, up for grabs without any control over his external environment, must have been extremely distressing for Mark, who was a very private person. I thought about how we'd had a bit of a tug of war at home about the wooden blinds in our upstairs bay windows at night when we sat in our lounge room. He wanted all of them closed, for privacy, which I countered with the observation that our house only faced the backyard from our neighbouring houses and was not visible from any street, not even by our neighbours, due to the position of their houses. It was actually not possible for anyone to look into our living room. We settled on a compromise, as I did not like feeling closed in, all of the light shut out, so we closed a couple of blinds near the sofa, which ensured complete privacy and allowed the city skyline glimpses to remain visible.

When I arrived at the hospital that afternoon, a nurse came up to me straight away. "I've got some big news for you." Her voice vibrated with genuine warmth. "Mark got a place at Shenton Park".

Relief washed through me and sparked some much-needed hope.

In order to be admitted to the rehab clinic, Mark needed to have more medical procedures. After the removal of the trache, a PEG was the second requirement for his crucial admission to the clinic. I learned that this was a feeding tube that is surgically inserted into the stomach so liquid food can be given on a long-term basis.

As I did not plan to go to the hospital until after the PEG surgery, I used the opportunity to go to the weekly Tuesday morning get-together at Headwest, an organisation dedicated to support people with Acquired Brain Injury (ABI) and to give these people a voice with the public and the government. Headwest happened to be located right around the corner from my place. I had driven past it on Canning Highway countless times.

As I wanted to get to know what living with ABI meant, the staff had invited me along to these meetings. The range of physical handicaps and speech impediments was quite scary. Most of these people had solely physical handicaps. One lady who had difficulty speaking, labouring to give sound to the words lined up in her mind, told me that people always assumed that she must be mentally handicapped and how incredibly frustrating it was to be spoken to like a small child. I found out that there were about 20,000 people living with ABI in Western Australia alone. That seemed quite a lot for a population of only two million people. An invisible, voiceless group of people, banned from centre stage, forced to live in the shadows of society.

So much seemed to be riding on the rehab clinic, the only place in the whole state with specialised ancillary staff such as physiotherapists and occupational therapists trained for ABI. Tight resources meant only a select few patients were admitted. The rest, some as young as teenagers, were banished to private aged care facilities that are unable to cater for the needs of young patients, and fail to provide the physiotherapy and other specialised care vital for preserving what health is left, stopping deterioration. Muscle tone is irrevocably lost if left to wither without physiotherapy.

Arriving at the hospital that afternoon after Mark's surgery, I was told that he would be moved to Shenton Park the next day.

Mark leaving the ward felt very strange. This was a place I knew. I was familiar with the routine. I had got to know and like many nurses. Some had gone out of their way to make Mark as comfortable as possible and to cheer him up with stories and little anecdotes. One incident that really stuck in my mind was when Tony, the Scottish nurse who had looked after him for weeks and always told him funny anecdotes, had made sure that Mark was still in his wheelchair rather than the hospital bed when the doctor from the rehab clinic was due to come and see him for his assessment. Tony would treat Mark to light-hearted Scottish banter. Such banter was right up Mark's alley. Everyone wanted him to improve.

When I walked alongside the ambulance drivers wheeling Mark down the hallway for what I assumed would be the last time, I was not sure what to expect at the other end.

7

Everything was different at Shenton Park, an L-shaped red-brick building, so unlike the massive, bleak, multistorey hospital.

When my dad and I arrived at the rehab clinic the following morning, cold sweat covered Mark's forehead. Though he was asleep, his eyebrows were drawn together. A look of agitation had replaced the peaceful expression from the previous day. I sensed that he had been shaken up by the move and that he had crawled right back inside to cope. He needed time to adjust to his new surroundings.

It also took me a while to adapt to the rehab clinic. After having been in a single room, Mark was now sharing with three other guys. It was so different from the hospital, where I had not met any other patients with acquired brain injury. Rather, I had witnessed countless patients who were up and walking the day after their brain surgery.

In Mark's case, there were no external signs of his injuries, apart from the staples in his head from the surgeries. His face, though, remained the same. Now I was in for a rude awakening. The young man in the bed next to Mark wore a helmet. I wondered why until I saw the helmet being removed for a sleep at lunchtime. A gaping hole in his head became exposed, with one third of his skull missing. A small gasp escaped my lips. I averted my gaze, feeling I had intruded on his privacy. Many of the patients seemed to be young and mostly male. It took me at least a couple of weeks to adapt emotionally to the atmosphere of permanence in this place.

This clinic had its own, very different routine. A nurse showed me around the ward. She stopped in front of the entrance door.

"This is a closed ward. That means that you need a pin number to leave," she said, stabbing her index finger at the number pad next to the door. "This is to protect some of the patients who're mobile but are in a confused state."

I swallowed as I noted down the pin number.

"How long do you think it might take for Mark's rehabilitation?" I asked as we strolled down the corridor towards the other end of the ward.

"After nine years of working on this ward I don't predict anything anymore. It just isn't possible."

There were two wings. The second hallway led to a yard. I poked my head around the doorframe and scanned the garden. It was surrounded by hedging and flower beds all along the fence line. I was relieved to see an outdoor area. Apart from a couple of inconspicuous concrete ramps near the entrance, it looked like any garden and did not reveal its alliance with the rehab clinic.

Next to the garden was a large physiotherapy room. At first glance it looked like a gymnasium, with its exercise balls strewn around the place. Then the nurse showed me the rehabilitation equipment. A standing frame that could be tilted electronically into a vertical position with a patient strapped onto a board drew my attention. It was designed for the most severe cases on the ward. Their bodies, I was told, had to get used to the sudden rush of blood that happens when they are placed into a vertical position after having been in a horizontal position for a prolonged period of time. Various leather straps dangled over hooks on the wall. This was the heart of the highly specialised physical rehabilitation, a chamber of endurance that required inconceivable courage.

Cold sweat collected on my forehead. I returned to my husband with a sense of foreboding of what hardships lay ahead for him.

On Saturday, I drove to the clinic with Rahel, who was hanging out to see her dad. I genuinely enjoyed going in with our little angel, as her dad used to call her. This time I was a bit apprehensive about how the environment and other patients would affect her. She gazed around the ward as we walked through, but did not have any questions. As soon as we entered his room, she wrapped her small figure around her dad's torso. Then she perched on the side of his bed and cradled his large hands in her soft, petite hands. All the while she talked to him about school, her homework, her friends and dancing. This prompted her to get up and show him the latest dance move she learned in her previous class. She stepped to one side, then the other, her eyes focused on her feet with great concentration. My eyes moistened as I marvelled at how naturally she behaved. There was no reserve, caution or holding back, as if we were all in our living room at home.

Society's relationship with the disabled is precarious, characterised by our own unwillingness to face our discomfort. Mark's confronting paralysis made others, myself included, behave differently, unsure. It is a striking example of how we show different selves not only to different people, but also to the same people in different situations. How disability and illness are not easily tolerated. Make us feel uncomfortable. Helpless. Expose our own vulnerability.

It seems curious to me now that I never thought of Mark as *disabled*, but rather as extremely ill. Even the term acquired brain injury sent ripples of disbelief down my spine. I could not make that term fit my image of him. My version of Mark had remained preserved in my heart. The die had been cast all the way back in the shadows of Tutankhamun, and medical evidence was not enough to discolour that picture.

My eleven-year-old daughter was the only person ever to visit Mark and behave utterly normally around him. This, I imagine, would have been the greatest gift possible.

Back in the car on our way home, Rahel told me excitedly that a patient had spoken to her when she walked back from the toilet. "Mama, guess what, he was also called Mark."

I turned my head to gaze at her beaming face.

"He said he sure hopes that my daddy, his namesake, will recover." She smiled at me, her eyes alight with hope. "He was a bit hard to understand," she added as an afterthought, "but really friendly."

Joschka did a recording on the dictaphone for his dad, amongst other things singing the Dockers' song, the anthem of his dad's favourite football team. His high-pitched, clear voice rang through the room as I pressed the play button.

"Freo, way to go! Hit 'em real hard, send 'em down below
Oh Freo, give 'em the old heave ho
We are the Freo Dockers."

My gaze focused on Mark. Tears welled in his eyes, like a green rock pool that overflows. Large drops slid slowly down his cheeks. My heart skipped a beat.

I grabbed the little purple, green and white pompon that Joschka had made for his dad from the bedside table and rubbed it against my cheek. Seeing the Dockers' colours reminded me of all the times Mark had taken the children to see a game the year we built our house. We had a family membership that season. The kids sported Dockers' paraphernalia. A bandanna and long scarf for Rahel that hung down to her shins. And little Joschka carried a purple plastic blow-up hand nearly as tall as himself and stabbed it in the air with each, *"Freo, heave ho"*, his smile beaming from ear to ear. As well as wearing an oversized jersey. When he climbed into the back seat of our Volvo station wagon, the blow-up hand always got stuck in the door. Mark would bend down to help Joschka into the car, and the three of them would wave frantically at me as they drove off. It was a little sad that the Dockers never won a game that they went to see. Even so, they always returned upbeat and buzzing from the vibrant atmosphere in the stadium.

I had successfully resisted all attempts by my family to compel me into joining them at the stadium. For years and years, I had heard the grinding high-pitched voice of the footie commentator and the shrill screaming of the crowd beaming through the TV in our living room at weekends. This was serious business for Mark. I was not allowed to say a single word during game time. Not even a "What would you like to eat for lunch?" – I had to wait for the ads to come on. I always watched Mark's reaction to a scored goal with unbridled fascination. He jumped to his feet, fist raised into the air, accompanied by a piercing, "Yes!" hissed through his teeth. And a particularly skilful mark earned a sharp slap on his thigh. Laid-back, quiet Mark morphed into an adrenaline-infused sports fan.

The Christmas before Mark fell into a coma, we had purchased a Dockers family season membership, which runs during winter from March to September. And now Mark was unable to take his children. Rahel and Joschka not being able to go off to the games with their dad, by now a family tradition and strong bonding between them, tormented me. I decided to take the kids myself.

At our first game, we squeezed our way into Subiaco Oval, Rahel wearing her bandanna and Joschka proudly raising his oversized blow-up hand. I wore the Dockers' scarf. If I was going to a live match, I was going to join in. Otherwise there would be no point in going. Being around the games on TV at home had rubbed off enough for me to know the basic rules. Mark had explained them to me during ads. Our seats were located in the membership stalls right behind the goals, surrounded by all the diehard Dockers' fans and immersed in a sea of purple and green.

Rikie, another true Aussie Rules footie fan, accompanied the three of us to one game. Later, giggling, she told me she had hardly watched the game as she found it more amusing to feast her eyes on me, screaming and yelling until I was hoarse. High-fiving Rahel and Joschka with each scored goal. After the giggles had died down, we glanced at each other, bereft. Would Mark ever be able to attend a match again?

~

The new routine of the rehab ward put a lot more pressure on my time management. While Mark was in hospital, I could visit him any time, which meant that I was able to pick up the children from school in the afternoon. Now my routine, my precarious house of cards, was in strife. I could not visit Mark between 12 and 2 p.m. Visiting in the morning was often not very effective. It happened many a time that I got there around 10 a.m. and Mark had not been showered yet. This would then take place during my visit, which cut our valuable time together right down. Also, the ward was very busy in the mornings. Most visitors came in the afternoon. Physiotherapy and speech therapy, aimed at strengthening Mark's mouth muscles for the purpose of swallowing more easily, generally took place in the mornings. Though I would have liked to have been present during these sessions, it was more imperative to keep him company during the long quiet hours of the afternoon.

It was a dilemma, juggling everyone's needs. If I went in the afternoon I could not pick up the children from school. That meant I had to make arrangements with two other parents to take Rahel and Joschka home for a play-over. Whilst I had a lot of offers of help, I did not want to have to rely on others all the time. This increased my stress levels. It all seemed very complex. I did end up going mainly in the afternoons because it was so important for Mark. The afternoon visit meant driving home in peak-hour traffic, exhausted to the point of having to force my eyelids to stay open, adding considerable stress and extra time to the drive home.

Having to accept help on an ongoing basis required a significant shift in my identity. I had grown up with a self-image of being strong and self-reliant. In fact, my mum had always said to me, "You're so strong, Katrin." Here, I'd hit a point in my life where I could no longer function without help from others. I didn't mind so much receiving practical help from the school mums with play-overs for the kids. I'd framed that in my mind as being for the children. But when it came to help for me, I cringed. Having to ask others to visit Mark so that he had more interaction than the four hours per day or so that I could offer him was hard. And most challenging of all, needing a shoulder to cry on. That I didn't do well. Looking back, I can see that while my internal strength served me well during this crisis, in terms of healing, it proved to be both a blessing and a hindrance. I thought I could get through the emotional distress by myself. Could deal with it within my own four walls. And that was to be my wake-up call. The extent of my trauma would prove to be too big to recover from on my own.

~

As my life was chewed up with my clinic visits, I started to feel overwhelmed with the repair jobs around the house that began to mount up, even though we had only built our house two years earlier. A leak in the reticulation, my car backfiring. And Rahel had accidentally leaned on the sink in the upstairs bathroom with such gusto that it came off. Everything was now resting on my shoulders. I was not sure how much more could fit onto them. I strained under the extra pressure.

Mark would have enjoyed seeing me silicone the sink back on with my dad's help. I rummaged through our chaotic laundry cupboard, until now my husband's exclusive terrain, before finding the long tube with the right adhesive. My dad and I stood side by side, shoulders touching. Whilst he supported the sink, I squeezed the silicone through the flaking yellow sealant gun onto the wall. As I glued on the hand-basin, gazing at our bright red and white tiles, I remembered the excitement and joy that had buzzed through my body during the designing and building stages of the house. Could this really only have been three years ago?

We had already lived on the block in a green, older suburb in Perth, within walking distance to the Swan River. We had moved into the old house with its white brick walls perched halfway up the block when I was pregnant with Rahel. With my protruding tummy, I stencilled red and blue teddy bears on the walls of what was to be our baby's room. Shortly after we moved in, Mark climbed on the roof top and exclaimed "Schatz, this is amazing, you can see the skyline from here." Peeking down on me standing in the garden, he added with his eyes lit up, "Well, when you've had the baby you must come up and have a look yourself." Once back down, he put both his arms on my shoulders. "With a two-storey house at the rear of the block we'd be able to see the skyline and the river. Amazing."

My eyes widened at his excitement. And thus, the idea of building a two-storey house one day in the future was born.

A decade later, we realised our dream. The new house was designed by us with the help of a skilled draftsperson and included unusual shapes instead of the ordinary rectangular building style, such as two rooms that protruded outwards, creating the visual impression of a triangle, which was further highlighted by using marine blue colour bond for the outside walls, in striking contrast to the cream limestone bricks. The house was built at the far end of the block to maximise the views. Whilst the original cottage had been small, we now wanted to treat ourselves to the luxury of lavish space, which we realised in our dream home, a two-storey building with the kitchen, main living room and our bedroom upstairs to make the most of our river and city glimpses. Many old trees, various species of eucalyptus such as jarrah and marri, surrounded our house. I loved waking up to be greeted by the green tree tops visible from my bed. Mark adored native flora, and he had planted our entire garden exclusively with natives, predominantly from Western Australia. In spring Mark walked around the garden, bending down to see the first flower buds erupting, delighted as a father watching his son scoring a goal at football. These plants were his babies and he nurtured them with loving care.

8

The ringing of the phone late at night crashed through the fog of my restless sleep, jerking my nerves to attention. Mark had been re-admitted to Sir Charles Gairdner Hospital, I was told, this time with infected shunts. I had no inkling of the extent of suffering that was about to befall Mark, that would sweep him up like a tornado and keep him locked in the centre of the funnel cloud for months to come.

On the way to hospital early the next morning, forced to stop on the freeway by peak hour traffic, I thought how unfair it was that Mark did not get the chance to receive rehabilitation at Shenton Park. This was already the second time that Mark had to be transferred back to Sir Charles Gairdner Hospital, as shortly after his arrival, a blocked shunt had been diagnosed. I hadn't even known that shunts could get blocked. Breathing in the dark fumes from the bus ahead of me, a wave of nausea overcame me. I remembered how, walking along the neon-lit hallway of Ward 52, I could not believe we were back in less than a week. And now, only a couple of weeks after the blocked-shunt surgery, during which time Mark had also contracted pneumonia, I was about to walk the corridors of the neurology ward yet again.

It took a couple of days for the pathology report to come back to confirm the diagnosis. Mark was already on intravenous antibiotics for the pneumonia, and now he was treated with another lot of antibiotics for the new infection. He was back in the High Dependency Unit. I kept thinking, what more does Mark have to endure? How much more can he endure?

The results of the pathology tests showed that Mark had meningitis. The magnitude of the repercussions of the brain infection, which Mark contracted in hospital during one of his brain surgeries, soon became evident to me in a conversation I had with one of the doctors.

"Katrin," he said, "we need to remove both shunts. They are both blocked because of the infection. However, when there's an infection we can't replace them straight away like we did last time with a blockage. We have to wait until the infection has cleared."

I slumped against the wall. After a moment I asked, "How do you clear the infection and how do you drain the blocked brain fluid if he has no shunts?"

"We insert two external shunts in the interim until the infection has cleared. And then, only then, can we place new shunts. There's no point in inserting new shunts until the infection has totally cleared, as otherwise the new shunts would also become infected."

"But this means two separate surgeries."

"I'm afraid so."

Two external shunts. A vivid image of Mark with one external shunt, a small plastic tube protruding from the left side of his skull, flashed through my mind. I pushed the back of my hand against my mouth to silence the wail that threatened to break out.

At home, I picked up the phone and dialled Ina's number. "It's not fair! It's just not fair. Other people live for ten years with the same shunt in place. Mark's already had one blocked shunt straight after the initial surgery, and now this." I sobbed into the receiver.

"Oh Katrin, I don't know what to say. This is heartbreaking."

I swallowed hard. "Fuck, the chance of having a serious complication from his previous brain surgeries is only about two percent." I hit the table with my fist, then bumped the back of my hand on the corner of the table. A blue bruise sprung up immediately. "This can't be happening. It's not fair."

"It isn't. It really isn't." Ina's voice trailed off.

Rahel and I went to visit Mark after the surgery. I was deeply shocked by the picture that presented itself to me. All of Mark's hair was shaved off. His entire head was bandaged. A small, clear plastic tube was sticking out of each side of his head and ran across the pillow to a machine next to his bed. I did not want my daughter to know how terribly upsetting it was for me to see Mark like this. It took all of my inner strength not to collapse on the floor. Mark himself was not only awake but very alert. His eyes were clear and held my gaze as I leant over him.

A few days later, when I came on my normal daily visit, I was unprepared for what I saw. There Mark was with the plastic tubes sticking out of his bare head, the bandages gone. He was propped up on his bed and had to remain in a particular half-upright position, as the shunts had to remain at a certain angle.

I fled to the grey concrete stairwell. In a corner, my body slid down the wall until I sat on the ground, my arms wrapped around my knees, crying uncontrollably. When I finally calmed down, I swore to myself that I would never, ever let this happen to Mark again. I would not let him endure external shunts again in the future.

~

We are locked into our hug, lost to the outside world, in front of the departure gate at Frankfurt airport. This is a very different goodbye to the last one at Cairo airport. Laid-back Mark has morphed into being emotional and teary-eyed. Having spent the last few months almost non-stop together in Bonn, tucked away in our seven square metres of heaven, we're about to be separated for three months.

Gesa's husky voice penetrates our island. "Come on, Katrin. We've got to go now."

I squeeze Mark's hand one last time. Once settled on the plane, I catch my breath, perhaps for the first time since Mark's arrival in Germany three months earlier. What an intoxicating romance we've had.

The last few days before my departure, though, Mark had grown increasingly restless. He started to worry about the long separation.

"I'll miss you so much," he sighed.

I had looked at him, remembering the flippant remarks that he'd made back in Egypt about love. Was I really the lucky girl who had banished all his sarcasm about love, who had captured his heart?

Looking out over the baby blue, cloudless sky through the small window in the plane, I bubble over with joy.

About a month later, Gesa and I arrive in Penang after an uncomfortable, sweaty train ride. The humidity is draining. I race to the post office and scan the building for the poste restante counter, passport ready in my hands. A thrill tickles my stomach when the postal worker turns around bearing the familiar blue and red striped borders of the airmail envelope in his hands. I rip the envelope open, exerting enough restraint to avoid damaging the fragile airmail paper.

25 July 1984
Mein Schatz,

When we parted, I would not have believed how it could affect me. … Alas how wrong could I be. I am constantly depressed, you come into my mind all hours of the day and night (the last three nights have been sleepless) and I am living with a great gap in my chest. Every day is just another day closer to seeing you. Often I wish I could just wake up and be on that plane to "my Katrin". If I had had any idea of how I would feel, I never would have left you. I could never have realised. … I've never chased or followed a girl before. If I have to follow you around the world, so be it …

You probably wonder, is this the same Mark I know? Well, it is. It's just that I never before felt this way. I'm constantly exploring these new feelings … You are my angel, my shining light.

I love you so much.
Mark xxxxxxx

The words buzz through my head all night. If only I could call him straight away. My concern for him alternates with thoughts of his declarations of love. Mark has adopted the German term of endearment *Schatz*, literally meaning treasure. I like that. Treasure. It seems more meaningful than darling.

I could not have known that this treasure of mine was to carry me off to a richly textured life down under. Or that this joyful life, tied to his presence, would be mine for only half my life. That I'd be left behind.

~

The high risk of blockage and infection of the shunts, and the external shunts themselves, made me contemplate the removal of Mark's cyst. I wondered if it was even possible. Then he would not need to live with shunts any more. I approached the neurosurgeon on duty and was told that the removal was too dangerous.

Prior to Mark's illness I had worked on a casual, seasonal basis as a tour guide for German tourists, showing them around Perth and close surroundings. On this occasion, I had decided to do a tour for the first time since Mark had fallen ill. I wanted to see if it was possible to do a little bit of work.

After visiting Mark in the morning, I picked up the tour group from their hotel and accompanied them on a city sightseeing tour by coach. Entertaining a whole group of tourists, happy and excited to be in Australia, in holiday mode, was overlaid with the surreal fact of Mark's suffering. As soon as the tour was finished, I returned to the hospital, as Dr. Nemeth had asked to see me that evening.

"I'm leaning towards the removal of the cyst," the professor told me.

Surprised, I asked, "How long would the surgery be and how high are the risks?" The other neurosurgeon must have spoken to his boss, I thought.

"The surgery itself might take about three to four hours. There's a four to five percent chance of serious complications, such as death or further brain damage." His voice was lacking intonation, flat, as if discussing a shopping list.

I stared at the green dusty leaves of the artificial pot plant. "I thought that the chance of something going seriously wrong would've been much higher. The chances of complications in a shunt operation are already one to two percent."

"That's right. One to two percent with each surgery."

"With each surgery ... That would mean repeated shunt operations carry the same risk as the removal of the cyst."

"That's correct."

"Can I think about this?"

"We need a decision by Saturday."

As I turned to leave the room, Dr. Nemeth spoke again. I swung back to face him.

"I want you to know that the removal of the cyst will not have any impact on Mark's cognitive state. That will remain the same. It will mean that he does not need shunts any more. That's why I'm recommending it."

My hand reached for the door handle. We were at eye level, his erect body rigid.

"By the way," he continued, "you also need to know that there is a very small chance, maybe one percent, that he might need a shunt despite the removal of the cyst."

That last remark went totally over my head. I stumbled out of the waiting room, numbed. My body found its way back to Mark's room, without my conscious attention.

I had two days to decide. My mind was going in circles, round and round the same issues. The responsibility stalked me, a constant shadow. It seeped into my sleepless nights. I don't want to have to make this decision for Mark. I want him to be able to decide for himself, I kept thinking. In the end, I informed the neurosurgeons' team to go ahead with the cyst removal.

On the morning of the surgery, Mark was distressed. All colour had drained from his face. He was frowning, ashen, agitated. He had developed a fever overnight and the surgery had to be cancelled.

~

A few days later I walked down the hospital corridor towards the High Dependency Unit. Lacklustre dark brown carpet squares doused in cold, bright neon lights. When I reached the entrance to the HDU, I heard a heart-wrenching moaning. A sound so excruciatingly painful that I had to stop, to hold onto the wall to steady myself. I intuitively knew that this was Mark. As I entered the room I saw his body distorted with pain, his limbs contracted and shaking.

Hearing his moaning and seeing his legs convulsing in pain took me to the limits of my endurance. My shock was magnified by the fact that I had not heard Mark's voice in months. The edges of my reality vanished. There was nothing to hold onto. I found myself on the threshold of an abyss, my toes edging forwards, curling around the cold rock.

9

The onslaught of Mark's intense pain attacks continued relentlessly. The cause was an acid burn on his stomach. Gastric fluids, I was informed by a nurse, had run out of the opening in the stomach around his feeding tube, the PEG. Mark's own body fluids had literally burned the skin on his stomach. The medical staff on the fifth floor of the hospital, the neurosurgery ward, did not have the expertise to deal with this crisis. Doctors from the gastroenterology ward did, which was located on the eighth floor. It took those doctors three days to attend to Mark.

During this time of the stomach crisis, I decided to visit Mark twice a day. I wasn't sure how I could make that happen – only that I had to. As it was a weekend, I needed someone to look after the children for the two daily visits. Witnessing Mark in agony twice a day for many hours evoked such despair in me felt my sanity seep out of me like sap out of a tree. I implored the staff to get specialist wound treatment for Mark's burn, time and time again. They tried their best to dress the wound. The burn continued to intensify.

Looking back at that time, I cannot grasp how I kept going. I was so close to my breaking point that I could feel the abyss sucking me in, threatening to annihilate me. I had lost the signature of the ordinary, all traces of normality erased. The ebb and flow of the everyday had been replaced with paralysing fear, shaped by prolonged uncertainty and ongoing life and death decisions. What vanished too in my fogged-up mind was the ability to reflect and contemplate. Simply acting was the modus operandi that was taking its place. Getting up, making breakfast and lunch for Rahel and Joschka, driving to hospital. What astounds me is that I am a reflective person by nature, and that the period of Mark's illness was the only time in my life where this trait disappeared. I did not seek solace in nature either – it was out of reach of my survival mode. My life had narrowed down to a tunnel with a faint glow of light in the distance that I directed my movements towards. Without an escape hatch, I had to keep travelling towards the speck of light. It was not until many years later that I found out that these were typical responses to trauma.

~

My boyfriend never disappoints me with mail in Asia. Every GPO that I had listed on a piece of paper bears a letter for me. Mark is an exquisite and witty letter writer with an astounding skill of observation. Pages and pages of thin pale blue airmail sheets spill out of his envelopes, covered in his small handwriting, the lines claiming all available space. He does not easily give voice to his emotions in person, but he expresses himself eloquently in these letters. If Mark feels shy or self-conscious, he doesn't show it. I live in a bubble of elation.

After several weeks, I receive a letter that makes me jump for joy: Mark wants to come to Thailand three weeks earlier, as long as it suits my friend Gesa. She's genuinely happy for him to join us. The three of us could not have guessed that this was to be the beginning of a special friendship, that we'd be living together one day in Bonn.

At Bangkok airport, I fly into Mark's arms as soon as I spot his mop of blond curls towering over the other passengers in the sliding doors of the arrivals gate.

We spend three weeks on the exotic island KoSamui. Blue skies, palm trees, white sand, clear, turquoise water. A lover's paradise. Back in Bangkok, it is time to purchase my plane ticket to Australia. I only have a return ticket from Thailand to Germany. Before my trip I went to the Australian Embassy in Bonn, just down the road from our little home, to apply for a tourist visa. The embassy officials declined my application on the grounds that I didn't have a return ticket for Australia, which I had planned on buying in Thailand, and simply handed me back my visa-less passport. Fair enough, I thought.

With the return ticket in hand, Mark and I weave our way right across the city of Bangkok to the Australian Embassy, negotiating the traffic abyss. After filling in the appropriate forms, I am asked to hand over my passport. The immigration official returns after some time, shaking his head.

"I can't give you the visa. Your passport has been blacklisted."

"What? How can that be and what does that mean?"

"Well, it means I cannot give you a visa until I know why the staff in Bonn did this. I'll send a telegram to the embassy in Bonn and find out why your passport has been blacklisted."

"When can I get my visa then?"

"I don't know. You'll have to wait for the reply from Bonn. I don't even know if I can give you a visa at all."

Mark and I just look at each other, stunned. *Blacklisted* sounds so political.

We're told to come back several days later. On the nominated day we return to the embassy, fighting our way again through the congested traffic, in almost unbearable heat. Tuktuks beep their horns incessantly.

"I'm sorry, but we haven't heard back yet from Bonn. You'll have to come back again in a few days."

There are only so many temples we can visit. Time drags on. On the third visit, things look up.

"Hello again." The government official greets us with a smile that extends right up to the corners of his eyes. "Yes. We've now had an answer from Bonn. The reason why you were blacklisted was because you didn't have a return plane ticket for Australia. So now that you do, I can give you a visa."

I can't believe it. All of this drama because I didn't have a return ticket.

"I'm glad to hear that I can have my tourist visa now," I respond, relieved.

"Actually," he says, looking at my Australian boyfriend, with a twinkle in his eye, "I can give you permanent residency right now if you'll get married within three months."

What is going on here? First, they don't want to let me into the country for a visit, and now they are throwing permanent residency at me.

"Well, I just want a tourist visa for now, thank you."

~

From the time of the stomach burn, Mark started to go noticeably downhill. His muscles contracted uncontrollably. First, it was the right arm. In time, it was both arms and both legs. His limbs could no longer be straightened after a period of time. I could not hold my anguish.

Every day I attempted to ease the muscle spasms, to massage Mark's limbs. Feeling the erratic muscle contractions and hearing his moaning was such an unspeakable experience that I was incapable of giving it words. My resilience bled out of me. The pain brought me to my knees, literally, at home, alone in my bedroom. I walked around in a daze, incapable of comprehending Mark's level of suffering. I despaired at my inability to ease his pain. This incomprehensibility, the absence of all meaning in this suffering, was to become my dark twin, and it was to overshadow, hijack even, my recovery from grief.

The contractions significantly changed the way Mark looked. His angelic expression was long gone. His eyes were squeezed tightly. A deep furrow etched into his forehead. His mouth was stretched open. Sweat accumulated on his forehead, trickling down his temples.

The physiotherapists at the hospital ceased working with Mark. Much later on, I found out from the physios at Shenton Park that this was the worst that could have happened as remedial exercise was not only helpful in treating muscle contractions but vital in avoiding permanent muscle damage.

I was ignorant of the ramifications of permanent muscle contractions. They came on so suddenly that it took a considerable period of time before I understood what was happening. At this stage I simply did not know, and no one explained them to me. My main focus was on healing Mark's stomach burn. The gastro registrar ceased feeds through the PEG. Complications with the wound continued. It was not healing well. I am not sure how Mark was being fed during this time. He had already lost about twenty kilos. His bones protruded and his face had a hollowed look, with dark shadows below his eyes.

Imprisoned in his own body, Mark's world had already narrowed into a thin slice of life. Paralysis is hungry. It constricts all flow. The insatiable, constant pain caused by the stomach burn and the muscle contractions robbed Mark of even that thin slice, turning it into a place of torment. Loss of hope began to linger in the shadows of my subconscious mind.

~

Meanwhile Mark still had the external shunts, infections and fever. Late on Monday, about three and a half months into his coma, the doctors thought that his external shunts needed replacing because of infections to the shunts themselves. On Tuesday, Dr. Nemeth asked to see me. He indicated that he was planning to schedule the cyst-removal for the next day.

"This is not ideal, but Mark is going to be as good as he's going to be. By tomorrow the external shunts will need to be replaced. As you know, they have a maximum life span of two weeks."

"So this means Mark has to have some form of surgery in any case. Either he has to have the external shunts replaced or the cyst removed. Is that right?"

"Yes, that's right."

"I don't want Mark to have another set of external shunts and then additional brain surgery. If you recommend tomorrow and all things considered, let's go ahead."

No more shunts, shunt infections and brain surgery. Only one more surgery. That was my mantra.

Dr. Nemeth nodded. He notified me of a long list of possible risks associated with this major surgery, then handed me a green clipboard with the consent form. I hated the signing of the consent form, the weight of responsibility, with a vehemence that choked me.

After the surgery, Ina and I walked through the milky sliding doors of the ICU. Mark was propped up on pillows, eyes closed, peaceful, attached to a multitude of tubes and machinery. His head was bandaged. We stood on either side of his bed, stroking his arms. He is alive, I kept thinking.

As Mark was still under the influence of the anaesthetic and therefore out of pain, this was the most relaxed he had looked since the infection of his shunts. A green-clad, bearded nurse looked after him, the strings of the gown barely long enough to wrap around his protruding body. Shortly after our arrival he talked over Mark's head as though he was not present and mumbled something along the lines of "vegetative". Ina and I looked at each other. She quietly went about taking the nurse to one side and explaining to him the incorrectness and inappropriateness of that behaviour. He was truly sorry and mentioned that he had been given that information in his brief.

We stayed with Mark for some time. The bright neon light was shining down on his face, which was framed by the stark white of the bandages. His arms lay by his side, still.

In the evening, Mark opened his eyes and moved his arms spontaneously, and also to command at times. I bent over his face, moved that he was coming to already and looking at me. This must be a turning point, I thought, hopeful that Mark's struggle for survival would be over.

10

After my eight months' holiday in Australia, we return to Germany. 1985 is the year of living happily in Bonn. Our apartment, which we share with Gesa, is located in the old part of the city, in the heart of a maze of one-way streets, among myriad quaint pubs and beautiful façades. Our favourite restaurant is Baffo, a cosy al fresco Italian place just around the corner from us, which makes the best lasagne I've ever eaten.

One Saturday night we walk arm-in-arm the five hundred metres from our apartment to the restaurant. I savour the balmy night, the warm breeze against the skin of my legs. Seated on a small square table with a white, well-starched tablecloth next to the window, we move the menus to the side. We already know what we want to order. The waiter places the brown, oval shaped oven-proof dish in front of me. I slide my fork into the béchamel sauce, bubbling and thick in texture, equally seduced by the alluring aroma of the freshly melted cheese and Mark's intense gaze in the soft candlelight. Stretching his long legs out under the table after the meal, he tells me that he loves living in Bonn. He leans forward and holds my left hand in both of his.

"I know you do and I'm so happy that you do." I twist my right forefinger around a particularly appealing curl. His soft, sun-bleached curls always make my heart beat faster. I cannot get enough of running my hands through his hair.

"Maybe it's to do with the fact that you're a man of leisure, that I'm the one working," I tease.

"Too right." He winks.

That year in Bonn is carefree. Mark adores living in the old part of town, right opposite a Lidl supermarket that houses a whole range of cheap, preservative-free German beer. Heaven for the Australian boy from the suburbs. I work on a part-time basis for a data protection company in an administrative capacity, and Mark uses his spare time to wander through the cobblestone streets or to read the German newspaper with a dictionary to hand. He often sits bent over the table under a large window in our apartment in a well-maintained heritage building, his left index finger pressed onto the newspaper, his right hand holding open the pages of the dictionary. No matter how many words need to be translated, he deciphers whole sentences and reads entire newspaper articles in this way.

At my parents' place, my mum and Mark spend a lot of time chatting and bantering.

"Hallo Mark, wie geht's Dir?" My mother raises her arms, beaming, and envelops him in a hug as soon as we've walked through their front door.

"Super, danke Ingrid." Mark leans down and holds my mum in a loving embrace.

She speaks only German with him, though she can speak a bit of English. Standing side by side in the entrance, she tilts her head back to look up at Mark, and underlines her story with large or small hand movements as required to explain individual words or phrases when Mark raises his eyebrows to indicate he doesn't understand something. Mark's eyes sparkle affectionately, sometimes accompanied by dimples or morphing into a full-blown laughter that erupts on both sides. I am fascinated and enchanted by their interactions and close connection.

The more Mark reads German and talks with my mum, the more his vocabulary grows. By the end of the year, Mark is able to hold a pretty fluent conversation in German with an adorable, unique accent that's coloured by a mixture of Australian and Dutch intonations.

Mark relishes his year of leisure. A permanent smile has settled on his face. I buy a second-hand silver 50cc Vespa, which I can park on the sidewalk of our narrow street where parking spots are scarce. Visiting my parents every weekend, Mark is always perched behind me with his long legs bent outwards and pushing against my arms.

My favourite German card game, called Doppelkopf, has been adopted by Mark as his favourite. It appeals to him because of its complicated rules, need for strategic play and the fact that each game brings up something unexpected. My mum and brother also love this game. Whenever my brother visits my parents, the four of us spend long Saturday afternoons playing Doppelkopf at my parents' round dining table, with my father preferring to read in the living room, happy that we're having fun. We also often play whole nights at my brother's place. He lives in an old mansion that's been converted to shared accommodation and there is always someone willing to play with us.

We travel a lot when we live in Bonn. We go skiing and hiking in the Alps. One memorable trip is to the city of Wroclaw in Poland, which used to be the German city of Breslau until the end of World War II, where my mother was born. My grandmother and her three children had to flee Breslau when my mum, the oldest of three siblings, was just ten years old. They arrived in Germany by fully enclosed cattle train carriages and were looked down upon as refugees, second-class citizens, by their fellow Germans.

Forty years after the war ended, Mark and I accompany my mother on a trip back to what is now Poland. My dad cannot come along because of a generic ban for all government employees that prohibits them from visiting the German Democratic Republic, which we have to cross en route. When we arrive in the city centre of Wroclaw, my mum parks the car and starts to walk. After four decades, she remembers the way towards the apartment building where they had lived. Once we reach the building, the three of us stand there staring at the grey house front still covered in bullet holes.

If my grandmother hadn't left with her young children on the last possible train before Polish occupation, my mum would still be living here now, and so would I...

~

The day after the surgery to remove the cyst, Mark was moaning with pain again. The contraction of his muscles had returned viciously in both his arms and legs. Mark could at times move his arms in response to pain. In the evening he was stable enough to be transferred back to the High Dependency Unit in the neurosurgery ward. The head bandages were removed. No more curls.

The gastroenterologist was concerned that Mark's stomach wound was not healing. PEG feeds had to be repeatedly ceased to deal with the infected skin. The contractions of his limbs worsened. When Mark was lying in bed, his knees were bent. I could not straighten either his arms or legs. As he was becoming more alert following the surgery, he also became more agitated. The muscles in his limbs worked continually. Vivid images of his contorted face played over and over in my mind during sleep-deprived nights, like a movie set on endless repeats. Day or night, I could not extricate myself from the barrage of images and sounds. I was locked into Mark's inescapable cycle of pain-racked suffering.

Rikie came for another visit from Melbourne. She had not seen her son since the shunt infections. I clenched both fists, the nails digging into my palms, as we walked into the High Dependency Unit. Her small frame lingered over her son's chest, one hand tightly grasping his upper arm, engrossed in gazing at his face. Then she straightened to an upright position and locked eyes with me.

I don't know how this was possible, but somehow Rikie was protected from having to witness her son in his worst throes of pain and moaning during the days she stayed in Perth. I still feel relieved that she was spared that image and auditory imprinting which can never be erased from memory again.

I was acutely concerned about our children having to see their father in this extreme state of suffering. It was evident that it would traumatise Rahel and Joschka, as it was bringing me, an adult, to my limits of endurance. I decided not to take them to visit their father while he was in severe pain. Rahel regularly asked to visit her dad. This meant I needed to give her an explanation for why she could not come that was truthful, but worded in such a way that it did not worry and upset her. She knew me very well and was able to discern what I was feeling.

Even without the overt suffering Mark was experiencing, it had been distressing to see him locked in his body. Joschka found it very difficult to visit his father. I admired his courage, for he kept visiting him regularly anyway. But knowing how hard it was for him, I had limited his visits to perhaps twenty minutes. I knew that I could not let Joschka witness his dad moaning in pain. I was also aware that Mark would not have wanted these images inscribed in their memories of him.

~

In an attempt to find some relief for Mark, I had asked around my circle of friends if anyone knew a practitioner of reiki, a Japanese healing technique. Jonathon, a friend of a friend's colleague, volunteered to come to the hospital. This stranger, an experienced reiki practitioner and teacher, walked into the hospital room one evening a week after the cyst removal while Mark's mum and I were there.

A serene expression and slow, mindful movements greeted us. Jonathon introduced himself first to us and then to Mark, and explained to him the purpose of his visit. He stood behind the top end of the bed and placed his hands gently on Mark's shaven crown. Large, masculine hands with long fingers. Mark's reaction was striking. Almost as soon as Jonathon's hands touched him, he began to respond. Sweat poured out, flooding his forehead and face. Within a short space of time he became remarkably alert, his eyes wide open, his irises clear and present. He tried to vocalise a response as well, opening his mouth, forming words with his lips, his jaw working hard. The unusual sounds that he managed to make were unlike his moaning in pain. Deliberate. Rikie and I sat stock still, observing the scene in front of us open-mouthed. We sat there in silence whilst Jonathon continued to give Mark reiki, repositioning his hands to the back of his head.

Afterwards he told us that he would be back the next evening. Rikie and I stared at each other, too mesmerised to speak. My mother-in-law had no experience with alternative therapies and was astounded by Mark's powerful reaction. She kept saying, "He only put his hands on Mark. Unbelievable. What a reaction."

True to his word, Jonathon not only returned the next evening, but the one after that as well. This remarkable man continued to visit Mark several times a week for many weeks. He would not accept anything in return. It was his gift.

Sitting in the hospital room one evening with Jonathan present, I smiled, thinking of what Mark's response would have been to reiki in the past.

"Katreen," he would have said, "what a lot of bollocks. Come on." This would have been accompanied by a light-hearted smile. I wondered if his illness might have changed his attitude in some way, when his body responded to reiki so strongly. Mark had been a confirmed atheist. "I only believe what I can see." His stance was firm and he did not want to discuss it.

I had always found it surprising that his passionate interest in philosophy, Plato, Hegel and Kant, was married to a lack of interest in discussing our opinions on the deeper meaning of life. When I met Mark in Egypt, one of the few possessions other than clothes that he carried with him in his backpack was a small, leather-bound volume on philosophers. I remember the yellowish, thin pages and small, old-fashioned print. Mark always preferred to read and think over debating. By contrast, I thrived on discussing meaningful topics and had found Mark's disinterest in deliberating increasingly disappointing over the years, missing a more intense sharing of this important aspect of my life with him.

However, at a time in our lives when we were preoccupied with child rearing, spending a lot of time with the kids and talking about them at length, not contemplating philosophy wasn't really noticeable in the flow of everyday life. It only became more visible to me later once I became more interested in spirituality.

My spiritual endeavours began slowly with weekly yoga classes when Joschka was a baby. The classes always ended with a meditation and Debby, our teacher, read out mystical or Buddhist poems or texts. It was the first dipping of my toes into waters that I was to explore in earnest a few years later when I joined a weekly discussion class in the Indian philosophy Vedanta, which is based on the Vedas, ancient Sanskrit texts. We debated concepts such as taking personal responsibility, being in the present moment, reincarnation and karma. I would return from these evenings intellectually stimulated and full of questions that I wanted to discuss with Mark.

A couple of years before Mark fell ill, I became interested in a personal development course. Though Mark was not interested in the content, he was very supportive and encouraged me to do it. I was somewhat saddened by his disinterest in talking about it, but at the same time I was mindful that his genuine encouragement allowed me to pursue my interest, and this outweighed whatever else I might have felt.

11

Mark's contractions continued and I still did not know what caused them, how he had gone so drastically downhill. The earlier days when he passed a ball from one hand to the next seemed a distant past. How did this happen? The masses of medication, repeated anaesthetics, surgeries, infections, antibiotics and, above all else, the pain had taken its toll on Mark's already severely weakened body. Nevertheless, the marked worsening of his condition was surprising and shocking. Now, there were only bad days. Previously, there had been "good" days, peaceful days where we could go to the courtyard together, enjoying the sunshine and breeze on our skin. I was unable to grasp what these changes meant. But at least after four weeks the various strategies by the gastroenterologists were starting to bear fruit. It had been a very, very long battle that was slowly, ever so slowly improving.

Despite the contractions, Mark was now alert and aware for longer periods of time. It was unpredictable, though, how he would be on any given visit. The possibility of another setback and not knowing if he might be in extreme agony was excruciating.

He could now be positioned in a wheelchair again. On the one hand it was good for his body to be upright. On the other hand, the contracted muscles made it almost impossible for him to settle for any period of time. Because he had yet another infection, I could not wheel him into the courtyard to catch some fresh air; we had to stay in the room.

Some time after the removal of the cyst, I raised the issue of returning to Shenton Park. For this to happen, I was told, Mark would have to be reassessed by the doctor from the rehab clinic. He had lost his place there. Two weeks after the surgery, Rikie and I were asked to meet with Dr. Jamison, the medical representative from Shenton Park. We went into a small waiting room on the ward accompanied by the social worker, and a doctor and a nurse from Ward 52. We all sat down. My voice trembled. I had to clasp my hands to stop them from fidgeting.

Dr. Jamison went straight to the point. "Mark is not an appropriate candidate for further inpatient rehabilitation."

"What?" Rikie and I exclaimed simultaneously.

My mind went blank.

"He won't be returning to Shenton Park."

"What? Why?" I shrieked. I wiped my forehead with the back of my hand, my fingers chilly against my burning skin.

"Look." She straightened her back. "I've made my decision. He failed the previous trial period of rehabilitation. There's nothing more that I can do." With that she stood up and left the room without turning back.

"This isn't fair. They can't just abandon Mark," Rikie exclaimed.

"Is there nothing we can do about this? It's so unfair ... wrong." The little hairs on my neck stood on end. I looked at Dr. Brown.

"Well, the decision rests with Dr. Jamison. But perhaps you could go and see Dr. Chong, the rehab specialist from Shenton Park," he suggested.

"This is just about money, isn't it?" I said. "There's only a limited number of beds in Shenton Park, and it's the only place for rehabilitation in all of Western Australia. So they have to leave the worst cases out because of lack of funding."

Rikie walked off. She kept saying, "They can't do this."

I feared the worst. That Mark would be shoved off to an aged care facility. Without any therapists at all, not even a physio which he was in such desperate need of. I couldn't imagine our children visiting their dad in an old people's home.

I went to visit Dr. Chong at his Shenton Park office. Rikie handed me a fervent, hand-written letter imploring him to give her son a chance. Dr. Chong, a short man in his fifties, a very experienced rehab specialist, was compassionate and understanding. He listened to what I had to say and then explained his position to me. Mark was not responding enough for rehabilitation; he would not be able to make use of an occupational therapist, a speech therapist, what they had to offer. In other words, those resources would be wasted, while another patient could make use of them. The difference here was that, unlike the cold, seemingly uncaring, brief response by Dr. Jamison, Dr. Chong actually listened to me and took the time to explain the situation. Also, he clarified that, in their assessment, Mark's neurological state had not improved in the four months since he had been admitted to hospital and that the rehabilitation ward was designed to help people who could and would improve. Although still shocked at these developments, at least I felt heard, because the consultant had taken the time to listen.

Where to from here for Mark? I lay awake at night, churning this question over and over in my mind. As soon as a residential care assessment was approved, Sir Charles Gairdner Hospital became pro-active. Apparently there was a private agency in Perth called Brightwater that ran many residential aged care facilities, as well as a "Young Disabled Scheme". The hospital contacted Brightwater regarding a possible referral. Brightwater promised to look into the referral, and – if found suitable – would send a doctor to visit Mark, with me present.

The doctor from Brightwater came to assess Mark. Again, the stakes were unbearably high. To complicate matters, on the day of the assessment Mark had a strong physical reaction to a medication he had been given. His whole body was shaking. Rivulets of sweat ran down his face. He sat in the wheelchair when the doctor arrived. I had never seen Mark shaking like that before. After talking at length with the nurses of the neurosurgery ward, the doctor agreed to give Mark a place.

I later found out that the only reason why Mark had been placed into a wheelchair despite being unwell was because Tony, the Scottish nurse, knew about the crucial assessment and wanted to help. I could only mutter a quiet *thank you*.

What got Mark into Brightwater was the fact that he could move his left foot slightly on command during the assessment. This was all that he had left. It was his ticket out of aged care.

~

I pulled my Falcon station wagon into the car park of Brightwater in order to have a look at the place. My eyes checked the clock and the tachometer. The thirty-kilometre drive had taken me over half an hour, outside peak-hour traffic. I sighed. At least it was in Perth, I thought, remembering that I had been told that this particular youth residential facility under the Brightwater umbrella was the only *private* care facility for people with acquired brain injury *in the whole of Australia*. This means that anywhere else in the country, ongoing care for people with ABI who have not been accepted into a public rehabilitation unit, who may be as young as their late teens, is provided in aged care facilities only. These facilities are set up to cater for the needs of the elderly and do not provide the specialist care needs such as physiotherapists and speech therapists that young people with ABI or other debilitating diseases such as motor neuron disorder have. There are simply no permanent care facilities for young people. They are hidden away from society, without a voice.

I entered the large complex of several buildings. As I searched for the right building, I walked past a spacious living room with large windows. My gaze settled on several people in wheelchairs, some of them tilted backwards with their heads leaning awkwardly to one side. I could make out vacant, far-away expressions in some of the eyes. A TV flickered. I gasped for air. It was evident, though, by the kind manners of the carers interacting with the residents and their gentle voices that the atmosphere was caring. A staff member directed me to the office where I was to meet the social worker.

Sophie greeted me with a strong handshake. Her musical voice seemed to add extra body to her petite frame. Unlike the social workers I had come across in the hospital, she was dressed not in casual clothes, but a dark grey suit. Her compassionate gaze was comforting. I took an immediate liking to her. This initial impression was later strengthened with every meeting. She asked me into the lounge room that was located in the same building as the office. I sat down on a green couch with small red dots. Another administrator from Brightwater joined us. I must have looked stricken, because Sophie placed her hand on my shoulder and told me to take my time.

"I'm sorry. I feel a bit shaken after seeing these people sitting there, just staring into the air or making noises."

"That's understandable. Most of us have never come into contact with people with acquired brain injury. It can be distressing at first."

"I don't mean to be disrespectful in any way. It's just that the thought of Mark being here is upsetting."

"You don't need to apologise. Let me explain to you how things are structured here. We have two different types of care facilities. There's the rehab facility. Patients in this stream are seen as having the potential to improve and will receive support services. That's where your husband will be placed. Then there's the permanent residential facility, which is the one that you walked past. Those residents are not expected to improve. They're here on a permanent basis and are very well cared for."

I crossed my legs the other way. My stomach was churning. "How long have some of these patients been here? Some of them looked so … young."

"There are patients who've been here for over ten years."

Please don't let this happen to Mark. Just sitting there, doing nothing, passing time, I thought.

"Would you like me to show you around so that you can see the house and room that Mark will be moving to?" Sophie interrupted my thoughts.

I stood up. "Yes, thank you, that'd be good."

"I'll start with this building that we're in. We have a common room here with a fully equipped kitchen and games. You can bring your husband here when you come visiting with your children. They'll be able to play here and you can spend some time together."

"The kids will like this. And it'll be good for their dad to see them playing. It doesn't feel so much like a hospital then."

We walked across a path leading past the original building that I had passed further along to another cream brick building, entering through the back door. I was greeted with the familiar, ever-present linoleum floors. The rubber soles of my shoes squeaked with every step as we walked along the hallway to the front of the building. Sophie showed me a room to the right that would be Mark's room. I could see green shrubs through the window. In the middle of the room was the bed, which faced a TV on a wall bracket. To the left were built-in cupboards.

"Patients wear their own clothes here. Please label all of Mark's belongings." She guided me out of the room. "Let me show you the kitchen and living room."

Several patients sat in their wheelchairs in the living room. It was lunchtime. Two women looked about nineteen years old. One man was engrossed in a TV program. Though confronting, the atmosphere was definitely caring.

I left the premises with mixed feelings. Relieved that I had found a place for Mark that felt kind. Unsettled from seeing the other patients in the rehab stream who looked pretty unresponsive. And concerned that there wasn't anywhere near as much rehabilitation here as in Shenton Park. In fact, rehab pretty much consisted of the occasional physiotherapy session with minimal equipment, a far cry from the modern, state-of-the-art facilities at Shenton Park.

Mark was moved from the hospital to Brightwater on the ninth of June, a day before my birthday. The house looked like a normal residential home from the outside. And, just like with any ordinary house, I always had to ring the bell to be let in. I expected not to have to return to the hospital.

12

Saturday morning, two days after my birthday. Out of all the birthdays, it had to be my 40th this year. My friends implored me to celebrate this significant birthday in some way and not to let it fall by the wayside. They planned a get-together for this evening, at my place. I was instructed not to prepare any food – they were organising everything.

The shrill ringing of the phone at 7 a.m. disturbed the chirping of the birds outside my window. In an instant, adrenaline pumped through my veins. A call this early in the morning could only mean one thing: that something was wrong with Mark. And that was exactly what had happened. His blood pressure had risen sharply, and he was clearly unwell, Brightwater staff informed me. He was agitated and sweating profusely. They decided to call an ambulance to transfer him to the emergency department at Sir Charles Gairdner Hospital.

Mark had only arrived at Brightwater three days earlier. Disbelief rose in my throat like green bile. As it was a Saturday, the kids were at home. I picked up the phone to organise friends to look after them, calculating in my head how long it would take me to drop them off and to get to hospital.

At the sight of Mark in the Emergency Department, I had nothing left in me to withstand this latest onslaught of Mark's unfathomable suffering, of witnessing it with all my senses. I could tell that he had hydrocephalus again, and I became saturated with sensory overload. Mark's eyes were filled with fear and anguish. He had the same symptoms as last time. The blood pressure monitor flashed in response to an alarmingly high blood pressure. A sense of *déjà vu* swept over me, with scenes from the first day vividly replaying in my mind – the screeching of the monitors, Mark thrashing around in bed, his agitation stark and overwhelming. Here I was in the same emergency department almost five months later, as if caught in a revolving door. How was it possible that this could be happening again?

It was clear to me, after taking one look at Mark's sweat-drenched, frowning face, that he was in urgent need of a CAT scan and treatment. He would need a shunt again. No! I heard the scream, unsure if my vocal cords had actually thrust the word into the room. My hands grabbed the cold metal rail of the bed frame.

The only reason why I had decided to subject Mark to the removal of the cyst was so that he would not need another shunt. Even a decade later, I tremble at the memory of the naked fear that spread through me. Although Mark's pain-induced moaning about a month earlier had pushed me to the very edge of the abyss, I had managed to hang on. But this additional emergency confronted me with an image that I was not able to endure. Because of Mark's recent major brain surgery, the hydrocephalus-induced swelling was visible. I do not know how I survived that day, dry-retching again and again, caught in a black terror that threatened to destroy me. The texture of this feeling of being crushed into nothingness was thick and sticky. Impenetrable. It literally felt as though I might cease to exist. My body. Me.

Gurgling and a sharp intake of breath from Mark jerked me out of my shock. I straightened myself up and raced over to him. Holding his hand, I leant right over his face, my nose almost touching his. Mark's fear-riddled eyes focused on me. His pupils were dilated, giving him a harrowed expression. I could feel his attention on me.

As another pain attack started, I instructed Mark, "Breathe. Keep breathing. That's it."

When the doctor on duty in the ED talked to me, he did not seem to be in any rush to treat Mark. Isn't he aware of the urgency of the situation? Because it was a Saturday there were no staff on duty to perform a CAT scan. This was a major public hospital, and no one was immediately available. It was unclear how long it would take the person on call to get to the hospital.

I came close to losing it with the emergency doctor, to screaming at him and making a scene. I knew that a delay in treating hydrocephalus could easily cause more brain damage, especially to an already traumatised brain that had just undergone major surgery. Anger, fear and disbelief choked me as if a large hand slowly squeezed around my throat.

"Look," I implored the doctor. "Mark urgently needs a CAT scan right now. Hydrocephalus is serious."

"Don't worry. It's all right. There's no rush. I've called the radiologist."

I made tight fists with my hands to stop them from throttling him. They were poised for action. "Actually, this is urgent. I know what the dangers of hydrocephalus are." I hoped the urgency in my voice would penetrate his casual attitude.

Out of the corner of my eye I saw Ina walking towards me. Intuitively, I knew that she was my lifeline in a very literal way. Looking back, I am sure that without her I would have cracked like a seed pod that spills its life force all over the ground, with only the broken shell left behind. My friend stopped that shell from shattering that day. There were fractures and spillage, but the shell, though damaged, remained in one piece.

Ina immediately grasped the urgency of Mark's renewed hydrocephalus and approached the doctor. At last, I was able to focus my energies on supporting Mark, who was in need of both emotional and practical help. His pain came in waves like contractions during labour. I walked back to his bedside, placed my face next to his, and guided him again to breathe through the next wave of pain. With his eyes wide open, he followed my advice.

Later on, Ina pulled me to the side. "Katrin, the doctor really reacted to seeing Mark responding to you. He paid close attention to the way Mark's eyes were glued to you and how he followed your instructions. Arghh." She raised her hands to her temples, shaking her head. "I know that the doctor thought Mark was in a vegetative state. When he saw the way you two interacted, he actually said that he couldn't believe how much Mark responded to you."

Finally, hours later, Mark was wheeled off for the CAT scan. Afterwards, a neurologist who I had never met approached me and, without introducing himself, confirmed what I already knew, that Mark had hydrocephalus again.

He turned to me, beckoning me to follow him into a quiet corner. Through eye contact, I invited Ina to come along.

"What do you want to do?" he asked.

"What do you mean?" I responded incredulously.

"Do you want to operate or not?"

A flash of hope surged through me. Maybe there was another alternative to yet another shunt operation.

"Well, if it's not absolutely necessary, then of course I would like to avoid it. What else can we do?"

The neurologist and Ina glanced at each other knowingly.

"Your husband needs the operation to relieve the pressure from the built-up brain fluid," he said, his eyes darting erratically about the room, avoiding my eyes.

My mouth opened, but no words escaped, my mind unwilling to comprehend the implications of what he had just told me.

"I want to operate of course," I said a moment later and walked off.

Ina caught up with me.

"I'm so angry with the doctor," I told her. "What he did was wrong. This is akin to euthanasia. He's asking me to withhold treatment. *To let my husband die.*" I held my head in my hands, pushing the palms into my temples. "The doctor has no right to throw something like this at me in such an ambiguous way. He didn't even make it clear to me that he's actually asking me to withhold treatment." I shook my head, over and over. "And there was no social worker present. I can't believe it. I just cannot believe it."

"It isn't active euthanasia, Katrin. It's withholding treatment, which is legal," Ina replied. "I do agree of course that the way he delivered it, so concealed, was dreadful. He was feeling extremely uncomfortable." She sighed. "It's so obvious that doctors aren't adequately trained to communicate compassionately with patients and their family."

"For crying out loud!" An involuntary scream escaped from my throat. "I still can't believe that this doctor is asking me to let my husband die."

I walked down the hallway, craving a moment alone in this large hospital full of patients, doctors and visitors. I stumbled outside. *How could he be so insensitive?*

I shivered. A strong wind penetrated my skin. Goose bumps ran down my arms. I did not want to move away, as if hoping the wind could sweep away what had just transpired. My disbelief. And my rage at the injustice of it all.

Suddenly it occurred to me that I must phone my mother-in-law to tell her that Mark was going to need another shunt. This would be a real blow to her. Now he would have to live with a shunt for the rest of his life, with all the risk that entailed. The future looked so much bleaker. *Was there even a future?*

When Mark was being prepared for surgery, Ina and I went outside, walking across the dark green lawn of a football oval across the road from the hospital.

"Ina, the chances of this blockage re-occurring after the removal of the cyst is only about one percent. One fucking percent!" I yelled, the sound echoing across the oval. "You know, several times they've said there's been a tiny, unlikely percentage of serious complications. And yet they've happened." My forefinger and thumb indicated a wafer-thin gap.

Ina pulled me into a tight embrace. I felt her heart beating against my chest. She stroked my hair. I let my head fall forwards onto her shoulder. We sank onto the ground. My hand swiped over the grass. I did not register the moisture on my palm. I looked up.

"Oh, Ina, what am I going to do about the party tonight?"

"Hmm. I don't know either. How do you feel about seeing your friends?"

I stared at the specks of soil on my palm. "Well, I think that if the operation goes well, I'll go ahead with it tonight. But I won't tell anyone what happened today or I'll crack."

"Ok. That's what we'll do."

We stayed at the hospital until Mark was out of surgery and back in intensive care. The shunt operation proceeded without problem.

It was 7 p.m. by the time Ina and I got to my place. Friends were there already with Rahel and Joschka. As I went to my bedroom to get changed, more people arrived. I did not tell anyone that night what had happened. It was so overlaid with unreality as to be obscured.

The atmosphere at my house was electrifying. Michael put dance music on. With the music vibrating, ten of us immediately took to the living room floor. Instead of solitary dancing, we threaded our arms around one another. We looked at each other, holding each other's gaze. Tears and smiles intermingled.

It still seems unfathomable, looking back with the buffer of a decade in between, that it was possible for me to experience such trauma and be able on the same day to feel love for and from my friends, to feel connected in the face of this level of vulnerability.

This paved the way for me to experience the extremes of emotion within a short space of time. Later, I consciously realised the significance of opening myself up to diving into the waters of love, for my children and my friends, of being really there in that moment of positive emotion, however brief. And for many months to come, that was how those moments were – short-lived, but nevertheless real. It surprised me when it happened. I allowed myself to sink into it, to breathe it in and to circulate it around my body with my pulsating blood. It no longer felt wrong, or dishonouring. I recognised it as an opening up to life.

Ina called me the day after the birthday party. "Katrin, I'm glad you had your party. It was so … special."

"Yes, it was incredible. I felt so close to you and the others. I've already had a few calls this morning. Everyone seemed to have noticed the strong connection." Chirping drew my attention. I turned my head and saw a couple of rainbow lorikeets sitting side by side on a branch just outside my window. A ray of sunshine lit up the orange feathers. "It took friendship to another level, don't you think?"

"Absolutely. It brings tears to my eyes just thinking about it." I could hear Ina blow her nose. "There was so much love. I felt the connection, too."

"I'll never forget last night." I paused, thinking about the traumatising day in emergency. "And it is especially unbelievable that it happened on the same day as Mark's second hydrocephalus … and the doctor's disguised prompting to let Mark die."

"Neither will I, Katrin, neither will I."

13

After a period of recovery in hospital following the shunt surgery, Mark was transferred back to Brightwater. I tried to settle into a new routine there, and usually arranged with staff that Mark was in a wheelchair during my visits so that I could take him to a nearby park.

On a sunny winter morning, I pushed Mark's wheelchair along the footpath. I struggled to navigate the heavy, squealing wheels over the curb. At the park, I turned Mark's chair around so that it came to rest next to a bench, which was nestled amongst gumtrees. I breathed in the faint scent of eucalyptus. Melodious birdsong filled the air.

"Look Mark, there's a butcher bird over there. I never knew them until you pointed the one out to me that lands on our balcony every few days." I stared at the bird. "I wonder if it still comes."

The white cotton blanket had fallen to the ground. I picked it up and, as I tucked it around Mark's legs, I said, "Remember when I migrated to Australia, I was so incredibly stirred up inside, and you were the one then to tuck a blanket around me in the plane."

The butcher bird continued its melodic song.

"Even though I never had any doubt that I wanted to move to Australia, that I wanted to live there with you, saying goodbye to my family was so bloody hard."

We had flown to Melbourne on the 28th of February, 1986. The preceding weeks had been decidedly emotional for my family and me. I was only twenty-one, and we did not know when I would be back for a holiday. Everyday life together and weekend visits would come to an abrupt halt. Despite my youth, I was certain I would never come back to live in Germany. The call of sunny, laid-back Australia was powerful, palpable and permanent.

~

Walking down the jet bridge at Frankfurt airport was the hardest thing I had ever experienced as a young woman. While I lingered in a last embrace with my dad, tears streamed down his face. I could not recall having seen my father cry before. His sadness fractured my heart more than anything else. My legs began to shake. I squeezed my parents' hands one more time, still holding on to both their hands as I began to walk backwards. My mum, dad and brother stood huddled together as I swayed down the endless passageway. I turned around every few steps, the outline of the three figures blurred in the distance.

"I remember that moment of wobbling down the jetway with such clarity," I said, stroking Mark's face. I lifted my head and saw the butcher bird taking flight. Its mate followed.

"Now that we have our own children, I find it even more remarkable how supportive my parents were of me leaving." Sitting on the end of the bench, I leant my head against the wheelchair. Our cheeks touched.

Mark had been aware of how remarkable my parents' support was. On 1 July 1985, he wrote to me:

I know how close you and Ingrid are and yet she encourages us so much to do our own thing, realising it's a loss to herself. What a great person!

I stood up and looked at my husband. His body was pushed even more against the side of the wheelchair. How can I possibly begin to comprehend that Mark is now locked in his body? I mulled over how I had been torn up inside at Frankfurt airport the day I migrated. If only I could have that kind of being torn up back again, I thought. With a bright future looming in the background.

If only I could free Mark. Give him back his vibrant body.

~

On the weekend, Rahel and Joschka came to visit their dad. The four of us went to the common room and the kids played games while I talked to Mark. Rahel interrupted her play at regular intervals to come over to us. Leaning on the armrest of the wheelchair, she kissed her dad on the cheek and smiled at him. I saw the light flicker in his eyes. Joschka, too, kept running up to his dad. He rested his small hands on his father's legs before dashing back to the toys. I knew that he was more relaxed than he had been in hospital because he pulled his sister's arm with his customary cheeky smile.

The periods when I could take Mark outside or to the common room were brief, though, as he could not remain in the wheelchair for long because of the involuntary muscle spasms, a source of ongoing severe pain. The staff put him in a side position in the mornings for a period of time to stretch his limbs, but this would soon become too painful. Something had to be done.

The physiotherapist pulled me aside. "Mark urgently needs a custom-made wheelchair that is capable of supporting his current body posture," she told me.

I looked through the door at Mark. His left leg hovered over the floor, stuck in between the two footrests.

"I've tried everything I can, but it's impossible to seat Mark in the standard wheelchairs available here." Her shoulders drooped forward and the lines around her mouth deepened.

I had observed that the physiotherapist had put cushioning at various places on the wheelchair as well as providing extra support to his head and arms. Despite all these efforts, Mark was only able to stay in the chair for about an hour a day. He could not join the other residents in the living room. He had to spend nearly all of his time lying in bed in his single room. Alone.

A cosmetic surgeon came to Brightwater on a voluntary basis to give any residents who needed pain relief some Botox injections, which is used in cosmetic surgery, but can also provide pain relief for muscle spasms. Mark received some shots for his bent neck. They did not help.

~

Financially, my husband was falling through the cracks in the system. As Brightwater was a private facility, everything had to be paid for, including the wheelchair and medications. Until now, the public health system had covered all the bills. The other patients at Brightwater generally fell into two categories: either they were on social welfare, or they had been involved in an accident and had been awarded a major pay-out.

As Mark was in receipt of a small amount of income protection payment, marginally more than the social welfare payments of the other patients, he was not entitled to public funding. Nor eligible to receive a wheelchair. I would have to find the money to pay for it.

Sophie, the social worker, was supportive. She had asked to see me in her office. As I entered, she stood up. Her slender frame moved across the room without a sound, the silence an eerie contrast to the noises outside. We sat down opposite each other.

"Katrin, I've been thinking about how we can fund Mark's wheelchair." Sitting on the edge of the armchair, she folded her delicate hands in her lap, her knees close to mine. "We could apply for a grant from the Lotteries Commission."

"Do you know how much it might cost?" I asked.

"About five thousand dollars." She leaned towards me. "But I don't want you to worry. We'll find a way to fund it."

I stared at the space between us, thinking about the trauma and life insurance we had applied for a week or two before Mark fell into his coma. How it must have rested on a desk, in amongst a neat pile of other forms when Mark's relative, who was our insurance agent, contacted the insurer immediately after hearing about Mark's illness. I wondered what would have happened if he had not done that. If he had not been a relative, he would have had no way of knowing. The trauma insurance would have enabled me to buy the wheelchair and pay for Mark's residential fee.

Sophie leaned towards me and placed her hand on my arm. My eyes focused on her.

"Katrin, I'm going to make a suggestion to you. This isn't going to be easy for you to hear." She paused. "I want you to think about officially separating from your husband."

I gasped and shook my head in small, slow movements.

"I know that this is very difficult for you, but it would help financially with the extra pressure of your husband residing away from home. You could apply for social security payments for yourself and the children, and on behalf of Mark as well when his insurance runs out. It isn't necessary yet, but I want you to know that this is an option in the future."

Separating from Mark?

As I stroked his knotted fingers back in his room, I thought about how excited we had been buying our first home. We had been living in a cottage close to Canning River for four years. Complete with regular glimpses of dolphins frolicking in the water while we had breakfast on our porch. The rent was astonishingly low for such a prestigious area, because it was a small, old house, surrounded by high-end large homes. Our landlord knocked on the door one evening when I was pregnant with Rahel. He told us that the cottage would be knocked down to make room for a new mansion.

Though we were upset at first, this prompted us to buy our own home before the arrival of our baby. My parents offered to lend us the necessary deposit. Mark had been in his current job at the City of South Perth for exactly the minimum six months required to be eligible for a home loan.

It was my dream to stay in the area where we lived, but this was financially out of reach. We looked at houses further afield. As my belly grew, so did my impatience. After having gone to home inspections together for weeks, one Saturday morning, I noticed a duplex in the neighbouring suburb advertised in the paper. It sounded interesting and it was just five minutes away. This was the first time I went without Mark to a home open. As I was driving up the hill, I remembered that I had previously thought I would really like to live in this street. I parked my car out the front and practically ran up the long concrete driveway, my belly swaying from side to side. The first thing I saw was beautiful wide jarrah floorboards and a quaint fireplace. Tears rolled down my cheeks. This is it, I kept thinking. I had to stop myself from jumping up and down in excitement.

I stepped outside and walked up to a low white picket fence, thinking that this would be the end of the garden. When I looked closer, I noticed that there was a large garden at the back of the house. I scrutinised the pamphlet that the real estate agent had handed me to double check the price. It had just been dropped fifteen percent and was now just within our range.

Having walked through the house, I forced myself to stroll out the door while the real estate agent watched me for giveaway signs. Once he turned away, I dashed to my car and jerked it into gear.

"Mark!" I yelled when I thrust our front door open. "Guess what? I've found our home. This is it. This is really it."

He gave me an amused look.

"Come on, you've got to see it. We've got fifteen minutes left of this home inspection."

We made an offer the next day.

I studied the familiar freckles on Mark's hand. That's twelve years ago that we moved into our own home, I thought, and now I'm meant to separate from Mark. As if he'll never move back home.

14

Mark's extreme pain attacks continued for months. His legs could no longer be straightened, as the muscles contracted unceasingly. It took all this time for me to find out what the cause of these muscle spasms was: following on from meningitis, Mark's brain was sending contradictory messages to both groups of muscles simultaneously, the contractor muscles and the extensor muscles. Both muscle groups tried to straighten and bend his arms and legs at the same time. It was relentless.

In hindsight, the fact that it took so long for me to find out the cause of the sudden, wild spasms that began more than four months into Mark's illness, and that I cannot even remember how I came to know, shows me how much my personality was affected by being in survival mode: I did not push for answers. The surreal nature of that time reminds me of a spiral-bound book I had as a child. Its pages were splashed with rainbow coloured, hand-drawn pictures of people and they were split into three parts that could be turned separately: one showed the head, the second the torso and the last the legs. All sorts of weird combinations were possible, such as a policeman wearing a housewife's apron on top of the spindly legs of a child. My life had morphed into a reality that was no longer recognisable, like a clown with a weightlifter's body and a ballerina tutu. Mark's current body state resembled surreal combinations – this should only exist in the imagination, the unreal.

At night, lying awake in bed, I couldn't shake off the image of Mark's face distorted in pain, perspiration collecting on his forehead, legs shaking furiously. It had settled into my mind with piercing vividness. And Mark's regular bursts of moaning echoed through my head with the same lucidity. My helplessness to relieve his suffering destroyed my sense of self. I no longer recognised myself or the world I inhabited. It was as if I were looking through the focal point of a microscope – existence had narrowed down to a pain-laden landscape.

There was nothing I could do to relieve his pain attacks; no amount of massaging, stroking, or love could make a difference. I was locked into the position of bystander, feeling his suffering with the nerves of my own body, aware day and night of his muscle spasms and torment, powerless to alleviate. It was all I thought about, even at home with the kids, unable to comprehend the cruelty of his suffering. This inability to make any sense of what was happening locked me into a pitch-black tunnel, without an escape hatch or sprinkle of light. Looking back, I don't know how I got through it without getting sick myself. But the drive to be there for Mark was so strong that getting ill, which would have meant being unable to visit him, was simply not an option. At the time, I didn't see it as resilience, but sheer determination. That's all I had left under my control.

By now, notwithstanding the muscle contractions, in a twist of fate, Mark was completely paralysed, unable to move deliberately in any way. Whatever minuscule movement he had earlier in his left foot which got him accepted into Brightwater had vanished. It was not until much later that I came to understand that he had *locked-in syndrome*, which is a very rare neurological disorder that causes almost complete paralysis except for eye movement. The patient is cognitively aware but cannot speak.

The repeated muscle spasms brought with them concerning weight loss. The amount of liquid food Mark was given through the PEG was dictated by a chart when he was in Sir Charles Gairdner Hospital that determined the nutritional needs according to body weight – but for an immobile patient. In a harsh twist of fate, Mark, locked in his body, unable to move, burned off additional calories through the involuntary muscle contractions. But his PEG feeds were not increased; the nutritionist at the hospital stuck to her charts. I tried to convince her to increase his food intake, but she refused. I was powerless again to instigate any change.

The rigidity of the hospital-system left no room for individual needs and circumstances. The institution as a whole constrained those individual nurses and doctors who tried to care for those whose situations were curved and could not be made to fit the institutional standard square boxes. As a wife of a patient who was one hundred percent dependent on the medical care offered by the hospital system, I had been disempowered to help him.

Years later, I still find myself unable to make sense of the reasoning the nutritionist gave me for not increasing Mark's feeds. Stabbing at her folder with her forefinger, her eyes fierce, she raised her voice. "I've told you before," she said, her voice vibrating with angry undertones. "This is what the chart says and I'm not seeing any need to change it. This is the correct amount of feeds."

When I confronted her with Mark's worrying weight loss, she refused to comment on it.

My outrage that Mark's stomach acid burn did not get attended to by the gastroenterology staff for three full days lives on. This was another hospital situation that shows up the alarming rigidity of an institution that categorises a patient according to their original illness, in Mark's case neurological, and that lacks the flexibility to respond quickly to care needs outside the particular ward. Many individual doctors and nurses who are highly professional and caring are constrained by the working of the institutional framework as a whole.

At Brightwater, the staff was well aware of Mark's pain. In an effort to address the situation, they took him by bus to a wheelchair specialist who was to build a custom-made chair with all the special padding that was needed. But before the ordering of the wheelchair went ahead, Mark's increasing pain had prompted the staff to liaise with the rehab specialist at Shenton Park who knew Mark from his previous stay there. The idea was born that a Botox pump might provide pain relief. Such a pump, I found out, is surgically inserted into the spine and gives off Botox at regular intervals directly to the nerves. They arranged for Mark to be transferred to Shenton Park for a Botox pump trial. It was explained to me that a pump costs $12,000 and that it would not have made sense to put him through the strain of the surgery if it did not work for him. If it did work, I would have to fund it myself. The social worker at Brightwater went out of her way to assure me that she would help me to find a way to raise the money.

Due to Mark's medical bills, I thought of writing to the insurer of our rejected life and trauma insurance. I explained our situation, that we had filled in the policy application form in good faith, and that I was asking if they would make a one-off ex gratia payment, a small portion of the modest trauma insurance component that would have been paid to us had the policy been accepted. I thought that it would have to be extraordinarily rare for people to fill in an insurance policy and a debilitating illness to strike while it is being assessed. I knew such a payment, made out of humanitarian compassion, would not carry any legal obligations, in case they were concerned about having to make future payments.

I received a reply from the insurers. I ripped open the letter, my palms damp against the paper. Not only was it a letter of rejection, it was an automated reply. The cold and impersonal language of the standard issue letter and the absence of any human note left a metallic taste in my mouth that lingered.

Early in August, not even two months after initially arriving at Brightwater, Mark was transferred to Shenton Park for the Botox trial. It was supposed to be a brief stay.

~

Here Mark was, back in Ward 1. Not as a rehab patient, but as an itinerant visitor passing through.

I needed to get the current pin code to exit the ward. My shoes squeaked as I walked down the stained linoleum floor towards the nurses' station. Yes, I was back in Shenton Park.

The highly trained physiotherapist pushed Mark's wheelchair into the large gym area. This is when I discovered how damaging it is to a muscle that contracts not to receive specialist physio treatment. From our conversation, it became obvious that targeted treatment by the physiotherapists in Sir Charles Gairdner hospital to counteract the contractions as soon as the muscle spasms had started would have been necessary in order to prevent permanent damage to Mark's muscles. Now it was too late. His muscles would never recover even if the spasms were to cease. I glanced at his contorted body, a mere shadow of his former self. He would never look like his old self again.

I could not endure to see Mark wrestling with his contracted limbs, locked into permanent pain, for much longer. I dragged myself through a hazy world that had become unbearable. A few remnants of hope, like spindly, solitary blades of grass sprouting from the ground, remained: everything now rested with the Botox pump trial. Would it provide the necessary relief required for Mark's chronic pain? Would it offer me a patch of solid ground, enough to stop me from falling down the abyss?

The day of the pump trial arrived. I caught up with the specialist afterwards.

"I'm sorry, Katrin, but the Botox didn't work in the way we'd hoped." He looked at me, his eyes soft.

"What does that mean? Did it work at all?"

"Well, not really. The response to the Botox was so minimal as to be insignificant. Also, I had to increase the amount of Botox to the maximum level, and still there wasn't really any relief. Certainly not enough to justify the risk of putting a Botox pump in."

Hot tears burned my eyes. Hope stopped whispering in my ear.

"I'm very, very sorry."

I went back to Mark, saw his face distorted from pain. Where to from here? What am I going to do to help you? The greyness of the little corner Mark's bed was in was overwhelmingly dreary. Mark, oh Mark. I don't know what's going to happen now.

Joschka's words, spoken about two months earlier, echoed in my ears. At eight years of age he had said, standing in front of me, at eye level with me as I was sitting down on our couch, that if Dad needed to die in order to be free from pain, then he would let him go. It had left me speechless.

At that time, I had not reached that point. Now, things could no longer go on like this. Yes, Joschka, you're right, I said to myself. If death is the only option left for Dad to be free, then I'm also willing to let him go.

I visited Mark in the evening. It was already dark outside. He was coughing, struggling. His breathing was laboured and wheezy. I sensed that there was something wrong with him. Immediately, I spoke to a nurse.

"What's going on with Mark? He's coughing and looks really unwell."

"Oh no, he's fine. We haven't noticed anything. There's nothing to worry about."

I left it at that. In the past they had always picked up when something was wrong with Mark. I was so tired. Exhausted to the point of having trouble staying awake, and yet at night I could not sleep. Maybe I was not as alert as normal because of the insomnia. I just could not think straight. I wandered out of the hospital that night, uneasy.

When I arrived at the ward the next morning, Mark had been moved to the opposite room. Even with an oxygen mask his breathing was laboured. The curtains were drawn around his bed.

A nurse grabbed me. Mark had pneumonia. I went back to his cubicle. Blank fear flickered in his eyes. I stood next to his bed, hearing the rattling in his airways, watching helplessly as he laboured with each breath. His forehead was covered in sweat.

Later on in the day, a doctor approached me. I was asked into a small, narrow room that functioned as an office.

"Mrs Den Elzen, Mark's pneumonia is severe," he told me. "We're currently waiting for his pathology reports to come back. We've put him on antibiotics."

The next day Mark's results were back. I was back in the tiny office.

"We have the results from pathology. It doesn't look good. Mark isn't responding to the antibiotics. The tests show that his body is not able to fight the pneumonia."

"Not able to fight the pneumonia?"

"His blood count cell is showing that his immune system isn't working anymore."

"What does that mean? What's going to happen?"

"If his immune system isn't able to fight off the pneumonia he will die, as the antibiotics are not working. I'm very sorry."

"I wasn't aware that his immune system is shot." After a long silence I asked, "Is there anything we can do to help him die in peace?"

"We'll call in palliative care and they'll administer pain relief and make Mark comfortable."

"How long will it take?"

"It could be as soon as forty-eight hours. Or maybe a week. It's hard to say."

"Forty-eight hours! I want to stay with Mark. Can I do that?"

"Of course you can. You can stay overnight. In fact, what we'll do is give Mark a single room and put another bed in there for you. Then you can stay with him the whole time."

Until this point in time, I had not realised that he was in danger of passing away. I had known for a while that he probably would have to live in a residential care facility, but even that had seemed unbelievable. He'd had pneumonia before. No one had spoken to me about the possibility that Mark might die.

I could see that his battered body, having endured multiple brain surgeries and masses of medication, as well as being malnourished, had nothing left to fight off this pneumonia. His body was defenceless. My sweetheart had given it his utmost, tried to stay alive for his children and me. I could not have endured what he did. Staying alive as long as he did.

Knowing that Mark's only chance of peace and freedom was death did not make it any easier to cope with it. I had never witnessed anyone dying. And now the first person I was going to support in death was my own husband. I was utterly unprepared for this task.

15

True to their word, the staff moved Mark into a single room. As I walked along the hallway next to my husband being pushed on his bed, I thought how a single room should indicate a victory on the road to rehabilitation. Not the collapse of it.

This was the first time in the nearly eight-month battle for survival that hope slipped through my fingers, irretrievable, like a mountain climber who holds her fellow abseiler on a single rope after he has lost his footing and dangles on a steep vertical rock face. She grips the rope beyond the limits of endurance, until it slips through her fingers, slicing skin.

Once Mark had survived the first week after his initial entry to hospital, I had come to believe that he would live. The question had always been in my mind whether he would ever be able to return home, but the possibility of death somehow had disappeared from sight. Looking back, it seems surprising that I didn't realise that, in his precarious state, death was always an option. But then again, the brush of ordinary logic cannot be applied to the canvas of crisis.

Unlike hope, death was a stranger to me. I had no idea what the actual process of dying entailed. After settling Mark into his new room, I had to go home to tell Rahel and Joschka what was happening. I struggled to keep my concentration on the traffic and ran into a car in front of me at a red light at slow speed. I had no words to respond to the angry barrage raining down on me.

At home I asked both children to come upstairs with me. They sat on either side of me on our blue couch, looking at me expectantly, their eyes wide open. I held their hands, looking from one to the other. And then I told them the truth, that their father had caught pneumonia again and that this time his body was no longer responding to the medication and that this meant that he would die. Rahel and Joschka both burst out saying that they did not want their dad to suffer any more, that they wanted him to be free from pain.

I told them that I would be staying with Dad overnight and that I did not know how long I would be at the hospital with him. And then a miracle happened. Joschka, who had not been able to spend a long time with his father because it hurt too much to see him locked in his body, spontaneously said to me, "Mama, I'm coming with you. I want to stay with you and Dad at the hospital."

"Darling, are you sure? I wouldn't be able to drive you home in the middle of the night if you changed your mind. You'd need to sleep with me in the single bed next to Dad's all night. Would you be okay with that?"

"Yes. I want to stay with you at the hospital."

Rahel stayed at home with my parents. The first night at the hospital was spooky. The hustle and bustle of the daytime now seemed other worldly. The regular whooshing from the iron lung next door pierced through the silence. This elongated metal contraption, the only remaining one in Western Australia, belonged to a man named Paul Berry. This ward had been his permanent home since the 1950s when he was struck down by polio.

The bathroom that I was to use at night was a large communal bathroom set up for the patients. When I went to the toilet in the dimmed down light, I had to wander past two large bedrooms. There was a lot of stirring in patients' sleep, rustling bed covers, coughing and snoring. Apart from those noises, there was an eerie silence.

Joschka and I snuggled up in our single bed that had been pushed right up against the windowsill. He was lying next to the wall and I was in the middle between my two "boys". Mark's bed was very close to mine and I held his hand. He seemed to like that. It calmed him.

The next day a specialist from palliative care arrived, a softly spoken man. Mark was going to receive a butterfly pump that would provide pain relief. The same day a nurse placed the pump under the skin on his chest. The change in Mark right under my eyes was phenomenal. His facial muscles relaxed. For the first time in about four months, he was pain free.

Over the ensuing days Mark was alert and able to connect with me again, focusing on me when I was close with breathtaking presence. He was awake and alert for hours on end.

Joschka stayed at the hospital for two or three nights. When I had been told that Mark could be passing away within two days, I had rung up all of his relatives. His family from Melbourne was only a plane ride of four hours away and they came over to Perth quickly. As did my parents from Germany. Within days, everyone had arrived to say their goodbyes.

There was one memorable evening that stands out for me with graphic clarity. Mark had his parents, me, the kids, and my parents present at the hospital, all circled around his bed within the small room. We made everyone fit and the rehab staff was very accommodating. Rikie sat on the bed close by her son's side, within his eyesight. In all the times she had visited him, she had never got to see him wide awake and truly alert, as I had experienced many times before the extreme pain had set in. Now Mark was present. Everyone in the room became aware of the connection happening and tuned in. The room fell silent. Rikie spoke to her son, and he listened. He responded through intense eye contact. His ability to remain present for an extended period of time was astounding. His body was full of morphine, yet he remained continuously alert for several hours.

Day after day continued with Mark and me in the room together around the clock. Our relatives took care of the children, who came to visit regularly. Most days Mark remained awake for hours. Seeing his face relaxed rather than distorted with agony was beyond words. After months of constant extreme pain, he had now been given some freedom to be a bit of himself again. We were able to weave threads again, the two of us, to connect.

One morning, after waking up by Mark's side, I let my gaze wander around the room, letting my eyes settle on each of the photos of us that I had pinned up all over the walls. All those happy memories from holidays, and moments from the children's lives, such as the first day at school, gleamed on the walls. No new memories would be added to these. Not with Mark in them. The thought was simply unimaginable.

A week and a half went by with me staying constantly by Mark's side. The surreal feeling at night of having been transplanted into another world or dimension remained with me. It always took me a while in the mornings to leave the nocturnal spaceship when the nurses and aides arrived, turning the ward from eerie silence into a buzzing bee hive.

After nearly two weeks, the palliative care specialist from the hospital came over to Shenton Park again and made an appointment with me.

"Katrin, I want to discuss something with you. I'd like to suggest to you to move Mark to a hospice."

I drew in my breath sharply.

"The thing is," he continued, his facial expression soft, almost tender, "that this is a rehabilitation ward, and the staff here are used to and want to see patients improving. Right now, they are getting upset about seeing Mark passing away. It's taking longer than the doctors had anticipated. This is difficult for the nurses."

"Oh." I pressed the palms of my hands against each other in my lap. "I understand what you're saying. But I'm very wary of moving Mark again. It's so unsettling for him and takes him days to get over." I looked down at my hands, not seeing. "This comes as a surprise. Another move was the last thing on my mind."

Dr. Kim's full attention rested on me. He was not trying to brush me off. "I understand your concerns. However, I feel that the move would be fine. There's a bed available at Murdoch hospice. They have wonderful staff there and are equipped and trained to help people die as comfortably as possible. That's what they do."

"Murdoch. My God. That's where Mark went to university. That would be the first time since falling ill that he'd be close to our home."

"What I would suggest is that you go to the hospice and have a look. How does that sound?"

The room was quiet for a moment. "Okay. I'll do that."

The small figure of the doctor left. Back in Mark's room, I let my eyes wander around the entire space. I felt torn between worrying about the effects of another move on Mark and understanding the emotional turmoil of the staff. They had been very caring, and I did not want to cause them any distress. I was grateful for the care Mark was receiving. The staff who worked in this unit, caring for people with acquired brain injury, clearly had a difficult job. However, it was very telling that the retention rate of staff was unusually high. The nurses cared and it showed. They stayed around for a long time, some even more than a decade. They were here to make things better. And they could not do that for us.

I picked up the piece of paper with the phone number of the hospice that the specialist had given me and dialled the number to make an appointment.

16

In the afternoon I went to Murdoch Hospice. Although almost adjacent to a freeway, it was sheltered from the world by a tranquil garden of native plants and flowers. A circular driveway right in front of the entrance made it feel more like a resort than a hospital or hospice. No visible sign gave its real purpose away. I saw a friendly, single-storey cream brick building. It was a large structure that weaved its way through its lush surroundings.

My first impression that this was not like a hospital continued as I entered the building. The atmosphere exuded calmness and friendliness. Whilst the receptionist called the nurse I had come to see, I let my eyes wander through the room. On the opposite side was a purple two-seater sofa. Soft lighting created the feeling of being in a hotel lobby. This impression was interrupted by three unassuming wheelchairs that huddled almost apologetically in the corner to the left of the entrance. One wheelchair was partially folded as if to take up even less space.

A middle-aged woman arrived, her eyes framed by an abundance of laughter lines, and took me on a tour of the hospice. As soon as we walked down a short hallway that opened up into a long passage, I was mesmerised by a large sculpture of a grass tree, forged out of rusty metal.

"We're having an art exhibition at the moment. It's being prepared right now and will open on Monday. That's why this area is filled with so many items. Normally it's empty."

Down the hallway, we turned into a passageway on the left. Here, the single rooms for patients were located along a horseshoe shaped corridor. All the rooms opened onto the garden. I decided that it would be a good place for Mark to be.

He would be coming back into our local area, just ten minutes down the road from home. It was meaningful to me that he had studied in the same suburb – Murdoch – that the hospice was in. The university and the hospice were located opposite one another, divided only by a road. Murdoch University … Mark had spent three happy years there. The campus was relatively small, with an abundance of giant ghost gumtrees. With Mark's deep fondness for native plants and trees, it was a pleasant environment for him.

After we had both finished university in Perth, Mark and I had lived in Taiwan for six months, where I had studied Mandarin. Upon our return, Mark had looked for work. A period of several years followed where he worked for local governments under contract, and then their funds would dry up and he would be out of work for a while until securing the next contract with the same or another local government. During this time, our family grew with the arrival of our two children. Rahel, with her blue eyes and round cheeks, was the spitting image of her dad. Joschka, on the other hand, with his brown eyes and olive skin, took after my side of the family.

Holding my baby girl in my arms, skin to skin, and breathing in her sweet smell, not of perfumed baby products but her own inherent scent, had evoked a deep level of contentment I had never known before. And I remember the four of us in bed, Rahel snuggled against me, lying motionless on her back, both arms tucked close to her body so as not to wake her brother, who was nestled onto Mark's chest, a proud *I'm a big sister* smile playing on her lips. Joschka's little body heaved up and down with each of his father's breaths. I gazed at my husband's face, moved by his serene expression. His cheeks glowed, lit up with a hint of dark pink, and his eyes sparkled, the usual cheekiness replaced with a soft brightness. This was a joyful time.

One of the things I admired most in Mark was his ability to be calm and understanding. I did not know anyone who was as non-judgemental as he. If I was upset about something he would say "Schatz, you don't know why that happened. There's probably a reason that we're not aware of. Let's see what we can do."

I was impulsive by nature, and Mark, calm and patient, anchored me.

Now I had to face his death without his companionship. I despaired that we could not talk about it and work through our grief together, as is the case with other terminal illnesses. He was moved to the hospice in September, having been locked into his body for over seven months. His room was spacious and had a sliding door that led onto the courtyard. Wood panelling gave the room warmth. The atmosphere at the hospice was quiet and calm, very unlike the squeaking linoleum floors of the hospital, the putrid disinfectant smell that settled into my clothes and nostrils, and the hurried activity of the medical staff. Here, all the floors were covered in a medium brown, loop-piled carpet that exuded cosiness. Nurses and volunteers walked without rushing. Doctors wore their own clothes. No white coats. Everything blended together. No invasive smells or sounds. There were no machines that beeped.

Apart from the bed, instantly recognisable as a hospital bed, the room and even the thick curtains were not unlike a hotel room. A timber chair rested in the corner for visitors. As our home was only ten minutes away and I was exhausted from having had broken sleep at the hospital for about two weeks, I consulted with the doctors and decided to sleep at home rather than in the visitor's chair. The staff assured me that if there was any change in Mark, they would call me straight away, any time of the day or night.

The move initially unsettled Mark again. New surroundings, new faces, voices, smells. At first his frown and tense face upset me. I went ahead and hung up all of our family photos on the walls yet again. After a while we both relaxed a bit. Only my parents were still with us in Perth. Mark's family had gone back to Melbourne.

There was a lot of caring in the hospice, down to small details. Mark's urine bag, which in the past had hung listlessly on the side of his bed, was now out of sight in a turquoise towelling cover. I appreciated the thought that had been put into making everyone feel comfortable and, even though it was not important, not seeing the bag and having the bright cover did make a difference.

On the third morning, a head nurse relayed a story to me that highlighted how important it was that staff took the time to properly communicate with Mark.

"Katrin, I wanted to let you know that the first time Mark was washed in the bathroom on the shower trolley he got very upset. He tightened up and he moaned. This was very disturbing for the nursing staff."

"What happened? Did they get to wash him?"

"Well, they did a bit, but not as thorough as they would have liked. I talked to the nurses to see what'd happened. Apparently, Mark was startled because he didn't know what was going on. I suggested to them that they should talk to him beforehand and to tell him throughout what they're doing and to take their time."

"Did that make a difference?"

"Yes, absolutely. Once the staff informed Mark what they were doing, he relaxed and stopped moaning."

I always knew that Mark could not only hear but also understand. Here he was after all this time, extremely weakened from being in a coma, surgeries, weight loss, medications, and still responding to instructions by nursing staff. And the neurosurgeons at the hospital had tried to tell me right at the beginning that Mark had complete brain damage.

By now, he had no strength left in his body and his muscle spasms had intensified even more. Both his legs were permanently bent and I could not straighten them, even the slightest bit. The same contortions inflicted his arms.

On the way home from the hospice, I pulled into a park and sat on a secluded bench opposite a small lake. A black swan swam past. I stared at the trail and gentle ripples he'd left in the water. The kids, I thought. Our beautiful children. How will they cope with their dad's death? What's life going to be like for them growing up without their father? The swan heaved itself out of the water and waddled past the side of my bench. Our eyes locked for a moment.

Over dinner I kept looking at Rahel's and Joschka's faces, wondering about their future. I woke up at night, heavy with fatigue, and looked at the red numbers of the digital display on my clock: 2 a.m. I got up, walked into the living room and reclined in the dark on our shell-back couch in the corner of our upstairs bay window, my head propped up on the armrest. I looked out the window and my eyes rested on the city lights in the distance. As my children and parents slept downstairs, I had this space to myself and began to sink into the quietude. I thought about Rahel and Joschka. My fatigue lifted and mental clarity arose. I wanted to give them the chance to grow up happily, not to be limited and defined by their loss during these pivotal years of growing up. I pushed myself upright into a sitting position and took a deep breath. It was clear to me that their chance at happiness hinged on my ability to find my own. And so, I dared to make the decision that I would find happiness again. It felt so far out of reach as to be unattainable, and yet I trusted that my bold decision would come true.

The next morning, the grass tree sculpture drew me to it at the hospice. The exhibition had been opened by now. Stroking the life-size sculpture, I thought about how much Mark liked native plants. I decided to purchase the artwork. Never before had I bought a large piece of art, and I let myself be guided by intuition. It simply felt right to bring that grass tree home. And it still does, today. For over a decade it has graced our spacious foyer, and it is the first thing my gaze rests on when I open the front door. It still holds the ability to make me smile at its sheer beauty and connection to Mark. Its sweeping metal strings that have been bent into the shape of the skirt of a grass tree clink when the kids brush past on the way to their rooms, the vibrations singing their way into the upstairs living room.

I received a note scribbled on tissue paper from a nurse congratulating me on my purchase. I had spoken to her about my interest in the grass tree. Warm tears welled up in my eyes. Light spread for an important moment into the dark spaces of my heart. These interactions with nursing staff, such as the note, and the occasional hug, connected me to the good stuff of our humanity, which was in danger of becoming invisible in the face of so much bleakness. I'm not sure if nurses are aware what a significant difference these connections they offered me made.

One particular memory of connecting has stayed with me. When Mark arrived in the Emergency Department of Sir Charles Gairdner Hospital on the very first day, I knew that he was on the brink of dying and that literally every second could make the difference between life or death. Inside, his bed was surrounded by one white coat next to the other, shoulder to shoulder, but no action seemed to take place. The need for speed was faded to slow motion. Aware that surgery was necessary to save Mark's life, time stretched on and on for me. A wall clock in the small room I had been asked to wait in announced each second with a loud vibration that pierced my consciousness like a jackhammer. Why wasn't Mark being taken to the theatre? The question tortured my mind. I felt trapped in the narrow room. A nurse entered with a plate of sandwiches. She took one look at me, put down the dish, and wrapped her arms around me in a tight embrace. I let myself sink into her arms, her heartbeat against mine. We lingered in each other's arms, strangers who had never exchanged a word. And yet she paused for a brief but eternal moment for me in a way that no words could have achieved. Such impulses bear the signature of our benevolence, which can get so easily drowned out by the shrill shrieking of the medical apparatus.

Another moment of compassionate connecting occurred at the hospice, when I visited Mark with both children on the weekend. The sun sent its rich rays onto Mark's left hand. As there was a sliding door in the room, I enquired if we could take him outside. This was more involved than I had anticipated. As he had lost so much weight, he was lying on an air mattress that was controlled by an electric motor. The nurse explained to me that this could not be turned off even for a short while. Then she stepped up to me, placed her hand with a gesture of utter tenderness on my arm and said, "Don't worry, I have an idea. Wait a moment."

She went away and returned with a long extension cord. Now Mark's bed could be wheeled through the glass door into the courtyard, attached to the power point next to his bed. The three of us surrounded his bed whilst a slight breeze caressed our skin. The children checked out a water fountain a few metres away from us, their laughter carrying in the wind along with the water drops they splashed into the air. It was comforting to be outdoors, to spend this time together as a family.

The hospice social worker approached me with a pressing matter: the hospice did not have the facilities to store the body of a deceased person. This meant that within a few hours of death a funeral parlour would need to come and pick up Mark's body.

I had to speak to and choose a funeral company while my sweetheart was still alive? My legs trembled. I froze. The social worker took a step towards me, placed her hands onto my shoulder and elbow, and guided me to sit down on a chair. How would I choose a funeral company whilst spending all my waking hours with Mark?

The hospice had a folder with several brochures from funeral companies. The following morning, I looked through them and arranged a meeting with one undertaker at the hospice, which took place in a windowless room. Why is it that all meetings everywhere seem to take place in windowless, depressing rooms, I wondered. A sombre-looking man dressed in a dark suit introduced himself to me. I could not believe that I sat there discussing Mark's funeral while he was alive in the room around the corner.

The man explained to me the proceedings of a funeral and left behind glossy brochures. I felt confused. It just did not feel right, but I could not tell if that was because it felt wrong to discuss Mark's funeral at that time or because it was not the right funeral company. The funeral parlour was located close to our home. On the way back from the hospice to our house, I took my dad along to see it. We were greeted by conservative religious surroundings. As soon as we walked in, I realised that this was not right for Mark. So I was back to square one. I had another look at the folder with shiny advertisements at the hospice.

The next day I drove to another funeral parlour that seemed a little more modern and neutral. Its décor was indeed more up to date, with purple walls and light beech furniture instead of the heavy dark carved furniture I had seen previously. There was the same procedure of discussing coffins and how I would like the ceremony conducted. And did I want to include the viewing of the body. Mark is still alive, for goodness' sake! Dry retching seemed to become my default mode.

The place did feel a lot better but still not quite right. I could not make a decision on the spot. The hospice urged me again to nominate a funeral parlour so that it could be noted down in Mark's medical records. I felt pressured and did not want to choose out of need.

Before I had time to make a decision regarding the second funeral company, I received a phone call at night at home. An acquaintance of mine had heard from a mutual friend that Mark was dying. She had recently joined a funeral company and was wondering if I wanted the funeral director to contact me. Later on that night, I received a call from the owner of the funeral company. We talked for a bit and I had a good feeling about her. She offered to come and see me in the morning at the hospice. I stared at the phone after the call. This is bizarre.

After meeting the funeral director the next day, I could see that she would be able to offer a service that represented Mark's essence. I was relieved to have found someone and to be able to provide the details to the hospice registrar.

That day, Mark was sleepy all day. He did not open his eyes once. When I got home, I was extremely upset. The doctor had told me that I should expect Mark to be asleep for some time before he passes away. They said that most people don't open their eyes again in the last few days. Now I will never see Mark's eyes again, I thought.

I grabbed my handbag, ran to my car, and took myself down to the river to be alone. Sitting in the car, with all of the windows closed, I sobbed uncontrollably, tears streaming down my face. Here it was, the "never ever". I don't know how long I sat there.

The following day Mark was again not awake. I took the children along to visit him and I had also arranged for them to meet the social worker to talk about their dad. Rahel and Joschka walked into their dad's room as soon as we got to the hospice. Then the three of us met with the social worker. Rahel was very articulate and did not have any difficulties expressing her emotions. It was an appropriate meeting that gave the children the opportunity to ask questions. Afterwards Rahel went back to say goodbye to her dad by herself. She told me later that Dad did open his eyes for her and that he focused on her. She was sure that he understood what she had said to him. By the time I went in to see Mark he was asleep again. Looking at Rahel was the only time in two days that he opened his eyes.

Shortly after Mark's arrival at the hospice, my father took me aside at home. He looked straight into my eyes and placed his hands on my shoulders.

"Katrin, listen to me. I want you to wake me up should the hospice ring you in the middle of the night. I want to be there for you and for Mark also. I don't want you to go through this alone. Promise me that you'll wake me."

"Oh, Papa. I promise that I'll tell you and I'm very glad that you want to come with me. I have no idea what it'll be like when Mark dies. I'm scared." I stared at the blue and beige stripes of the carpet. "But I do know that I want to be there for him."

The call came on the sixth day of Mark's stay at the hospice, at 5 a.m. I woke my father. The children and my mother woke up as well. The kids climbed into bed with their grandmother. My father and I drove off in the darkness. We had to ring the bell at the front door. Everything was whisper quiet. When I got to Mark's room, he was wide awake. I was completely taken by surprise. I had not expected to see him looking at me again. I sat down at the side of his bed and held his hand, bending down close to his face so that he could see me.

"I love you," I said.

He blinked once in response. Yes.

"Mark, I want you to know, Rahel and Joschka are going to be fine. I can do this. I'll do everything in my power to make sure they're well!" Even then, on his deathbed, Mark managed to respond a second time, blinking once for yes again.

We were so close, so connected. Knowing that he was aware of my presence meant everything to me. Mark was awake for a long time in the morning hours. He passed away that afternoon.

17

I am leaning against a worn, grey, laminated counter at the Social Security office, staring at the form in front of me. I am asked to tick the marital status box: *married, divorced, single, widowed.* My tears drop onto the paper, blurring and smudging the printed words. The box marked *widowed* remains in pristine condition.

A widow at forty? Is that the box I now inhabit?

Widowhood is alien to me. It has been dumped into my unwilling lap and rests there uneasily. It is a label that hangs off me like a pair of oversized overalls. It is a label used to describe *old* women with faint moustaches in Mediterranean villages who wear black for the rest of their lives, thus denoting to the rest of the world, and themselves, their now permanent status as widow. It is a label that I refuse. But is it as simple as that? Labels are rarely consciously chosen but imposed on us by others. Can I just say, no, that's not who I am? I don't even know who I am. I've lost myself in the terrain of the surreal landscape that I can neither recognise nor read.

I sigh and tick the box in black biro. It is a solid mark. I am beginning to grasp that there is no easy way either to inhabit or to refute this alien box, to grasp what I am feeling, or who I might be.

I am fatigued after months of daily hospital visits, where life had hovered. Exhaustion has curled up in my bones. The initial period following my loss is marked by impenetrable grief. It infuses every cell of my body, every nerve and dendrite. At home, alone, my body shakes.

~

Though I knew – with all doubt erased – that Mark had to be released from his torment, this did not lessen the despair that engulfed me following his passing. I realised that the potency of my intense grief had to shrink before I could begin the task of my recovery and decided to face my outer landscape first. Gazing into the remains of my bleak internal landscape was beyond my grasp.

When Mark was in hospital, I had promised Joschka that I would not work, that I would be there to pick him up from school every day. I kept that promise. My previous work as casual tour guide for German tourists involved shifts that I would not have been able to do as sole parent. Emotionally, I would not have been up to putting on a happy face anyway. I realised that I needed to give myself time to heal my desolate inner landscape. That without active grieving and recovery, I would not be able to realise my goal of raising my children not defined by their loss and offering them a chance at happiness.

As I stood in front of the stove one evening, mid-week, my vacant gaze directed towards the boiling pasta, my mind was flooded with images of Mark in hospital. The ringing of the phone brought me back into the kitchen.

"Katrin, we'd like to invite you over to dinner on Saturday night." Tina swallowed audibly on the other end. "We're hoping you can make it ... It's been a while, you know."

Images of a succession of shared dinners, with the four of us, the two couples, surfaced. I spun around and stirred the pasta, pushing the memories aside.

"I don't know ... maybe." I could not stop remembering our shared dinners. "Can I let you know in a couple of days?"

"Yes, sure." Tina hesitated. After a moment she added, "It's not good for you to spend Saturday night at home. You need to get out. Please, think about it."

Saturday nights and Sundays, they were the hardest. Families everywhere you went. Families everywhere you looked. Fathers with their children in shopping centres.

After I tucked Joschka into bed I went upstairs. I let my weight fall against the back of the sofa and pulled my knees up to my chin. I thought that I should open myself up to some distraction and decided to accept the dinner invitation. My friends' home was safer than a restaurant abuzz with animated people and shrill noise, the world ticking over at its usual pace as if nothing had happened to change its pulse.

This first solo invitation has embedded itself into my memory with photographic clarity. The two of them sat on one side of the table across from me. Should I stay on the left or should I shuffle into the middle to fill the space? The empty spot next to me expanded. The conversation faltered, repeatedly. The palpable absence of Mark's ready banter and his wit, delivered at lightning speed with his eyebrows raised so slightly as to be barely noticeable, hung thick in the space between us. I left early. Curled up into a ball under my doona.

Later, I turned over in bed and fumbled my way in the dark past the polished metal of the desk lamp on my bedside table. In the faint red glow of the digital clock, I could make out the scarab artefact nestled amongst a biro and a water bottle. My fingers caressed the outline of the carved, cold stone, gliding along the smooth ridge on the back that marks the wings of the beetle. I cradled the small sculpture in both my palms until it gradually got warmer, the texture of the hieroglyphs imprinted on the bottom pressing against my skin. A faint aroma of cardamom seemed to cling to the air. I drew a deep breath, savouring the smell. For a moment, I was back in Egypt right there on our last day of sightseeing in Luxor, when Mark had asked me if I'd like to travel with him.

I placed the scarab on the empty pillow next to me. She was barely recognisable now, that young woman who had travelled alone to Egypt, carefree, filled with unquenchable exuberance, and became swathed in the knowledge of her love, an exciting future luxuriously stretching ahead of her. She could not have known that they would spend twenty years together from the moment they met on the train. And that she would be left behind.

~

My daily hospital visits and Mark's survival had been my all-encompassing focus for the last eight months. It had been traumatic and physically exhausting, but it was the life I had led for that period of time, propelled forward by hope. After Mark's death, this intense life morphed into a vortex of grief and a terrifying void as my daily routine fell away.

Shortly after Mark had passed away, Rahel and Joschka, who had slept in my bedroom with me during their father's illness, moved back into their own bedrooms. It was not a difficult transition for them. For me, it symbolised the end of Mark's struggle for survival. And it signalled the beginning of life with just the three of us.

My new, unknown life revolved around Rahel and Joschka. At first, spending time with them provided short windows of relief, and later, longer ones – relief from being sucked into grief. Early on, I was able to let the warmth of their love enter the dark spaces inhabiting my body. To feel my love for them with tenderness.

Walking towards Joschka's classroom, I was greeted by the other mothers. This was a long-standing routine that had been put on hold for me for the duration of Mark's illness. Reconnecting with that sense of regularity, and starting the day with smiles and small talk with the other women whom I'd known for years grounded me, and at the same time, felt surreal in its semblance of normalcy. A momentary brush with fiction, as normality was no longer the texture of my life. I was abruptly jolted out of it when the conversation turned to *my husband said* … Even so, for a moment the routine made me feel part of the school community again. They all knew what had happened, and if I had wanted to, I could have asked for a hug. But that would have been too hard, here, exposed, out in the open. No, the routine, at that time my only routine, provided some patches of solidity in an otherwise fluid ground.

After dropping the children off at school, I returned home to my private hell of grieving. I slowed down my pace on the way back, taking in the impossibly blue spring sky. And the flower buds bursting forth with a surge of energy, their vibrant life force so at odds with my inner landscape. I walked haltingly, aware that my respite from grief was short-lived, on hold out in the sunny open space. The closer I got to my front door, the more I could feel the pull of my four walls. It was my sanctuary, yet also my territory for mourning, where I was in my personal bubble of emotional pain. The intensity of my grief, trapping me like a morass, was unbearable. But the alternative, to pretend I could run away from it, would have damaged my and the children's chance of future happiness.

At home, I cried for hours. In the bathroom, I sank to the floor, the tiles icy against my cheek, hugging my knees. Later, as I lifted myself up into a sitting position, leaning against the wall with my legs stretched out on the floor, a conversation at school the previous afternoon replayed in my mind.

"You'll get over it, just give it some time," Jane had said as she leaned towards me, patting my back.

I recoiled under her hand.

"I know how you feel." Sandra walked up to us, joining in the conversation. "My mother died two years ago and it was horrible. It will get better. You just can't see that yet."

In the afternoon, I walked to the bathroom and splashed my face with cold water. Saw a woman in the mirror I faintly recognised, as if meeting a school friend decades later, the resemblance worn so thin as to be barely visible. As I ran the brush through my hair, the intensity of my emotions began to subside. At 2.50 p.m., I walked to school, pacing myself down the hill, still feeling the echo of my inner world and startled by cars whizzing by, by life around me.

Outside Joschka's classroom, I chatted with the other mothers.

"Oh hi, Katrin. How are you going? I was just telling the others that the annual school bush dance is coming up soon," Sandy said.

"That's always a lot of fun," Julie remarked. "Are you going to come?" she asked me.

A memory of last year's event flashed by. Mark bent forwards, holding both of Rahel's hands and skipping sideways up and down the dance floor with her.

"Yes, I think I will. I hadn't realised yet that it's that time of year already."

Despite the painful memory, it felt comforting to be part of the school community.

The constant knowing of Mark's death pulsated at the back of my mind and melted – dreamlike – into the soothing life around me. Joschka ran past me, pencil case and books in hand, to his school bag and tucked his belongings inside.

"Mama, I'm playing soccer with Aiden," he announced.

I quickly grabbed his arm and planted a kiss on his cheek.

Rahel strolled over from her classroom. I bent down to hug her, and then leant back, holding onto her shoulders. We smiled at each other. Her sweet embrace sent waves of warmth through me.

This routine repeated itself over and over for weeks, months. The interplay of grieving at home and re-entering life in the afternoon. On the walk to school, I transitioned from being immersed in my internal landscape to opening up to the external landscape around me. I genuinely switched modes.

I always looked forward to seeing Rahel's and Joschka's smiling faces. In the evenings we played a lot together. I dedicated my afternoons and evenings to them because I wanted to. When I was with my children, I focused on them and enjoyed their company. Was present emotionally. I did not suppress my grief in order to engage with Rahel and Joschka. I gave it all the space it needed during the day when I was alone, and in the darkness of the never-ending nights. Sometimes, sadness overcame me, triggered by a reminder, a song on the radio, an expression on Rahel's face, so like her father's. And then, I did cry in front of the children. Pools of tears collecting in my eyes, rolling down my cheeks. But not wailing, being knocked over. No, not that.

The wellbeing of my children was my first and foremost priority. It was what mattered, what I really cared about. The school routine was beneficial for Rahel and Joschka. It gave them a focus, structure and a lot of interaction with their friends, which continued into the weekends with play-overs.

Looking back, I am surprised how well both of the children handled their grief. At the time, I did not think about this. Perhaps I was too deeply steeped in my own grief. Years later, I came across bereavement literature that warned of the possibility of nightmares, debilitating anxiety or anger tantrums in children who lost a parent. Rahel and Joschka slept well and continued to play with their friends and applied themselves to their school work. But their way of coping with grief differed decidedly. Rahel, three years older than Joschka, talked about her feelings with me and with her friends. She was very open about it. By contrast, Joschka has not talked about his feelings. His strategy for dealing with his intense feelings was to keep himself busy. Playing at friends' places was central to his life after his father's death.

My nights were battle zones. The continuous playing of the high-definition movies in my inner mind were the weapons that attacked me, stealing my sleep. Lying awake in bed, as my breathing stuttered in shallow spurts through the stillness of the night, I thought about the extent of my physical exhaustion. Katrin, you cannot recover from this place of sheer fatigue, I thought. You need to do something to lessen this excruciating exhaustion.

The next morning, I rang the hospice where Mark had passed away. It had a support centre for patients and their families which was staffed by volunteers. I made an appointment for a remedial massage the following day. On the way to the hospice, I felt uncomfortable about accepting help from the centre. I didn't have cancer, I wasn't dying. I didn't know then what a lifeline Jane, and the centre, was to become in the early period of raw grief.

As I pulled into the laneway leading to the hospice, images of Mark lying in bed, no longer breathing, bore down on me. I deliberately drove to the entrance door of the support centre so that I would not have to walk through the main part of the hospice. When I entered the large room, hesitant, Jane, the co-ordinator who ran the centre and knew me, got up from her desk, crossed the room, spread her arms and pulled me into a tight hug. I closed my eyes, allowing myself to sink into her embrace. Tension drained out of my neck and shoulders. The warmth of her body soothed mine.

"It's good to see you, Katrin. I'm glad you're here."

Her open, affectionate gaze, devoid of pity, drew me in as much as her embrace had. I was relieved not to have to say anything, least of all how I felt.

"Can I make you a cup of tea while you're waiting for Agnes?"

As I cradled a mug of green tea in my hands, a middle-aged woman greeted me, the small lines around the corners of her mouth suggesting a readiness for laughter.

Stretched out on the massage table face down, I peered through the large hole onto the grey carpet. My eyes focused on a small brown stain.

"I use a method called trigger point massage," Agnes explained.

She turned on the CD player and sounds of the rainforest began to fill the room. Agnes placed one finger on a point on my back. A sharp pain pierced through my flesh. I yelled out, could not stop myself. A while into the massage I asked her how much pressure she was applying. She assured me that she hardly exerted any pressure on me, yet it felt like a searing force.

On the drive home, I reflected on the acute sensitivity of my body. I shook my head, thinking about how much tension I held in my back, especially my neck and shoulders. A particular trigger point on my shoulder blade had sent a sharp, agonising pain all the way to the top of my head, as intense as labour pain. Only I was not giving birth to new life and hope. Instead, I had to release the loss of hope, the loss of my life with Mark. And our future together.

"I want Mark back," I screamed in the solitude of my car. "I want to grow old with you!"

As I watched a large truck packed with sheep driving past at the traffic lights, their woolly flanks bulging through the slats, and random cloven-hoofed legs sticking out into the air, the stench of urine and panic penetrated my car.

"I don't want Mark dead. I want him back!" I screamed until I was hoarse.

Thank God I had shut the windows at the lights. I had to laugh at myself, worrying at a time like this about what other people might think. The laugh had a hysterical, tearful edge to it. The outburst, though, released tension from my agitated stomach.

I had neglected my body the entire time Mark had been sick. There had simply been no room to attend my weekly yoga class, to go for walks through Wireless Hill Park or along the river near our house as had been my habit beforehand, to buy fruit and vegetables at the greengrocer rather than the supermarket. All that time I was like an elastic band that had been stretched to its outermost limits, continually, without ever easing off, even marginally.

Looking back on that time now, I am stunned that I did not get sick. Adrenalin had continually surged through my body for three quarters of a year. This hormone is not designed for such duration, but for a short-term fight-or-flight reaction to danger. I know now that the long-term levels of adrenalin had put enormous pressure on my system. It showed in my fatigue. And the tension which was locked into my shoulders and neck.

For months and months, the trigger points on my back did not ease, but continued to inflict intense, shooting pains along my nerves. I persevered with the massages at the hospice. Taking care of my body seemed like something tangible, doable.

18

A nicotine yellow A5 unmarked envelope perched under my windscreen wipers. I spotted it, barely visible in the dim light of the undercover car park. It was a day or two after the funeral. I walked back to my car after having spent time with Mark's family. Amongst them was Mark's relative S, who had flown over from Melbourne to attend the service and who was also our insurance agent. Startled, I vaguely recalled him mentioning something about necessary forms. It must have been him who had placed the forlorn envelope on my windscreen, I thought.

At home my hands shook as I ripped open the envelope with my thumb. As I glanced over the first few sentences of the paperwork a chill shot down my spine. The pages slipped out of my hand and fell onto the floorboards with a thud. A cover letter written by S informed me in a couple of short paragraphs that I had to go to the Supreme Court to receive my life insurance payout. He had attached forms and noted that he would not be further involved in the process.

I rang S in Melbourne. "What do you mean I have to go to the Supreme Court? It's a straight-forward life insurance claim, isn't it?"

"That's what you have to do."

"But why? Why isn't the policy paid out to me? We've had this life insurance for such a long time."

"You are not named as beneficiary. That's why you have to go to the Supreme Court."

"What? What're you saying? Of course I am. I remember filling in the forms. Mark and I put each other down as sole beneficiary."

"That's not the case now. I can't help you. That's how it is."

"How come this isn't the case now?"

A prolonged silence punctured only by his laboured breathing seeped through the receiver.

"As I said, that's how it is."

And that was the end of the conversation. I gaped at the telephone in my hand, unable to take in what had just happened.

The following morning, I sat in front of my computer and stared at the white letters on the black keyboard. I lifted my head to look at the screen, the cursor pulsating steadily on the blank email. My nerves throbbed in sync with the cursor. My fingers began to type: why was I removed as beneficiary? All throughout the day I kept checking my computer for emails. My cold hand grabbed the mouse and clicked the cursor onto the inbox. The silent folder amplified the sensitivity of my chafed nerves. Finally, the next morning, the Inbox lit up. My hand shook, jarring the little wheel under the mouse, missing my mark as I tried to open the email.

I leaned toward the screen and scrunched my tired eyes at the bright light. It was early in the morning and I had barely slept. The explanation that S gave was that the removal of beneficiaries was due to the recent addition of income protection insurance, which he had linked to our life insurance. "What?" I screamed. What was that supposed to mean? I'd never heard of such a thing. It didn't make any sense at all. My fatigued brain yearned for a precise explanation.

Initially there were emails back and forth between us. I repeatedly asked S how it was possible that our life insurance had been linked to Mark's income protection insurance. Two such different and unconnected types of insurance. One personal and one professional. We had the life insurance in place since the beginning of our relationship over fifteen years ago. The income protection insurance was only taken out recently in the last few years when Mark became self-employed. Unbeknownst to us, S had removed us as beneficiaries of each other. As he put it, the linking of the two insurances had removed the *option of naming a beneficiary*. To this day I cannot understand how it was legally possible for him to do this.

The illogical nature of this justification clogged up my brain like a syrupy liquid. Removing the beneficiaries goes against the very purpose of taking out a life insurance policy. I repeatedly asked S in my emails why he had linked the two insurances, but he never answered my questions. Having silently delivered the forms to my windscreen wipers when he was in Perth, he would not communicate with me when he was back in Melbourne.

After my early emotions of abandonment, anger took over. I could not unleash my feelings on S, who had removed himself from me. Repeatedly I shouted at the top of my voice, alone, my fists clenched. Until my throat dried out and ached. I knew that S loved Mark. He was what could best be described as a *nice* person. A family man. His friendly face and ready smile made him likeable. This made it even harder to reconcile his inexplicable actions, his unwillingness to help.

I recoiled from having to draw on my meagre inner resources, by now wafer thin, to deal with this, because it felt like such a betrayal that I had to at all. I could not understand how this had happened. I could not make sense of the whole thing. I could not even begin to grasp S's behaviour.

I contacted a lawyer friend of ours, Tom. Inheritance law was not his area of expertise, but he put me in touch with a colleague from his law firm. The first thing she said to me when I met her in her office was that the insurance company was legally free to distribute the insurance funds to me, even in the absence of me being named as beneficiary and in the absence of a will. She contacted the insurance company and was met with a wall of resistance. They would not release the funds without a court order. This takes time, which saves the insurance company money in the form of interest, by delaying the inevitable pay-out.

I returned home and bolted up the stairs into the living room, where my parents sat on the couch, and explained the situation to them.

"For God's sake, Mark and I've done everything right by putting the policy into place. And through no fault of my own, I'm now faced with this mess."

"Katrin! I don't know what to say. This is ..." My mother turned to my father. "Werner, what do you say to this?"

"Tell me again exactly what happened and what you've got to do now." My father's calm voice was in stark contrast to my mother's agitated intonation, yet it was underscored by a slight tremor, barely audible. After hearing the details, he replied, "This does sound very odd. But this isn't my area of expertise, and I'm not familiar with Australian law." He exchanged a glance with my mother. "But you know, I'm sure this can be sorted out one way or another. It will take time though, these things always do."

I was suffocating in a sea of bills and now there seemed no end in sight. I was on edge. As I looked at the window across the lawn, an image of a real estate agent, folder and biro in hand, scrutinising every room in our house and taking notes, flashed through my mind. I feared for our house. It was more than a home. It was our anchor, our emotional safety zone. Without this refuge I did not know how to cope emotionally. The house was much more than a physical space. It had Mark's love for us imprinted in it.

My distress not only delayed but derailed my process of recovery. What really got to me, grinding me to a halt, was how *unnecessary* this was.

The legal process dragged on for about six months. The fees mounted until I received the pay-out of the policy. In the meantime, I had to continue making the repayments on my mortgage. My financial situation was made worse by the fact that I was not entitled to receive parenting payments because of the investment home, which was yet to be completed. I felt deep gratitude for my parents, who had been helping me with the mortgage payments. Without them, I would have lost the house.

At night, I woke up after a short spell of restless sleep. I turned over onto my left side. A sharp pain speared deep into my shoulder blade. I clutched it, and eased onto my back, staring into the darkness that weighed down on me. My eyes burned with fatigue. The blackness was only broken by a slither of pale orange light shining through a slight gap in the curtain. I kept thinking, if Mark knew right now what was happening to me, he would be horrified.

At this hour, even the birds were muted. I yearned to hear Mark's breathing next to me and moved my arm across the bed. It landed on the bare pillow with a thud. The emptiness prompted me to think of the many injustices that had happened in the last nine months. Could all that have really taken place in such a short time? Mark did not get a CAT scan from the GP. The neurosurgeon at the hospital had wanted me to withdraw treatment within a week of his strokes, only to retract his recommendation of the withdrawal of treatment with an "anything is possible now". And then Mark's inexpressible, endless pain for four months in the absence of specialist pain management.

With my arm still on Mark's empty pillow, the memory of his moaning echoed in my ears, haunting the silence. And now this. On top of everything else. S's injustice, the last in a string of incomprehensible wrongdoings, left me unhinged. Would some faceless bank snatch away the very roof over our heads? No. Every brick and splash of mortar was imbued with a tangible connection to Mark. We could not lose this house, our sanctuary.

I got up the next morning before the kids and walked into the bathroom. My gaze was drawn to the reflection in the mirror. I could not reconcile the image of the pale, waxen face and dark-circled eyes with the woman I had known myself to be only last summer. I navigated the stairs like a sleepwalker. Time to get the children up for school.

I did not know then that these unanswered questions and the illogical nature of the whole thing would cause me fierce anger, rage and hurt for a long time to come. Following the tenth anniversary of Mark's death, I reflected on the decade that had passed in a conversation with Ina.

"You've had to face so many injustices. I can't even begin to imagine." My friend picked up her fork and twisted the linguini on her plate. "That reminds me, I've been meaning to ask you – have you ever spoken to S again?"

"No." I shook my head and looked across the table, watching Ina poke her fork into a king prawn. "You know, the absence of any explanation from him has pained me so much. It's driven me crazy. That, more than anything, has made it really hard to accept the whole thing, to let it go."

"Yeah, I understand that. How do you feel about it now?"

"Well, I don't know if I'll ever be able to make peace with it." I sighed. "I know that my bitterness is toxic for me, but because it still feels like such a betrayal, I just don't seem to be able to let it go. The thing is, I really don't want to carry this resentment around with me, but it sticks to me like …" I stared outside, searching for the right words to capture my feelings, "like an invisible skin."

"What'd help you to let go, do you think?" Ina put down her cutlery on her empty plate with a clunk.

"I'm not sure. Maybe if it didn't feel so disloyal?" I looked down at my plate of pasta, barely touched. "I've often wondered what S made of it all. Maybe if we could've communicated, if he'd expressed his thoughts and feelings, something, anything."

That night I thought about how I still felt so angry with S. Realising how much the emotional fallout continued to haunt me, I yearned to be able to put it behind me. I knew early on that my deep-seated anger stifled my recovery and I had made the conscious effort not to ruminate about it. This had proved to be helpful, though the anger and hurt reignited if it got triggered by some reminder.

It had taken me ten years to give up my inner struggle to fight the fact that it did happen, because it *felt* so wrong to accept it. While I knew intellectually that holding on was bad for me, I couldn't help myself emotionally. Simple acknowledgement felt like condoning what had happened. The insurance policy was something concrete that we had put in place. After everything else, Mark's undiagnosed cyst and all that followed, events outside my control, the life insurance policy should not have been taken out of my hands by removing me as beneficiary without my knowledge. That stung so much.

The conversation with Ina was a catalyst for me to deliberately focus on letting go of my anger towards S. It became clear to me that I needed to process the whole disastrous event in order to move beyond my strategy of not giving it any attention, which had served me well until now, but was no longer enough. I consciously made the decision that I didn't want to hang onto this anymore. Writing was instrumental in helping me to voice and process the entire insurance fallout, which had had such detrimental financial and emotional consequences for me. I realised I needed to let go of seeing S's decision to delete Mark and me as each other's beneficiaries from the life insurance policy as unnecessary, because even though it should never have happened, it locked in my resistance to the fact that it actually *had* happened. I have come to recognise that I will never know why S made the choices that he did and have learned to let go of needing answers. I no longer make my inner peace dependent on finding those answers. Accepting no longer feels like condoning. It took a lot of work to get there, but the freedom I now feel means it's been worth it.

~

With Mark's death, the attitude of some of the people around me changed. During his illness, I had received a lot of support, especially with the children, and was met with gentleness. This morphed into a matter-of-fact detachment. Within a few weeks, *you must get on with your life* seemed emblazoned on some people's foreheads.

This mindset startled me. It was as sudden as it was unexpected. I felt vulnerable and exposed. The periods of weeping alone at home left me emotionally depleted and physically exhausted. My raw grief felt like being ill. It was emotional rather than practical support that I was in need of at that juncture. And physical closeness, the reassurance that only the warmth of a touch can bestow on the wounded body. A hand lingering on my arm for a moment, to say, I'm here with you. You're not alone. What I needed more than talking was an arm around my shoulders from my girlfriends.

But I didn't know that myself then. Seeing me in the grips of grief was difficult for everyone. Much harder to deal with, and much less tangible, than offering practical help to a friend whose husband is in hospital.

My closest friends were there for me, with hugs, visits and phone calls. But the expectation that I should move on with my life brought some harsh experiences with it. A friend of mine, whose son regularly played with Joschka, criticised me when he had two sleep-overs in a row at their place. She reprimanded me for saying no shortly after Mark's death when they had asked me if I could have their son stay overnight; she was angry, her voice sharp, laden with accusatory undertones. "This doesn't work for us, you have to let our son sleep over as well."

My jaw dropped. I stared at her, speechless.

That night in bed, I contemplated my friendships. A cold terror made the fine hairs on the back of my neck spring upright at the realisation that my friendships were already shifting. Now that Mark was gone, many of those friends who we had socialised with as couples no longer felt the same to me, and it seemed that I didn't feel the same to them. Almost all of our friends were couples, with the exception of a few single female friends, who I mostly saw in a group of friends or at school.

And those couple-friendships morphed quickly. The void left by Mark's absence was a black vortex that unsettled everyone. The scenario of the triangle inscribed me as the odd one out and I felt marked, as if my forehead was emblazoned with neon letters. I stopped accepting couple-invitations. Perhaps they stopped being offered. It's hard to tell.

I realised I would need to forge new friendships, especially with other single mothers. That they had to reflect the layout of my new external territory. This did not mean that all our friends would fall away. I had always caught up regularly with Ina on my own, so there was no difference now in our friendship. On the contrary, it had been strengthened by her unwavering support for me throughout Mark's illness and now during my recovery as well.

Much to my relief, our German circle of friends also stayed almost the same. We usually met up as a group. It did not feel awkward to be at our usual get-togethers. But it did feel lonely. To walk up to the park with the kids, picnic in the cooler box, without Mark, clawed at my heart. At a BBQ, Mark had always brought a plate with my cooked chicken over to me. "There you go, Schatz," he would say to me with a twinkle in the eye.

Now I was no longer anybody's *treasure*. The longing for that intimacy affected me physically. My body responded with aches. A continually sore shoulder. A stiff neck. Stomach cramps.

I wanted to meet women in the same situation as me, but that turned out to be fruitless. There were no other young widows around. I could not find a support group in my age bracket. Not being able to connect with other women who could understand what I was going through evoked a strong sense of isolation.

19

My ears refused to reveal Mark's voice to me. But without invitation, they played the tape of his moaning over and over. Every night, but also sometimes during the day. Why can't I get to his voice? I've heard it for twenty years, so how is it possible to lose it? Not being able to dwell in the memory of Mark's melodious, humorous voice, to draw comfort from it, was yet another painful loss. The silence of his voice was deafening. I didn't know what was worse, the incessant replaying of his moaning that I had no control over, or this deafening silence of his voice. I tried so hard to reach into every track of my memory, but I was blocked at every turn by a flood of memories from the hospital. As if faced with the closed boom gate at Checkpoint Charlie in Berlin during the Cold War, I was denied entering the land of happy memories. Photo albums were not the solution. Looking at photos was too painful. Instead of actually being able to take in the joyful holiday shots, it unleashed a flood of memories of Mark locked in his body. I wanted to gain entry to those joyous memories so badly, craved to see Mark's smiling face, to have him make me laugh again. Yet I was surrounded by the shadows and darkness of his suffering that had wrapped itself over me like a cloak.

I could not bring myself to play a video tape that would have offered Mark's voice to me. I was too scared and did not think I could handle actually hearing his voice through the loud speakers. We had a lot of video tapes. And because it had been mainly Mark who filmed the children, his voice and commentary were recorded in most of the scenes from our old life.

~

Then came our first Christmas without Mark, just three months after his death. Thinking that the children would find it too hard to be at home, I suggested that we could spend Christmas with friends in the country.

"No!" they both exclaimed in unison.

"Christmas should be like always, with the tree and presents at home," Joschka blurted out.

And so I bought a conifer and decorated it with the traditional Christmas decorations from my childhood that my mum had brought over from Germany.

On Christmas Eve, a colourful assortment of presents covered the shiny Jarrah floorboards around the tree. We stuck to our family ritual, a melding of German and Australian traditions, not opening all the presents at once, but giving out one gift at a time. Every time Rahel and Joschka received a present, they made sure that it was my turn next. Aware that their dad was not there to buy me presents, they had bought me several gifts to fill the hole. Joschka passed me a rectangular present, with green Christmas trees on red wrapping paper and a red ribbon. I carefully pulled the sticky tape from the wrapping paper. Six fish dangling from thin clear tubing, attached to a shiny metal lamp, looked up at me. I kneeled down and stretched my arm to plug the cord into the power point behind the cabinet. The fish lit up in iridescent blue – my favourite colour. I gasped in awe.

The children's eyes shone with expectation. "Mama, do you like your presents?" Had they bought the right things?

They were beautiful, I told them truthfully. Later on that night I cried tears of joy and sorrow; it was a special Christmas that I will always remember.

I am still a mother, I thought as I went to sleep.

The most important anchor point in my life was my children. This continuation of identity, in what was otherwise a fragmented terrain, rooted and soothed me. It was tangible and real. The three of us felt like a family to me, though a much smaller one that had been unwillingly reshaped and still carried the imprint of the old contour.

Mark's death had altered my identity of being a mother but had not made it unrecognisable. On the contrary, it remained strong and visible. I did not resent being alone with the children. What did cause me gruelling pain was the loss of sharing the delight in our children. That look that used to pass between us when Joschka scored a goal on the football field. The "that's our son" look that you cannot share with anyone else. Or when Rahel stood on stage at the end-of-year dance concert. When we saw her face of intent concentration and her sparkling costume. The absence of that sharing, of us as parents raising our children together, left a permanent void. Parenting with Mark had been forcefully taken from me. I missed it.

Another loss was in the realm of raising our children bilingually. Because Mark had devoted the same enthusiastic attention to learning German as he did to travelling, his language proficiency had thrived. This made it much easier to raise our children bilingually. After our daughter's birth, I started to read about how to raise children bilingually and there was general consensus that the most important aspect was consistency. So, we began to embrace what is known as the one-parent-one-language approach, whereby each parent chooses the language they wish to communicate with their children in and consistently uses that language. When we sat at the dinner table, the children would look at me and speak German, knowing that their dad understood everything, and then look at him and switched effortlessly to English. Only when other children or people were present did I speak English with them.

Not long after Mark's death, Joschka told me that he only wanted to speak English at home from now on, the seriousness of his expression startling. I was so stunned by his certainty – he had clearly thought about this – that I decided to sit with it. Some time later I asked him why, and he said that he was worried that he would forget to speak English properly. My heart ached for him. The unspoken subtext was, I felt, that speaking English at home would be a palpable connection to his dad. And I thought that this was a trauma response. I respected his wishes. This meant that I also spoke English to Rahel as well. It became our family language and a habit, though I sometimes spoke German with Rahel when we were alone, and we all continued to speak it with my parents. No longer speaking German with the kids as our home language was a significant loss that further leached colour from our home life, already devoid of Mark's presence.

～

The large expanse of grass overlooking the Swan River was moist. I sat down on the lawn, right on the water's edge. The cold dampness edged its way through my shorts. A shiver ran through me. My gaze came to rest on a group of black swans that huddled on a sandbank. Families, I thought, as I noticed the smoky grey feathers of some adolescent birds, not yet black.

It made me ache for what we had lost. Our family would never be the same again, whole. I missed the bantering at the dining table.

Whatever the shape the three of us would become, it could never recapture what we had been. Though my sense of being a family was still intact, its texture no longer had the same softness to it. It had edges and serrations now. What is the shape we have morphed into, I pondered. A triangle, in a way, but that did not even begin to describe the complex layers we now inhabited. What shape would we become, the three of us? Would it always feel like a triangle, with so much missing? I felt like an amputee whose limb had been cut off. Phantom pains occur because the severed nerves do not recognise that the limb is gone, still sending their electrical signals to the brain as if the missing bones and flesh were still attached. Grief is like that. The heart is simply incapable of recognising that part of you is gone. And like the nerves which still perceive the separated limb, I could remember. Mark could no longer talk to me, but I knew what he would say in almost any given situation. Twenty years of companionship does that. It can make you finish each other's sentences, at least in your own head. How long would this knowing last for, though? Months, years? And then? How long could the past survive inside of me? The details will surely fade, I thought, as they were already beginning to thin here and there.

My gaze wandered from the swan family on the sandbank to the wide expanse of the river. How could the water still flow when my life was not? Instead, I stared at the void in place of our joint future. The past could be preserved, at least to a degree, the fundamentals if not all the details. But there was no longer a future to be carved together. The future only belongs to our children and me now, to the living. I knew what Mark would say in so many situations, but could this extend to new events beyond the edges of what he got to experience? He would never parent his children as teenagers. I could not know what he would say to them as adolescents.

Every morning when I woke up, with my consciousness still lingering in the in-between zone of sleep and wakefulness, I began to shed the short reprieve granted by my brief bursts of sleep. The realisation dawned on me anew that I had lost Mark, part of me. Half the bed was empty. My body seemed to bleed then, unwilling or unable to seal the blood vessels that leaked its scarlet mark onto the white sheets. The sensation of bleeding scared me. Will this ever stop, I wondered?

New Year's Eve loomed ahead. I did not want to spend it without friends, the first one in twenty years without Mark. I yearned for the end of this year, and for a new year to rise, in the hope that it would bring some relief and ease. We visited friends in the country, saw the year out at their place with a luxurious dinner.

The first of January came. The three of us went for a walk with our friends. It was hot. The flies buzzed around my head in a black cloud. I had been in the rear when everyone stopped to scan the ocean in the hope of sighting a humpback whale. As soon as I stood still the cloud of flies descended upon my eyes, nose and ears. I shooed them away, but there were too many. So I walked on along the narrow sandy track that was lined by low shrubs on either side. I was now at the front of our group. As I made my way downhill, the path was littered with sharp limestone rocks. I gazed at the ocean for any sign of whales, and just as I looked back down onto the path I saw the shiny brown body of a snake right in front of me, one step ahead. Its body spanned the width of the path, its tail end and head hidden on either side in the shrubs. My right leg was already in motion and hovered in the air close to the body of the snake. I pulled it back, turned around and ran back up the hill. In my panic, the tip of my foot caught on a rock. I stumbled and fell. My left shin scraped over the ragged edge of the limestone. Thick blood oozed out and ran down my leg. I looked up and Joschka stood right in front of me. He saw the blood and all the colour drained out of his face. He began to shake, his eyes wide open. I realised in an instant that having just lost one parent, he was in shock at the sight of my blood, afraid another parent could be taken from him. Because of Joschka's reaction I focused all of my attention on him, which cushioned my own fear for my leg. I needed to reassure my son.

"Joschka." My voice quivered but I looked straight at him. "It's okay, I'm all right."

My friend took me to hospital, as the wound required stitches. Over the next few days, the pain was searing. The painful, potholed start to the New Year jarred me. I had clutched to the hope that it would bring new beginnings, a new energy, something positive to hold onto. My leg, with its piercing pain throbbing through my nerves, proved me wrong. Nothing was going to be that easy. How naive of me to think otherwise, I admonished myself.

Driving us home all the way by myself with my aching leg proved the indisputable fact to me: I'm alone now. I've got to do everything by myself. I oscillated between self-pity and acceptance. Rahel and Joschka were caring; they did not fight once on the way home and helped me to carry our luggage inside. Looking back, it strikes me that the intense physical pain gave expression to my grief in a way that words, and even crying, could not.

My friend Gesa, with whom Mark and I had lived in Bonn for a year, flew to Australia to spend time with me. During the summer school holidays, I put my children on a plane to Melbourne to visit their grandparents and cousins. With this, I started the tradition of flying them over to see their dad's family every summer. It was important to me to make it possible for Rahel and Joschka to have an ongoing connection with them.

Filling out the unaccompanied minor forms at the airport made my hand shake. It was surreal to separate from them. I ached to keep them close and not to put them on a plane that would send them to the other side of the continent. But I was aware that it was a good thing for them. They had cousins the same age in Melbourne and would have a lot of fun together.

The next day I drove to the international airport to pick up Gesa. I relaxed when I saw her smiling face, and soaked up being wrapped in her warmth and kindness. Here we were, both apart from our children and feeling weird about it. I had suggested to Gesa that I show her the southwest, and to visit my friends in Albany. One of them, Uwe, was a diving instructor and had his own business. I was not taken with the idea of scuba diving and had never been drawn to it. But Gesa, who'd always had a keen sense of adventure, was eager. And so the two of us went ahead and did the course. My passion was to see the rare sea dragon, this wondrous creature of the ocean, much larger than the sea horse, which inhabits the waters around Albany. On the second last day I spotted the elusive, leafy sea dragon through the bubbles escaping from my breathing apparatus. Even though it was nestled in amongst dense kelp, perfectly camouflaged, waving to and fro with the current, I noticed it. Despite the mouthpiece, I managed a cry of joy.

20

Death had inscribed a fixed and unbending demarcation line in my life: B.M. and A.M, before and after Mark's death. The space between the *before* and *after* that I found myself in immediately after my loss was a no man's land, like the strip of land behind the Berlin Wall.

On a recent trip to Berlin, over a decade after my loss, I returned to the city for the first time since my visit there with Mark twenty-five years earlier. I went to Checkpoint Charlie. Although it was June, heavy rain bore down on me and I had the hood of my jumper pulled tight around my face. A strong gust of wind nearly ripped the umbrella out of my hands. Despite the cold weather, my attention was focused on a row of display boards with black and white aerial photographs of the Wall. I pulled the umbrella onto my shoulders and held it tight with both hands. The photographs showed in detail the no man's land behind the wall, known as the death strip, scattered with landmines and spiked with barbed wire. I bent closely to make sure that I was seeing right. There was a second wall parallel to the famous graffiti-emblazoned wall, about 150 metres apart. I hadn't been aware before that there had actually been two walls in the divided city, one on either side of the death-strip.

Following Mark's death, I was stuck between two walls, like the separated Berlin: a wall behind me that marked my husband's death, and another wall in front of me that I needed to climb in order to reach my future. I was locked into the death strip, a terrain filled with the memory of suffering.

My nights continued to morph into a battle-zone. Instead of sleep and rest, they were filled with incessant images of Mark's face, scrunched up, sweat collecting on his forehead, his right leg, paper-thin, contracted into a right angle. Akin to distant machine gun firing, his moaning tortured my ears. There was no escape from the piercing eyes of the specialist, marked by cold indifference. I pressed my palms against my eyes to block out the image, but that failed to erase it.

The chain of wrongdoings that had happened to me and Mark were like landmines deposited just under the surface, waiting to detonate. I knew that if I did not pay attention to those landmines, if I made a wrong move, the distress held in my body, stored in the lining of each cell, would explode. A violent explosion could only destroy. Not only me, but my children as well. I had to tread carefully.

I did not feel burdened by fulfilling the task of raising two children on my own. But I felt the weight of responsibility, being the sole carer and decision maker, bearing down onto my shoulders.

Would I be able to offer my children a happy future? There were no grandparents or siblings living in Perth whose support I could draw on in everyday life. I thought a lot about raising my children on my own. By far my strongest motivation at this point was to allow them to grow up to be happy. And I did not want them to be defined by their loss. It was crucial to provide them with the environment that would make it possible for them to explore their own identity. As the sole person raising my children, I had to be able to offer that environment and also to support them in their grief. It was clear to me that I had to embody it. But I was depleted. Physically, emotionally, mentally and spiritually. I needed nurturing myself. The word *sole* was spinning around in my head in an endless loop. There's only me. Only me.

A few weeks after Mark's death, I inadvertently drove within the vicinity of the hospital on my way to a girlfriend's house for lunch. As I found myself in the right-hand lane that turns into Thomas Street, I suddenly realised that I was about to pass the hospital. It was too late to switch lanes. As the lights turned green, my throat constricted. I drove down the double-lane road and caught a full view of the hospital. I was forced to take in the car park where I had pulled up countless times, anxious about how Mark would be. I immediately jerked my head towards the road. Cold sweat made my hands clammy on the steering wheel. I gripped it tighter until my nails dug into the rubber. Dr. Nemeth's arctic eyes devoid of sympathy stared back at me from the tarmac, freezing my spine. "Your husband as you know him is gone," echoed through the car. Delivered with the precision of a scalpel slicing skin. The words bounced off the windows, increased their tempo and spun around my head. My breathing sped up, my heart pounded in my chest.

I was sucked into the vortex of his freezing cold detachment. Even though it was summer, goose bumps ran down my arms and back. Only after I had passed the hospital did I reach a side road that I could pull into. I brought my car to a sudden halt and collapsed onto my steering wheel, sobbing.

"Go away, please, go away," I pleaded with the images.

They refused. It took a long time for the stare of those emotionless eyes to recede. I picked up the phone and dialled Susan's number.

"It's me. I'm so sorry but I can't come any more." My voice trembled.

"Are you all right? What happened?"

I swallowed hard. "I just drove past the hospital and was barraged by all these images of the specialist's eyes from the meeting when he urged me to withhold treatment, right in the beginning back in February. I'd completely forgotten I'd be driving past the hospital if I took Mounts Bay Road on the way to you."

I stayed in my car for about half an hour, still clutching onto the steering wheel. Then I turned on the ignition and drove home, in the opposite direction. After this incident I avoided driving past the hospital for a very long time. Those chilling eyes had the potential to destroy my precarious foothold on the no man's land I was in.

It made me realise how embodied memory is. The physical reminder of the hospital and the roads leading up to it jerked my cellular memory awake. The traumatic memories had clawed their way into the very fabric of my body, my tissue, nerve cells, blood vessels. The only way that I could parent my children the way I wanted to, nurturing and facilitating happiness and joy, was to heal myself from this trauma. I realised that without traversing this abyss with awareness I would not be able to reach a future that had any real quality of life.

How could I achieve this seemingly impossible task? I lay awake at night, cold sweat collecting on my forehead. In the midst of my sleep-deprived nights, I could not begin to imagine how I could release all these traumatic memories. It felt impossible.

I did, however, know how *not* to do it: by numbing my pain with drugs or alcohol. I wasn't tempted anyway. I'd always avoided medications if at all possible. The spiritual journey that I had embarked on a decade or so earlier and personal development courses that I had attended had taught me the importance of feeling my painful emotions and not suppressing them.

As I stared at the ceiling at night, my eyes too tired to follow the shadows across the room, terror always arose in me when I thought of the extreme physical pain Mark had endured. I was locked into my suffering, stuck. I vaguely understood that the key to unlocking the door was to give up pushing against the fact that all these injustices had happened, unable and unwilling to accept them. What you push against emotionally doesn't go away but actually sticks to you. In pushing against past events, the endless mental loop of *this should not have happened* locked my emotions in a box so I could not process them. I did open myself to feeling all along – I was not repressing – but I didn't realise at the time that I was often feeling the intense emotional pain of resisting. That is, my unwillingness to accept what to me were avoidable causes of Mark's suffering, especially the GP's failure to order a lifesaving CAT scan, was actually locking me in to my own suffering.

I couldn't stop it because to me it meant I was honouring Mark, his almost superhuman effort to fight for his life. It felt impossible to stop thinking that this should not have happened, and to accept that all these injustices had taken place, which had led to such inhumane suffering for Mark and his death. Acceptance felt like condoning, which I was vehemently opposed to. All the shoulds and shouldn'ts kept leading me down the rabbit hole to my suffering. They were the signposts of pushing against.

This evoked a strong inner conflict between my emotional landscape and my beliefs. I understood intellectually that resistance, the internal voice that screamed *this should never have happened*, would condemn me to remain stuck in this cycle of the endless replaying of memories of Mark's suffering and the cold detachment of the neurologist. But this clashed with the actual reality of my intense feelings. My body simply needed to keep resisting in order to keep what Mark had been through alive, so the memories of his heroic fight to stay alive would not become obliterated. I need to dare to break from the suffering I'm locked into, I realised. But how do I do that?

I began again to delve into spirituality and personal growth, which had been put on hold during Mark's illness. Now, my spiritual quest took on a new level of intensity. It no longer was an interest, a drive, to nurture my soul in order to lead a meaningful and integral life. Now it had become existential. How did Mark's suffering fit into my idea of a universal higher intelligence that is far greater than the world we inhabit?

Ina had invited me to ring her up any time I needed to talk. One morning in spring, even the bright blue sky and sight of the vibrant red flowers of the bottle brush tree in my garden could not cushion the pain that began to flood me on the way home from dropping off the children at school. As I walked up our red recycled brick driveway, I stared at the native plants Mark had planted. How much joy it would give him now to see his plants blooming. As I unlocked the front door, images of Mark leaning over the yellow flowers of his kangaroo paws, a smile of deep contentment lighting up his face, caused a flood of grief.

I dialled my friend's number.

"Oh Ina, I don't know what to do about all this pain." I waited for the sobbing to ebb down enough to continue speaking. "I know that I have to feel this pain, but right now that just feels like theory, mind stuff. How the hell am I actually going to do it?"

"Yes, it's so unbelievably hard to do, and you have experienced so much trauma." Ina took in a long breath. "I guess you can just take it one day at a time, or even a moment at a time." The line went silent. "I wish I could help you."

"You are helping me, Ina, more than you can possibly imagine. You're there for me, and I don't have to hide anything in front of you, worrying how you might feel." I stared outside at the cloudless sky. I had fallen in love with this sky the first time I came to Perth, and the love affair continued, but now it was no longer a comfort. "It just hurts so much. The pain brings me to my knees. It's literally so strong that my body can't stay upright." I shuffled my bare feet from side to side, the rough wool of the crimson carpet scraping against my bare skin.

"I'm so sorry, Katrin."

"You know, I'm so scared of the next pain attack. One moment I'm okay and then the pain will just come out of left field, triggered by all sorts of things, like the flowers Mark planted, or a song playing on the car radio. Or even a stranger who's got the same curls as Mark. And of course, those bloody memories of the specialist." My fingers twisted the white cotton strings attached to the end of the rug. "I feel so vulnerable."

In hindsight, I cannot believe that I never went to see a grief counsellor. However, no one had mentioned a specialised grief counsellor to me, including the support centre at the hospice, and I don't even know if there was one in Perth at the time. Also, I had this self-image of being strong, and this had been mirrored back to me all my life. First by my mother, who always said, "you're so strong". And later, all throughout Mark's illness, almost on a daily basis, friends and acquaintances said to me "Katrin, you're so strong. I couldn't do what you're doing."

My stomach always contracted in response to this comment. I knew that it was well-intentioned, but it served to create a distance between me and the other person. It set us apart. I came to dread it. I didn't know myself that I would be capable in such a crisis, but no one can possibly know how they would react. Something inside me propelled me forward. I simply acted and did what was required. I did not and could not stop to contemplate anything beyond the immediate decision making required by the surgeries and where Mark would be moved to.

If I had known then the way trauma works and is locked into the body, I would have looked for a trained trauma counsellor. As it was, one part of me thought I could do it myself with the help of personal development courses. I was naïve about the complex nature of trauma. Another part of me feared I would never be able to achieve resolution, that making sense of Mark's torment was simply impossible. But more than anything, I did not even recognise that I was traumatised for over a year after Mark's death. His suffering had become my inner yardstick, and compared to being locked into his body and his extreme pain, I did not see myself as suffering. How could I not have recognised that I was traumatised, with the incessant inner movies playing the scenes over and over? It strikes me as odd now, but perhaps it is simply the signature of trauma itself.

Who I was now was unknowable to me in the no man's land of early grief. It was obvious to me that my own path of addressing my grief required me to face my recurring images in order to have a chance of moving beyond them. If I wanted Rahel and Joschka to be happy, I had to somehow be able to carve some happiness for myself. There was no other way.

But having clarity and achieving my goals were two different things. In my darkest moments, the road that I had set for myself seemed unattainable. The strength required to deal with my intense emotions as well as knowing that a single CAT scan at the time of Mark's initial headaches would have averted all of his and our suffering was, at times, too hard to take. I could not imagine ever being able to accept Mark's suffering, but I wanted to reach a place where my visual images and auditory memories stopped tormenting me.

Perched on the sofa with the sun shining onto my face through the bay windows, I closed my eyes, intent on conjuring up happy images of Mark. But his smiling face was out of reach. I realised with panic that I could not remember Mark's face without dragging myself through the images of his distorted body. Not only had I lost Mark, I had lost access to twenty years of memories. How is it possible that the last eight months imprison my memory, that they won't let me past to see what's beyond, I wondered.

I could not move or think without the remembered suffering seething in my consciousness. A constant battle raged within me. Everything in me yearned to fight Mark's torment that continued to be so real, despite the fact that death had stopped it, though not for me.

I faced a blank concrete wall ahead of me in the death strip I found myself in, high enough to block out my beloved blue sky, and without an end in sight to my right or left. There was no way to navigate around it. To move forward, I had to climb this barren wall. I felt a barrage of questions bubbling under the surface. Do I have the ability to scramble up this barrier that has no footholds or anything tangible to hold onto? How can I confront my memories?

21

"Umdiada, umdiada ..." A chorus of voices, tiny high-pitched children's voices intermingled with the clear ringing of several sopranos and the low vibrations of a baritone, echoed through the vast arid land scattered with spinifex in the remote countryside.

I put my lunch box with left-overs from last night's vegetarian pasta and salad into my day-pack, zipped up the tent and strode across the parched ground to the centre of the campsite. I joined in the morning circle and Rahel's smooth, warm hand slipped into mine. On my right, a calloused hand offered a firm grasp. My gaze wandered around the circle. Colourful rainbow hoodies, purple floppy hats, striped pants and giggles immediately brightened up my day. Joschka stood on the opposite side of the circle, next to a couple of boys his age, and his cheeky smile told me that he was happy.

After the singing stopped, a deep voice bounced around the group. "Good morning everyone, we've got spectacular walks planned for today."

"Yeah!" Cheering and clapping erupted.

The voice continued, laden with a chuckle. "So we're walking around the granite outcrop today. There's a long walk of about fifteen kilometres and a shorter walk. Let's do a show of hands for who wants to do the long walk."

Fifteen hands shot up into the air. "One, two, three, four ..."

Under a canopy of a postcard-blue desert sky we headed off into the bush half an hour later, led by our front guide. Ripped strips of crimson red material spilled out of a worn calico bag tucked under his belt. They were going to be tied to branches to show the route. A signature of the Great Walk Group and subject to many jokes. The rear guide would collect them later on, as well as making sure no one was left behind.

After a kilometre I paused to drink some water. As I screwed the lid back onto the bottle, I stopped to take in the scenery. The sweeping ochre granite rock towered over an endless expanse of spinifex and low bushes.

The fine red dust settled into my clothes, backpack and hiking boots. Joschka's nose was covered in freckles and specks of red dust. He raced off to catch up with the other boys, his black backpack swinging from side to side.

Back in camp in the late afternoon, squealing and high-pitched laughter erupted. I sat up, the imprint of little rocks lingering on the bare skin of my arms, and screwed up my eyes to make out the source of the laughter. A bunch of kids was involved in a mud-fight at the shallow waterhole we camped alongside. I saw Joschka bending down and scraping a handful of mud off the ground, his T-shirt smeared with a mixture of mud and red dirt. I broke into a big smile, and a surge of warmth, like the rays of the midday sun, radiated through my stomach. It was so unusual to feel this surge of warmth instead of the ever-present, gut-wrenching stomach cramps and deadly void, this embodied signature of my grief, that my body relaxed, truly let go for a moment for the first time since Mark fell ill.

The Great Walk became a lifeline for me in the wake of Mark's death, and over the years, it turned into an indispensable feature of my personal landscape. For the first time in my life, I experienced being a member of a community.

The Great Walk started in 1988 as a protest walk against the logging of the state's precious old growth forests, from the country town of Denmark on the south coast of Western Australia to the city of Perth. Twice a year, the Great Walk organises a camp during the school holidays in the bush. We cook over an open fire, often on the properties of farmers, away from all technology. The logistics involved in a ten day camp at about three or four sites for up to fifty people, without refrigeration, running water, toilets and showers are phenomenal. As is usually the case with community groups, a few people put their hand up and dedicate a lot of time to organising. Among the group, the odd person who was not coordinating a camp would pipe up and tell others what to do. Tempers flared at times, but settled quickly as well. The surroundings, usually tall trees or granite boulders, were too beautiful and serene for us to remain angry for long.

Although there was an early morning wake-up call at 6 a.m., there would be the odd straggler who was late coming to the bus that would take us to our walk, with the whole group sitting and waiting. Patience was an essential ingredient, something I was not endowed with by nature. But over the years, I mellowed and got used to the idiosyncrasies of the group.

Instead of getting impatient, I would just "drop into Great Walk time". Relax and chat.

The evenings around the fire, often under a star-infused night sky, were as much fun as the spectacular walks throughout the day. The food, prepared by a handful of alternating volunteers, was delicious. Much to the dismay of many of the women on camp, we never lost any weight despite the long walks because of the luxurious desserts. Apple crumble eaten around the fire, in the spotlight of the head torch, the smell of cinnamon intermingling with the smoke, was a sensuous feast. The absence of refrigeration notwithstanding, we always had plenty to eat, and the odd raisin or pumpkin seed from the much sought after snack-bags with dry fruits and nuts would continue to linger in the crevices of my backpack pockets for months afterwards. In the evenings we formed a circle around the blazing fire, snuggled up in warm jackets and woollen hats.

Rahel and Joschka hung out with the other kids throughout the whole walk. When we moved camp, which involved taking down the fire-pit, marquee, massive cooking pots, tables, crockery and packing it up in the truck, and then reversing the whole process at the next camp site, Joschka would attach himself to an adult male and help with the digging out of the fire-pit or other jobs. The Great Walk was an opportunity for Joschka to spend time with men, something that was missing in his life, which became more and more obvious the older he became. He learned how to light a fire, take care of the solar lights and other equipment, how to secure a tent in a storm. And even how to eat vegies for a week, something he resisted with great passion at home. The group brought out the best in him.

I remember one walk where Joschka learned how to make knots from one of the older men, who had offered a knot-making workshop to the group. Joschka leaned over the thick, dirt-crusted rope that the man's weather-beaten hands tied to a metal bar on the old truck, his expression intent. At the next camp site, he snatched the tent rope off me that I was about to tighten around a peg. With a big grin, his brown eyes alight with sparkles, he puffed out his chest like a mating peacock in the throes of courting and proceeded to display his newly acquired knot skills. I was impressed.

This special group was to become a pillar in my recovery from grief. And an important part of the lives of Rahel and Joschka as well. It showed them, and me, another way of being, away from computers, mobile phones and iPods. And running water – we learned the art of performing a bucket wash.

I forged new friendships, meeting people from all walks of life that I would otherwise never have had the opportunity to come across. They came from all over Western Australia, not just Perth. There were few couples in the group. The Great Walk was a magnet for single mothers, and I became friends with some of them. My partnered friends couldn't relate to the problems and emotional challenges of being a single parent, and I was relieved to have made friends with other women I could share the ups and downs of being a single parent with.

Some very special friendships have been forged out of the Great Walk camps, with some spilling over into everyday life back in Perth. The connection with the Great Walk, the land and the people, and the friendships that have grown out of that connection, have provided a colourful and soft new texture to my post-loss landscape.

~

Two years after Mark's death, I had made noticeable inroads into my physical recovery. My emotional onslaught from the recurring images at night, though, continued. As did the torment I felt at the memory of my husband's suffering and the level of pain endured by him.

After much deliberation, I decided to attend a personal development course overseas in the January school holidays, knowing that the children would be well looked after by their relatives in Melbourne. I felt out of control in the face of the nightmarish movies set on endless replay that appeared in my mind every night. I could not turn off the internal video recorder by myself and knew that I had to find a way to address my inability to work my way through my memories of Mark's suffering. And so, I turned to the course, a longer and more intense one than the one I had previously attended a few years before Mark fell ill, in the hope that it would help me on my path of recovery.

It had felt unsettling to have been at opposite ends of the Australian continent to Rahel and Joschka during the previous summer school holidays. Now it was outright scary to be in two different countries.

My main intention for attending the course in the US was to make some sense of suffering. Mark's suffering, but also the suffering in the world, which had come into sharp focus for me following his death. I began to take the first steps towards some relief from my trauma. I didn't expect this path to be quick or evolve in a straight line. I had found the first foothold on the concrete wall I needed to climb.

Early on following my loss, I recognised the importance of developing new friendships and I met several new female friends through the Great Walk. In the first couple of years after Mark's death, I forged a particularly strong friendship with a male friend.

I had met Wayne on a previous personal development course, and then did not cross paths with him again until years later when I went to a get-together in Perth for people attending the upcoming overseas course. I immediately recognised him, standing in front of the kitchen bench, wearing a red, blue and white flannel shirt tight around his broad shoulders. Rolled-up sleeves exposed brawny arms dotted with sun-bleached freckles, testimony to a life lived on the land.

At the airport a couple of weeks later, I walked into the departure gate and spotted Wayne's distinct broad frame lounging on a seat. Much to our surprise, we were on the same flight. This trip marked the beginning of our friendship.

During the course at the venue, we ran into each other at least once a day and always stopped to say hi and grabbed a moment to find out how things were going. One morning half-way through the course, I was extremely tired and could barely keep my eyes open.

"Katrin, I see you need to have a bit of a sleep during lunch." He placed his hand on my shoulder. "I know your hotel is too far away to walk there and back during the lunch hour, so would you like to come back to my hotel for a nap?"

The thought of a bed within a stone's throw of the venue was tempting. "Are you sure – what about your lunch? You need to eat something?"

"No worries, we can just grab a sandwich here and then bring it with us."

We took the elevator, which was panelled with mirrors. Dark rings under my eyes stared back at me.

Wayne swiped the card and we entered his room.

"Ah, my roommate seems to be out. Looks like you're gonna have a quiet sleep." He pulled back the down doona and fluffed up the white pillow. "Do you want to eat your sandwich first or go straight to sleep?"

I took off my shoes, nodded towards the bed and fell onto it. Wayne pulled the doona over me and tucked it under my arms and back.

"Sweet dreams. Don't worry about the time. I'll wake you."

I went to sleep with a smile on my face. It had been a long time since I had been tucked into bed.

I was particularly impressed by the fact that Wayne never made a pass at me. The absence of sexual innuendo was refreshing. It also made it very safe to become friends. Wayne had recently lost his farm as a result of several years of drought, and he was coming to terms with this painful loss. His broad frame conveyed groundedness and carried a calming imprint of the land he had cultivated. Following the course, a strong bond developed between us. It was an emotional connection, stripped of chemistry, that became as close as the friendships I had with my best girlfriends.

Not long after returning home from overseas, Wayne invited us to his father's farm, where he went for a holiday, staying at a fishing shack perched on a cliff facing the sloshing waves. Having navigated several dirt roads, I pulled my Elantra into the long, unpaved driveway of the farm. Tractors, broken farm machinery, rusted drums and cables spilt out of several large sheds. Diverse tools, tins and tables covered every inch of the dusty ground that was interspersed with shiny patches that had been licked by oil. My jaw dropped. A black and white dog jumped up at me, barking. Rahel bent down to stroke the dog and Joschka raced towards the farm machinery, eyes wide, repeatedly uttering "Wow."

Wayne leant against an old, battered jeep with the left-hand window missing that looked as if it had not been licensed for a couple of decades. I introduced him to the kids, who were suitably impressed with their surroundings.

"We've gotta drive down a pretty rough track to the fishing shack, so we'll chuck your gear into the back of this old lady and get going."

As I hopped into the four-wheel drive, I ducked my head to avoid the clusters of grey spider webs that covered the inside roof and the sun visor. The dirt track turned out to be marked by deep potholes and we could only go down the steepest bits in first gear. As we mounted the top of a hill, a view of the ocean opened up. There was a silver lining on the horizon, where the frothing swell met the flawless turquoise sky.

We stayed a couple of days at the fishing shack with Wayne and his brother's family. The tin walls rattled in sync with the wild ocean. At night

I relaxed in my sleeping bag, inhaling a mixture of the sharp chemical smell of insect repellent and salty seaweed.

The next afternoon, when all the kids played on the beach, Wayne and I scrambled up a steep hill. The sandy path offered no solid footholds and I slipped more than I walked. At the top, panting, we sat down. The echo of the rumbling untamed ocean reached us. Tiny white flowers with the tips of the petals painted in crimson bloomed amongst the dense, dark green ground covers. My body responded to the beauty of the scenery, the frothing waves sloshing against a seemingly never-ending pristine beach framed by white, flawless sand dunes. The tension in my shoulders eased off and my muscles relaxed. We sat there in silence, breathing the salt-laden air deep into our lungs, until the sun began to set, casting its golden glow onto a massive, off-shore rock. Strands of radiant light stroked the waves, bathing the sea in an orange glow. With the fading light we began to talk. Curiously, unexpectedly for a man raised in the harshness of unyielding land, Wayne was sensitive, and an attentive listener.

22

Back in Perth, I stared outside through the wooden blinds in our living room. Though my gaze rested on the yellow flowers of the Acacia hovering right in front of the window, it was unfocused, not taking in my surroundings. A single CAT scan would have saved Mark's life. Would have averted all those months of his torment. Images flooded my mind of Mark bent over the kitchen bench, his jaw clenched, clutching the mobile phone, his knuckles white. He had called all of his relatives in Melbourne individually, his mother, father, and both sisters, asking them if there was any history of headaches in the family. In all the time I had known him, he had never rung them on the same day. He only contacted his mum regularly. Did not call his dad.

All of Mark's brain damage and the whole state of being locked in was the result of the hydrocephalus, the increasing build-up of the brain fluid. As this was not diagnosed, it caused the strokes which led to Mark's brain damage.

I had never seen Mark in naked fear before. He'd always been my rock, had soothed my fears with gentle reassurance. Had taken on life's challenges with patience. Mark's unconcealed fear had frightened me. Even humour had deserted him.

Not only did the GP decide not to pursue diagnostic tests for Mark's severe headaches, she actually did the opposite: she had reassured Mark he had tension headaches. This was evident from a printout from the internet, several pages long, that she had handed him during the consult. It featured headings such as "what causes tension headaches", "what are the symptoms of tension headaches" and "how can I prevent frequent tension headaches". It made no mention of other, more serious possible causes.

As soon as Mark had walked through the front door, coming home from the consultation with the GP, he had called out to me, his voice unusually loud, swelled with urgency.

"It's nothing serious," he called up to me, "only tension headaches." Mark steadied himself on the handrail while walking up the stairs. I raced down to meet him.

We hugged each other tightly. I placed my hands onto his shoulders and gazed at his face. I could see the strain and fear leaving his body; his shoulders dropped down and relaxed. The frown that had been inscribed on his forehead over the last week eased off.

Then Mark produced the printout he had been given. This, to him, was the proof that his headaches were not serious. He studied the paperwork, his attention focused, unwavering. This seemingly definitive information prompted him to go back to work.

The next day he put on his polo shirt with the logo of the rising sun, walked over to me, his grey workbag dangling over his shoulder, and bent down to give me kiss.

"I'm going to work today, Schatz."

I looked at him, surprised. "Are you sure? I mean, are you really well enough?"

"I've read the information the doctor gave me a few times and I'm going to give it my best shot to get better."

"I'm really worried. I don't think this is a good idea."

"Don't worry, I'll be fine. I really need to do this, to work towards getting back to normal."

I remembered how he had clutched the pages, crumpling the edges of the paper in his need to believe its content that shielded him from anyone's doubt, especially his own.

Only two hours later I heard the low humming of his van coming up the driveway. Through the window I saw Mark opening the car door and easing himself out. He took slow steps towards the front door. I raced downstairs and flung it open. His face looked ashen and his normally bright eyes looked dull.

"I had to come home. The headaches are too strong. I couldn't concentrate." He forced a smile. "Alas, I tried. That's what matters. I'm going to bed to have a lie down. I'll be right, don't worry." He walked to the top of the stairs and turned around again to face me. "I'm going to try again tomorrow. I need to learn to get my normal life back with these headaches. They're not serious, but it looks like they might be here to stay. I've just got to adjust to them."

Even a couple of hours seemed proof to him that he was giving his best shot in resuming his normal life, following the advice given in the information sheets. For life had not been normal over the last week. On the contrary, the severe headaches had forced Mark to stay in bed; he had to remain upstairs all of the long Australia Day weekend as he was too weak to go downstairs. He could not even tuck the children into bed at night. Mark's debilitating headaches had arrived out of the blue. One day he had been fine, then he could barely get out of bed the next day.

I perched on the edge of the bright blue sofa that was tucked into the corner of the bay window in our upstairs living room. The same sofa Mark had been sprawled on that Australia Day weekend, his forehead scrunched up, shiny with droplets of sweat. I stroked the arm of the couch, my fingertips following the textured lines ingrained in the material.

All Mark's suffering, all that time locked in his body, would not have happened if he had that single CAT scan. The knowledge that Mark's torment could have been avoided with one simple, easily available diagnostic tool crushed me like a surfer caught beneath a gigantic wave, tumbled underwater, unstoppable, until my lungs threatened to burst. I bashed the padded arm of the sofa with my fist. I yelled out, "One single CAT scan!" Over and over.

Knowing that Mark's cyst had been operable magnified my despair. Even in the extremely poor state that Mark had been in by the time the cyst was removed, the surgery did not inflict further brain damage. Given that the surgical removal of the cyst was undertaken without problems in Mark's paralysed state, the most likely scenario if it had been discovered earlier was a full recovery.

Time after time in the hospital, on a daily basis in the High Dependency Unit, I had seen other patients get up out of bed just one day after extensive brain surgery, after the removal of a tumour, their heads swathed in white bandages.

I looked at the empty seat next to me. Mark would be sitting here today if he had been given that CAT scan. That was all that was needed to diagnose the pressure on his brain brought on by the increasing hydrocephalus. At that point in time, it was not important to know what caused the hydrocephalus, just that he had it.

I felt very strongly that the GP should have ordered a CAT scan given Mark's history of sudden, unusual, severe headaches, being woken up by the pain, the absence of an obvious explanation and the fact that he returned for a second consultation within a few days, because rest had not alleviated the headaches over the long weekend. To me, this was a case of medical negligence. Not a slight error. This mistake by the GP, her decision not to order a CAT scan and instead to reassure Mark with information on tension headaches, had caused extreme trauma, both to Mark and to us all. I simply could not fathom why she had not ordered such a simple diagnostic test.

It was important to me to follow this up and not to let it disappear into nothingness. I did not want anyone else to go through what we had endured, most of all what Mark had suffered. I had sought expert opinion on the professional conduct of the GP whilst Mark was in hospital, about two months after he fell into his coma. I lodged a complaint with the Office of Health Review. The role of this government organisation, I was told, was to provide impartial resolution for complaints about health services provided in the state of Western Australia.

I was assigned a complaints manager, B, who remained a faceless scrawled signature. She wrote a letter to inform me that she was seeking an opinion from an independent advisor on the case, a GP. And then I heard nothing for almost six months until mid-September, when I received a letter in the mail. Mark had just been moved to Murdoch Hospice. I ripped open the white envelope and began to read.

The letter dated 10 September 2004 informed me that the complaints manager had received the independent opinion from a GP in relation to my concerns about Mark's doctor. The complaints manager paraphrased the report by the independent GP and outlined that, although Mark's doctor seemed to have taken a good history and sound notes, she did not appear to have found a cause for the headaches and might have found a CAT scan to be of use for the purposes of making a diagnosis. According to the complaints manager, this needed to be put into context. She explained that the independent opinion stated that the suspicion of tension headaches was appropriate given that they are the most common form of headaches. The letter concluded that B intended to make further enquiries regarding the issue of diagnosis and the CAT scan.

While I was at the hospice, the complaints manager rang our home to speak to me. One of my children answered and told her where I was. Mark passed away the following day. The next contact B made with me was about three weeks later. My hands trembled when I saw the sender's address on the white business envelope. I ran up the driveway to the privacy of our house. The letter dated 30 September stated that the complaints manager had closed the file. It explained that she had obtained an independent opinion from a senior neurosurgeon who confirmed that it was too early for the GP to have ordered a CAT scan when she saw my husband. This letter acknowledged that B was aware that Mark had passed away. She expressed hope that I would find reassurance in this information. Rage detonated like a land mine and tears of anger streamed down my face. I was appalled with her deliberate choice of timing and the notion of reassurance felt like mockery. After my husband's funeral I did not have the strength required to attend to the abrupt closure of the complaint. I did not know then the extent of B's actions.

It was not until the following year that I re-read the correspondence by B. I thought about the timing of her one and only phone call to me and the closure of the case. She knew that Mark was close to dying when she called and yet she closed the case shortly afterwards, aware that he had just passed away. The timing of the whole complaints process struck me as odd. It had initially been a lengthy process. A lot of time had been given to the independent advisor to respond, who took nearly half a year to reply. I scanned the dates of the two letters I had received from B, 10th and 30th of September. How dare she close the case immediately after Mark's death, and without ever speaking to me? Apart from the dreadful timing, the whole thing did not seem right. For several weeks, I agonised over what to do. Finally, I decided to contact a lawyer.

Thus began my foray into legal territory.

~

I sat at my desk downstairs in the study overlooking our lawn. Memories of Mark and the kids playing cricket in the garden flickered like old movies in my mind. I had no idea how to find a lawyer who specialised in medical negligence. I had asked around my circle of friends, but no one knew of an appropriate law firm, not even our friend Tom who was a lawyer himself.

I grabbed the Yellow Pages and flicked through the thin paper to the section on lawyers. One advertisement for a local law firm specialising in medical negligence caught my attention. I dialled the number, not knowing what to expect. The receptionist put me straight through to a lawyer named

Jane. I briefly explained the situation. Jane invited me to her office to discuss the case.

The morning of the appointment with the lawyer in the city, I walked the children down the hill to school and then returned home to get changed. During Mark's illness and in the weeks and months following his death, I had not given any particular thought to what I was wearing. I was not dressing up for anyone, including myself. But now, for the first time, I was dressing for a specific purpose. A tangible event rather than one day of mourning blurring into the next.

It felt strange putting on a fairly formal navy skirt, the static polyester lining foreign on the skin of my legs, so unlike the cotton skirts I normally dressed in. I caught the bus into the city, unsure what lay ahead. Gazing out the window onto the heavy oncoming traffic on the freeway, my determination strengthened. I did not want any other family to go through what we endured. What I wanted was for our case to somehow force clear guidelines for GPs in relation to serious, potentially life-threatening headaches. At this stage I did not know that a name exists in medical terminology for such dangerous headaches: Red Flag Headaches.

Perched on a grey office chair, I relayed my story to the lawyer. My heart pounded in my chest when she said that I appeared to have a case for medical negligence. When she took down some details, including Mark's birth date, she mentioned, "Oh, the same birthday as mine."

Sitting in my living room at home that afternoon, contemplating what I should do, I thought about the weird coincidence that the lawyer had the same birthday as Mark. And not only that, she also had a Dutch surname. I took these synchronicities as a positive sign that I was on the right track.

After several nights of tossing and turning, I phoned the lawyer to say that I wanted to go ahead with the case. On my first visit to the legal firm, Jane had explained the procedure for pursuing a claim against a medical doctor. The course of action would be to instigate mediation with the medical insurer of the GP; the outcome that was sought was a settlement. I read between the lines that the medical insurance company would fight this case hard. Any headache case would send their alarm bells ringing because of the widespread nature of headaches and the potential of a precedence case.

The phone still in my hand, I sat on the carpet with my back resting against the couch and considered the significance of a precedence case.

Yes, this is exactly what I want, to set a precedent which forces GPs to order a CAT scan in cases of serious, otherwise unexplained headaches.

At the second meeting with my lawyer, I explained that I had filed a complaint with the Office of Health Review and produced the two letters that I had received. Jane asked if I had seen the actual report by the independent adviser. I stared at her in disbelief.

"Could I actually read that report?" I asked.

"Yes, of course," she replied. "You are entitled to obtain that report. In fact, you can apply to receive the report by the independent adviser under the Freedom of Information Act."

"Freedom of Information Act," I echoed. I took a deep breath. I actually have some rights here, I thought. I'm really glad that I'm sitting here, pursuing this case. I'm actually going to get some answers.

23

My naked feet caressed the smooth, shiny surface of the wooden floorboards of the hall. I closed my eyes and let the sound-waves pulsate through my body. The black, oversized loudspeaker stood tall and upright in front of me, fearless. The drumming echoed through my stomach, which expanded and contracted in sync with the music. Five-rhythm dance mirrors the rhythms of life, slow, staccato, chaotic, lyrical, stillness, the instructor had said.

My mind relaxed and slowed down its rapid thinking. I trembled with the sheer joy of letting go. I began to move, swaying from side to side. The room oozed calmness. I opened my eyes and gazed around, noting how everyone seemed absorbed in their own world, becoming one with the music.

My skin was stroked by the soft breath of the music, the first of the five rhythms played on the night, tender and melodic, like the gentle ebb and flow of a bathtub filled with steaming water, bubbles caressing alert skin aching for touch. I began to feel my body moving. The tight grip my active mind exerted on me, continually searching for answers, was gradually loosened.

The speed of the music changed. I hovered for a moment. This was the chaos phase. A cold shiver ran down my spine, leaving goose bumps in its trail. Should I lie down at the edge of the dance floor, I wondered, out of the way of chaos's destructive path? A moss green mat beckoned me with its peaceful softness. I ran my hands over my skirt, from the top of my thighs to my knees, resting there, unsure. My hands dropped and my arms flowed from side to side, finding their own rhythm in the absence of any discernible rhythm of the erratic song that offered no direction, speed or sense. Legs clad in fisherman pants stomped wildly next to me.

My body followed suit, dropped all need for control, for direction and intention, and started, tentatively at first, to listen to its own tempo, absorbed in the present moment. The irregular screeching beat, constantly changing, unpredictable, forged its way into me, now less guarded and surrendering. My body swirled, my feet stomped, my arms flailed around me, cautious at first, then more daring, surrendering, deeper and deeper. The muscles in my stomach, always tense, softened, despite my dislike of chaos. I gave in and let my body lead, swaying, twirling, my feet stomping. Diving into the present moment.

~

The report of the independent GP that I had requested under the Freedom of Information Act arrived in a mustard-coloured envelope. I ran up the long driveway to the front door and bolted upstairs, taking two steps at a time. I grabbed a pair of scissors and opened the envelope as I perched on the arm of the couch.

My hands shook, rustling the paper. The report was dated mid-August. Stunned, I pored over the pages:

- I am a little surprised that the patient was not directly questioned about the effect that the headache was having on his ability to work and what steps he was taking to remedy the headache and the success or otherwise of this.

- I am concerned that no actual diagnosis was offered on this second consultation. I would have thought that given the fact that the patient had returned complaining of ongoing headache and that there were, at the doctor's admission, no significant stresses in his life, further investigation would have been appropriate at this point. ... In my opinion a one-week history of undiagnosed persistent headache in a man who was not a frequent headache sufferer suggests a sufficient possibility of underlying pathology to warrant a further investigation or at least an opinion over the telephone from a neurologist.

- I do feel it reasonable to expect a General Practitioner to be able to investigate or refer on someone with ongoing and undiagnosed potentially serious symptoms.

I could barely breathe. The pages slipped onto the floor. I leaned forward and held onto the back of the sofa. And I wailed at the insanity of it all.

I was in the middle of cooking that night when the report forced itself into my thoughts. A wave of emotion swelled up. Rahel sat on the couch reading a book. Joschka played with his Lego downstairs in his room. I turned off the spaghetti bubbling on the stove and ran into my bedroom. I closed the door and sank onto the bed. Mark's side of the bed, I noted. I lay down on top of the brightly patterned orange doona cover, his last birthday present for me. My tears soaked the material. I pressed my palm over my mouth to stifle the sobs, acutely aware of Rahel next door. Disbelief magnified the intensity of my anguish. "Mark," I whispered. "Why did you have to suffer so much? Why? When it could have been averted."

I remained on the bed until I calmed down. I thought of the uncooked pasta on the stove. This clash of realities, cooking dinner and the content of the report, was unbearably surreal. I splashed my face with cold water and walked back into the kitchen. Rahel immediately looked up from her book.

"Did you cry, Mama?" She dropped her novel onto the couch, came over and wrapped her arms around me.

I nodded. "Yes I did, sweetness. I'm okay though. Really. I just thought about Dad."

Rahel tightened her embrace.

After the children had gone to bed, I re-read the letter to grasp the enormity of the information. I punched the couch, angry and in disbelief. How could she have done this? Closed the file after this report by the independent GP? A sentence from the report echoed through my mind. "I do not know the geographical location of the doctor's surgery and thus am not aware of the availability of specialist and radiological services." Availability! Fucking hell. There's a large radiology centre five minutes down the road from us. How easy would it have been for Mark to go there. Five bloody minutes away.

Here was confirmation that the GP should have ordered a CAT scan, and the complaints manager had withheld the information. The room disappeared and all I could see was the paper in my hands. I got up, went downstairs into my study and rummaged through the paperwork until I retrieved the two letters from B. I scanned them for an explanation of what had happened.

The first letter stated that the independent advisor found that the GP *may* have found a CAT scan of diagnostic use. May have. Are you kidding me? I carefully re-read the report. And then the letter by the complaints manager. It claimed the report stated that the GP's suspicion of tension headaches was appropriate. *There was no such statement in the report.* I gasped, incredulous.

I studied the second letter in order to find out what reasoning B had used to justify closing the file in the face of the opinion voiced by the independent GP. She referred to an independent opinion from a senior neurosurgeon. Hang on, I thought, on the 10th of September she had informed me she was following up the report by the GP which had taken six months to be submitted. And now, on the 30th of September, she claims to have obtained an opinion by a neurosurgeon. That seemed odd. I picked up the A4 envelope again and looked inside. There was another piece of paper inside. I pulled it out. It was entitled "Memo". It detailed that B had spoken to a neurosurgeon *over the phone*. The specialist's opinion had not been obtained in writing then, but simply in a phone conversation. The neurosurgeon is said to have confirmed that if Mark had returned after one week, as suggested by his GP, then that *may* have been the time to explore a CAT scan referral.

How many times was Mark meant to return before his headaches were taken seriously? This memo was dated 30th of September, the same day as the letter she had sent me to say that she was closing the file. It had taken half a year for the written report by the GP, and now, in a hurry, another opinion had been sought over the phone and the file closed immediately.

I wondered if this was proper procedure. I tossed and turned that night, unable to go to sleep, wondering what lay ahead, where legal representation would lead me. Was there any justice out there?

24

My gaze wandered from the bright yellow custard that hugged the sides of the apple strudel over the alpine panorama all around me and lingered on the sheer beauty of the majestic mountains. I feasted my eyes on the luscious, vibrant green of the trees and grass that is so noticeably absent from the West Australian summer landscape. I was drawn to the strength and steadfastness of the exposed rock. Then my gaze drifted back to the eager faces of my kids nestled next to their smiling grandparents on the wooden bench, savouring their dessert. We were already high up at a quaint Austrian *Alm*, a rustic alpine restaurant, and yet the mountains towered above us. In the background, the irregular ringing of cowbells added to the magic of the scene and soothed my senses.

It had been nearly two years since Mark's death, and this was the first time Rahel, Joschka and I visited my parents overseas in Germany. They lived near Bonn, a long way from the Alps, but their love for the mountains went back a long way. When I was growing up, our three-week summer holidays were always spent in the mountains, hiking all day, walking uphill for several hours, before being rewarded with the three-hundred-and-sixty-degree mountain panorama at the summit. I always loved the clear air, heavy with the scent of freshly cut grass, which symbolised summer for me.

In the last few days, the mountains had proved themselves to be calming. Immersed in the beauty and immensity of the landscape, some of the layers of my intense emotions began to soften. More than that, I could reconnect with the little girl inside of me who remembered her parents taking care of her. I snuggled into my dad, perched on the timber planks of the restaurant. As a child I had relished stroking his face, shaven and more textured than the softness of my mother's skin. Something about that hint of coarseness was comforting. My dad's gentle masculinity, his hand lightly placed on my elbow when we entered restaurants, and his compassion glowing deep in his kind blue eyes nurtured me. It made me realise how much I missed that masculine presence in my life. But it also made me enjoy the rare opportunity to sink into my Dad's presence.

We got up from the table, not a speck of custard left on our plates, and the others went outside. I walked to the toilet in the belly of the functioning farm, with the unisex lavatory placed next to the cow shed. I caught a pungent whiff of cow dung as I closed the door behind me. I struggled to turn the key. As I undid the belt of my shorts, I noticed that the windowless space was tiny, tomb-like. The whitewashed walls were uncomfortably close. An uneasy feeling settled into my stomach. As I reached for the key in order to open the door, it did not turn. I rattled the door handle, frantic. The door remained shut. In a split second, my body was awash with a wave of panic that set my nerve endings on fire and made my heart pound in my chest, hammering against my ribcage. My breath was reduced to a shallow, rapid intake of air. All I could think was *I need to get out.* I hammered my fist against the door and yelled for help. A baritone voice answered immediately, "I'll get the innkeeper."

A laid-back voice asked me in a thick alpine accent to pull out the key on my side. It eased out in one smooth swift movement. My trembling hand dropped the cold metal key, and it fell to the ground with a clonk. The door opened from the outside. I looked straight at the innkeeper's felt hat with its elongated tip dangling down the side of the young man's head onto his shoulder.

My legs took me outside, through a dark passageway past the cow shed to where my family stood waiting for me. My tongue lay thick in my mouth, unable to form the words that would give some shape to this surreal experience. I have always had an affinity with words and yet I could not describe my turmoil. I turned to look to the left to see a pair of large brown eyes gazing lazily back at me from the cow paddock. The presence of my family, the cow and the pristine surroundings were in stark contrast to my emotions.

I swallowed hard. My parents did not seem to notice my agitation. They simply remarked, "Oh, there you are."

We resumed our walking tour for that day. I looked down to the ground as I set one boot-clad foot in front of the other. A multitude of still steaming greeny-yellow cow pats were strewn across the path, forcing me to pay close attention to where I set foot.

That night, I lay in bed awake. My mind wandered over the incident in the toilet. That was an anxiety attack. It was unlike anything I had ever felt before. When Mark had been locked in his body, I had come to know the blackness of despair. This was very different, even unlike the shock I experienced in Intensive Care. I was overwhelmed by the memory of the intensity of my panic. Instinctively, I knew that it would take ages to comprehend.

Over the coming weeks, I grew more and more concerned about my inability to make sense of the anxiety attack. I experienced flashes of my emotions when I had been locked into the lavatory. That I had lost control like that rocked the foundations of my sense of self. Though I feel my emotions fully, I can equally identify strongly with my intellect and with logic. The temporary mental paralysis sparked off a fear in me that burned a hole in my persona. Even when I had stood facing the abyss of Mark's torment, my toes curled around the precipice, I had not lost control, had kept myself together. How is this possible, I asked myself over and over, that I did not fall apart then, but lost it now?

Meanwhile, this new part of me was entrenching itself in my life on a regular basis. From the first panic attack onwards, whenever I entered windowless, fully enclosed public toilets, I could not bring myself to lock the door. In the cubicle, at the very least I would check if the key would turn smoothly before shutting the door. I felt deeply unhinged in these spaces, my heartbeat speeding up. When we returned to my parents' home, an apartment on the top floor of a high-rise, we entered the lift as usual. As soon as the doors shut, I broke into a sweat. As the elevator rattled along, I could not concentrate on what my parents were saying as I waited in agony for the doors to open. With elevators, there is a suspended moment between moving and the opening of the door. First, the movement slows down. Then there is a hovering stillness before the doors open. That is the worst moment.

I left the elevator, the very elevator that I had used all throughout my childhood hundreds of times, swamped with clammy anxiety. I had a problem. It took quite a while to name this problem to myself: claustrophobia. Following the full-blown anxiety attack in Austria, overnight, I hated being in enclosed spaces, toilet cubicles and elevators. In my everyday life, this did not occur too frequently. But on holidays, I was confronted with my inability to be in confined spaces on an almost daily basis. To my relief, I was all right on planes, as long as I had a window to look out of – except, of course, for the dreaded tiny toilet.

Whenever I entered one of these spaces, my self-image as a rational, independent person was shaken. Who had I become? What was happening to me? It took me a long time to confide in others. I mean, I grew up with an elevator.

Surprisingly, I did not see the connection to Mark's illness immediately. It was not until about a year after the sudden and powerful arrival of this phobia in my life that I recognised the link to Mark's locked-in state. I was sitting cross-legged around a fire on a friend's property in the country, celebrating her birthday, when the man next to me, who I had never met before, began a conversation with me, his deep voice soothing, like the narrator of a nature programme. Somehow, the subject of my deep discomfort in windowless enclosed spaces came up. And the nature of my husband's illness. During this chance encounter, he observed: "It seems to me that your fear of becoming locked inside an elevator or other small space is linked to your husband's locked-in syndrome."

As I looked into the licking flames of the fire, feeling the softness of the earth underneath me, the relationship with Mark's imprisonment became obvious. I shook my head. How could I have missed this connection? When I had spent so much time thinking this over. With relief, I noted that at last there was a logical explanation. And yet, I still found it impossible to accept this irrational fear in myself.

25

The motor of the bus hummed under my seat. If the brilliant blue skies unmarked by clouds were anything to go by, the upcoming mediation meeting might deliver an outcome that acknowledged the importance of GPs employing diagnostic technology in the face of debilitating, severe and unusual headaches, known as Red Flag Headaches.

I yearned for the GP to be held responsible for sending Mark home reassured with a diagnosis of tension headaches and her decision not to send him for a CAT scan.

My lawyer had explained the process of mediation. I was no longer represented by Jane, who I had spoken to initially, as she had left the law firm. My case had now been taken over by the owner of the firm.

"The GP has handed her case over to her medical insurance company, which will be represented by lawyers acting on their behalf," he told me in his office. "Cases first go to mediation, and the majority are settled that way." He leaned back into his chair.

I cradled a cup of green tea in my hands, listening intently.

"What would happen to the GP if we settled?"

"Her premiums would go up."

"That's it? Well, that's good. I don't want her to have any negative professional consequences. But I do want it recognised that, with Mark's severe headaches and return visit to the surgery, she should have ordered a CAT scan." I was relieved that a settlement at mediation would not endanger her career. "I'd like a wake-up call for GPs that they shouldn't ignore the warning signs of severe, sudden headaches." I sighed deeply.

"Settlement does not constitute any admission of guilt; you need to know that." His voice was underscored by a serious tone.

I nodded. But I didn't really take that last bit in until I thought it over at home. In the quietude of my own four walls, I contemplated how I felt about not having any admission of wrongdoing. There would be no precedent for future cases then, which is what I wanted most of all. It would give some sense of, well, not closure, for that was unattainable, but perhaps … I grappled to put my thoughts into words. What was it that it would give me, us as a family? Recognition. Some recognition that Mark had deserved to be taken care of with much more diligence.

The bus pulled into St. George's Terrace. I looked at the house number on the nearest building and then at the letter bearing the location of the meeting room. My hands trembled. Only a few buildings to go. My gaze wandered up the high rises ahead of me. The appointed building was located opposite Perth Concert Hall. How many times had I driven past and pointed out the concert hall and neighbouring Governor's residence to the German tourists on my city sightseeing tours?

Upstairs, my lawyer led me into a waiting room until we were called in. The meeting was over nearly as soon as it began. Not even routine pleasantries were exchanged. I stated my name, the mediator read out what the case was about. The opposition stated that they would not enter into any settlement proceedings.

With that, we were dismissed.

Back outside, the innocent, brilliant sky belied the hostile, unyielding mindset the medical insurer had adopted. Bile bubbled into my throat. They refused to enter into any discussions. This was unusual, I was told.

Like so much else that had happened.

Not long afterwards, I received a letter from the insurer warning me that they would pursue court costs if I took this matter any further. Startled by the combative tone of the letter, I let it slip out of my hand. It was a clear indication of the hostile attitude employed by the medical insurance company.

I was now faced with the distressing decision of whether to go to court or not. I agonised over this during sleepless nights and endless discussions with family and friends. My body responded with cramps and diarrhoea. In the stillness of the dark nights, I asked Mark: what should I do?

With the obvious aggression of the medical insurer and the massive funds at their disposal to spend whatever was needed, such as top legal representation, I knew it was a David against Goliath case.

After two weeks, I made up my mind. I was not going to be bullied by their muscle power. I knew without a doubt that the GP should have ordered a CAT scan. Though I considered her decision not to order a scan medically negligent, especially her diagnosis of tension headaches, I did not see her conduct arising out of disinterest or malice. It was a mistake. A human mistake with deadly consequences. I owed it to Mark, and to our children, not to drop this case because of the threatening attitude of the insurer. If they refused settlement, I was left with no other choice but to go to court.

Yet I was shaken by their intimidating letter. Scanning the white pages for consumer information advisory groups, I came across an advisory body for medical issues. I made an appointment and was told that they had never heard of a case whereby the medical insurance company had "chased a widow for court costs."

Preparations for the trial ensued. Expert witness reports relating to the consultation conducted by Mark's GP and sent to me by my lawyer tumbled into my mailbox, and kept rolling in. Whenever another report arrived, my hands trembled, unwilling to expose the contents. The continuous flood of expert reports dispirited me.

"This is the nature of legal proceedings," a lawyer friend told me. "Don't take it personally. It's all calculated strategy; emotion doesn't come into it."

Don't take it personally. This advice came from a few sides. I had no intention of not taking it personally, even if I could have. I was way too emotional by nature, and this case was personal. I had lost my husband. My children had lost their father. And one CAT scan would have meant that he would be alive now.

26

The trial started on Monday, the 11th of June 2007, at 10.37 a.m. in the District Court of Western Australia. I know this to the minute because I have the trial transcripts.

Plaintiff: Katrin Den Elzen

Defendant: Dr. Sharon Hart

My sandal-clad foot got caught under the heavy metal door that guards the entrance to the courtroom. I limped into the windowless space. Neon lights cast their impersonal hue across the room. I sat down on an uncomfortable, fixed plastic chair in the second row, my toe pulsating with heat. I looked down, saw purple patches spreading, and felt the throbbing ache of the swelling.

I was there to get answers, to hold the GP accountable for what I saw as carelessness. For letting herself be distracted by Mark's youthful skin, tanned instead of ashen. For failing to make sure that he did not continue to walk along the precipice of brain damage.

How was she going to defend herself, her decision not to order a CAT scan? What had made her think that it was tension headaches?

At the time of the court case, I was in a relationship that didn't last that long but that I had wanted and expected to be long-term and sincere – until I found out that these intentions were not shared, despite earlier promises to the contrary, adding new, agonising hurt to my already wounded self. Things were already rocky between us. He came to the court on the first day for support and chose to sit in the row behind me.

My friends Ina and Wayne were seated on either side of me. Ina shuffled in her seat. I turned to look at her and she tilted her head towards the row in front of us. I gasped. There she was. Petite with shoulder-length brown hair. It had to be her. She was the only other female in the room apart from us. My body sat upright on the chair, not touching the supportive backrest, startled into an agitated alertness. The air in the confined room, hidden away amongst towering concrete buildings, was stale. I tried to take a deep breath, but my lungs seemed to close up. It was not innocent, this courtroom air.

~

"All rise," the clerk bellowed.

I looked at Ina. She grasped my hand and squeezed it, her warmth soothing my shivering arm. Wayne's solid frame was comforting.

"Your Honour, I appear for the plaintiff in this matter," said my barrister.

Plaintiff. That's me. How bizarre.

A legal discussion ensued between the judge, the barrister for the defence, Mr. Lockwood, and the barrister acting on my behalf, Mr. Dawson. Phrases spun around my head – *the plaintiff's evidence – in my respectful submission – plaintiff's book of evidence – Mr. Usher – defendant's book of evidence – amended statement of claims – amended book of papers* …

The three-way discussion went on and on. The white curly wigs, reminiscent of a period drama set in a castle, gave the setting a surreal air. It was difficult to concentrate, as I was going to be called up first. The legalese bouncing off the courtroom walls stirred up the butterflies in my stomach. I did not dare whisper to Ina. We exchanged a sideways glance.

My barrister summed up our case. Then the defence barrister started a debate about the issue of *hearsay*. Specifically, he aimed to pre-empt what "the plaintiff" might say in regard to what her late husband had told her about his consultation with Dr. Hart. Physical sensations he had described to me were admissible. Anything else was not.

"If the deceased came home and said, 'I told the doctor such and such', that would be hearsay," Mr. Lockwood asserted.

I'm not even on the witness stand yet.

At 11.42 a.m., I was called up. I wiped my damp palms on my thighs.

With my toe, now yellowish-green as well as purple, still throbbing, swelling over the edge of my sandal, I made my way over to the witness stand.

"I swear by the Almighty God that the evidence I shall give shall be the truth, the whole truth and nothing but the truth."

I scanned the room, took in the barristers and several men in dark suits. Out of the corner of my eye, I glimpsed Dr. Hart's face. There was nothing about her features that stood out. With the exception of her slight build, which startled me.

I pulled the chair back, sat down, and placed both my hands, palms down, onto the polished wood, as if the grain could steady my nerves. All my senses were poised, quivering.

"Mrs Den Elzen." My barrister looked at me, his expression neutral. "Your full name is Katrin Den Elzen? Katrin spelt K-a-t-r-i-n?"

"That's right."

I took a deep breath. My voice sounded clear but strangely unfamiliar.

I answered questions about my personal particulars, and about Mark's university qualifications and work history. The inquiry moved to the time Mark's headaches started and the consultation with Dr. Hart. The discussion about hearsay at the beginning of the trial notwithstanding, the issue reared its head as soon as I gave evidence about what Mark had told me.

My barrister asked, "How do you know that your husband was taking painkillers?"

"I saw him taking painkillers. I saw an empty packet of painkillers on his bedside table. And on the weekend I asked him, 'How often are you taking painkillers?' He told me …"

Mr. Lockwood interjected: "I object to that."

My mouth had already formed the next word and my lips hovered half-open.

The judge replied, "I think that probably would be hearsay."

A debate about precedence cases regarding hearsay followed.

"What did you observe from your own eyes how your husband was feeling?" Mr. Dawson asked.

An image of Mark's furrowed eyebrows and pearls of sweat collecting on his forehead flashed through my mind.

"He was clearly unwell. And he was very worried about the headaches and told me so repeatedly. What struck me most was that he wasn't even reading. He wasn't watching TV. For him to just sit down, without a book in his hand, or a newspaper, that's something he'd never, ever do."

I stated that I observed and overheard Mark ring up every family member in Melbourne because he was so worried about his headaches. I gave evidence that Mark spent the long weekend between the bed and our couch, lying down and mostly sleeping. That he did not come with us to the Australia Day fireworks at the river, as was our family tradition. That his headaches worsened considerably on Monday.

I kept looking only at my barrister. Did not let my gaze wander to Dr. Hart, who sat in the front row behind the two or three suited representatives from her medical insurance company.

Then I was asked about the pages from the internet that Dr. Hart had given Mark at the consultation, entitled "Tension Headaches". I told the court how he had asked me to read them and how he had felt reassured by them.

"Do you tender them?" the judge asked.

"Yes, I seek to tender them," Mr. Dawson replied.

"Exhibit 1, thank you Mr. Usher." The judge addressed the attendant.

My evidence covered the days after the consultation with Dr. Hart, how I drove Mark to Fremantle Hospital, the rush by ambulance to Sir Charles Gairdner Hospital, his emergency operation, up to the point where Mark had an MRI brain scan almost a week into his coma.

"And there was a meeting with the professor?" My barrister's expression remained neutral.

"Yes, about the results of the MRI scan, which showed the extent of the brain damage. He was advising me to consider non-treatment."

Here I was, talking about the meeting with Professor Nemeth in a court of law. This meeting that had left me in shock in the Emergency Department. The horror of the neurologist's words had haunted me on countless nights. My painful memories of the professor's cold demeanour were in stark contrast with sitting there in the court, giving evidence, calmly, as if I was talking about my shopping list, loaf of bread, butter, chicken fillet, bananas ... That was even more surreal than sitting among wigs and black robes.

"So, the professor said ..." My barrister started to ask me.

"Is this a convenient time?" the judge interjected.

"Indeed, Your Honour."

"All right. 2.15."

I looked at the barrister, who had turned his back to me and walked over to his seat. It took me a moment to realise we had broken off for lunch mid-sentence. Moisture collected along my spine. The sombre room transformed into a chatty hub. My gaze brushed past Dr. Hart. She stood next to two suited men towering over her. Her eyes were cast to the ground. This must be hard on her too.

I got up, my mind still on the meeting at the hospital. I stumbled and my big toe began to shoot sharp pains up my leg. I'd forgotten about it. Now that I looked at it, I noticed that it was even more swollen.

After the lunch break, I continued to be questioned by my barrister about Mark's illness, his various hospital stays, and his passing away at Murdoch hospice. The questioning by my barrister finished off with me reiterating how relieved Mark had been by the diagnosis of tension headaches, and how he had clung to the advice outlined in the internet pages he had been given by Dr. Hart.

At 3.10 p.m. my barrister said, "I have no further questions."

Without a break or pause, the defence barrister got up and began his cross-examination. There was no greeting. Not even a slight nod.

He stood a few metres away from me. Big-framed and tall, his black robe hung loosely by his side and the wide sleeves swayed with every gesture.

"Could the witness be shown exhibits …"

I was asked to look at Mark's invoices and work diary and was questioned about them for about ten minutes. Later Mr. Lockwood asked me about the start of Mark's headaches. There what felt like aggressive undertones in his voice.

"Just answer my question."

I was shown another exhibit.

"Mrs Den Elzen, if you could look at that document on page …"

I looked down at the paperwork that the court clerk had placed into my hands. They were medical notes from 1995.

"It says there that your husband had headaches. And it mentions him having a cold."

"Yes."

"Do you remember that the headaches were associated with a cold?"

"Well, I was just reading that here as you were pointing that out."

I looked up from the paper and stared directly at the barrister. A shudder went down my arms. It was as if I could see green slime running down his body. His posture remained the same, but a slight flicker in his eyes showed that he probably did not expect that answer.

Questions turned to the start of Mark's headaches, and whether he worked or not after seeing Dr. Taylor in relation to his headaches on Friday the 23rd of January 2004. I stated that he did not work afterwards, that he came straight home.

"You're sure about that?"

The barrister employed the cold, calculating tone of voice and attitude you would expect in a criminal case, alien in this civilian court. I was the plaintiff, not the defendant, and yet, as his eyes stared me down, I felt as if I was on trial for murder.

"Yes, one-hundred percent sure."

I was asked to look at Mark's diary, at the jobs he had written down for that Friday.

"As you said to His Honour earlier, this diary shows the work your husband does on a given day. Doesn't that mean that was the work he did that day?"

"That means he was planning to do that work, but he didn't do it because he didn't leave home again after he came home from the surgery."

"Are you sure about that?"

"I am one-hundred percent sure."

"You're not getting confused with the other consultation, when he came home from seeing Dr. Hart?"

"No, I'm not getting confused with that."

The questioning continued until 4.15 p.m. and then the trial was adjourned until the next day. I was to return to the witness stand the next day.

Outside, I went to a café with Ina and Wayne. The man I was seeing left to go to his house – he said he disliked being in court and did not return the next day. My hot chocolate arrived in a black mug. I stirred the froth absentmindedly, the spoon clonking against the rim of the porcelain.

"What a day." I put down my spoon and wrapped both hands around the warm mug.

"Ah." Ina took a sip from her cup. "God, I need this, after that cross examination."

"Did you see how the barrister tried to discredit me with these headaches Mark had in 1995?" The mug shook precariously in my hand and I nearly spilled some milk on my top.

"Well, let me tell you it didn't work." Ina nudged me. "You did really well answering his questions. Staying focused."

"So tomorrow morning you're not first up, are you? They're having expert witnesses first?" Wayne asked. His calm voice was just what I needed to reduce the intensity of my anger.

I nodded. "Yeah, it's via video-link from over east. It seems that's the time they've booked her."

"How many expert witnesses are there altogether do you know?" Wayne inquired.

"Mmh, let me see. I think it's three for each side. We're both having two GPs and one neurologist, so that's six altogether." I put down my empty mug. "And then there's a psychologist appearing for each side. This is in relation to me, to identify the effect Mark's hospitalisation and death has had on me."

That night I tossed and turned. Legal jargon spun around my head.

Just answer yes or no ... I turned over to my left. *My learned friend ... what I put to you was* ... I pressed my palms onto my ears ... *just confine yourself to the question.* I threw back the quilt ... *Your Honour ... just answer my question* ...

I could not stop these phrases from looping around in my head. The more I tried to go to sleep in order to be well rested for the next day on the witness stand, the more the phrases burrowed into my consciousness.

~

The next morning, I met Ina outside the court building. She knew that I was anxious about riding in the elevator and made sure she was there in the lift with me. I hobbled inside, my toe pulsating. Wayne was already waiting for us outside the courtroom.

The trial started at 9.30 a.m. with one of our medical expert witnesses called via video-link, a professor of neurology from Melbourne. My legal team had to go outside the state of Western Australia to get an expert witness. She gave evidence that if a CAT scan had been taken on the days prior to Friday the 30th of January when Mark was hospitalised, that the hydrocephalus would have been seen on a scan. The reason for this, according to the specialist, was that the scan taken on the 30th showed that the hydrocephalus was not acute, and that it had been there for a while.

She also explained that hydrocephalus, or literally "water on the brain", did not increase in a linear manner. She held up a diagram which showed that the pressure increases slowly initially, but there is a point when it rises steeply. This, she said, was a typical pattern. She concluded that the scan taken on the 30th showed that raised intracranial pressure was the cause of Mark's headaches leading up to that day.

In cross-examination, Mr. Lockwood put the following history to the witness: mild to moderate headaches that had been improving, relieved with analgesia, and no other symptoms.

Rage snared its spindly fingers around my heart, squeezing it tight. It was very difficult to remain mute.

At 11 a.m., after a short break, another one of our expert witnesses was called, a GP.

Mr. Dawson questioned him on the way he would take a patient's history.

The witness gave a whole long list of questions he would ask about the history of the headaches, the onset, duration, location and type of pain the headaches caused.

"History becomes especially important where examination findings are minimal or absent. If you didn't know the patient, then history taking needs to be more detailed."

Mr. Dawson continued his line of questioning. "If the analgesic use extended to nighttime, would that come within your description of responding to analgesia?"

"No, if a patient wakes up with the headache and then has to get up in the night, that would indicate a more severe headache."

Following the cross-examination of the witness, the court adjourned for lunch.

"All right. 2.15. Thank you." The judge set the time to resume the session.

I stared at the lacklustre fried rice on a white chipped plate in front of me. I picked at the food with chopsticks, but my stomach rebelled when I tried to eat a mouthful.

I looked at Ina and Wayne. "I cannot believe how Lockwood presented the facts. For God's sake, to present the headaches as mild? And being unable to work and having to lie down means no other symptoms now?" I gagged on the rice.

Both of my friends shook their heads. "It's unbelievable, outrageous." Ina hammered her fist onto the table. The plates vibrated and clonked.

"I like the way the GP made a point about being self-employed and not working," Wayne said. "He reckons self-employed people tend to drag themselves off their death-beds in order to go to work."

"Yeah, that should've set her alarm bells off." I shoved the fried rice into one pile.

"Dawson asked him if it would increase his index of suspicion if he was unable to go to work." Ina drew quotation marks in the air to indicate the legal jargon. "And naturally he answered that it would. A busy, self-employed man who was rarely ill, and who came in with sudden headaches would be uncommon, he said."

After lunch, Ina and I returned to the courtroom and sat down waiting, silent. The defence barrister lounged in his chair a mere three metres in front of me. His upturned wig rested on the table, exposing a bald head. He turned around to a suited insurance representative and held up a diagram of a brain. Waving the piece of paper in the air, his face distorted in disgust. "Ugh. Gross."

We stared at this scene, and then at each other, open mouthed.

Straight afterwards, the court resumed and I was back on the witness stand, facing Lockwood. An image of his disgusted expression, nose scrunched up, lips pressed together, was still with me.

Just before 3 p.m., I was released from the witness stand. And then the judge made an impassioned, unexpected speech.

"I would approach a mediation, and I would be very disappointed if the parties failed to sort out their differences."

My hands gripped the armrests.

"There are many cases where settlement represents a fair outcome in a way that a result in the favour of one party never can. This matter is most unfortunate, and I recognise that. There's always a sadness felt by judges that matters of this kind end up at this point when there're other ways of resolving differences."

I was stunned. After a moment, a flash of hope reared up its head that perhaps we could have a settlement.

Ina noticed my expression and leaned closer in to me. "They never brought anything to the table at the mediation meeting," she whispered, "they probably won't now either." She looked at me, her eyes soft. "I'm sorry to crush your hopes."

27

The video screen flickered and a female face appeared upon it. This was our expert witness, a professor in general medicine from Sydney. Questioned by my barrister on what constitutes a sound consultation, she stressed the importance of history taking, especially in a patient not seen before.

"A lot of people have difficulties describing pain, because they're not used to it. So one way of measuring the pain is to ask if it interferes with their functioning on a day to day basis. For example, have they gone to work? Did they leave work early? Have they participated in their normal family activities on the weekend?" The face of the witness was gigantic, framed by the screen. "I'd ask if they've been well enough to eat, would ask about their lifestyle, did the headache interfere with their sleep pattern, did it keep them awake, did they have energy?" she continued.

In cross-examination Mr. Lockwood seemed impatient with the expert's approach. "Can you just assume the history that I gave you? That is, not a persistent headache, but a headache fluctuating, improving, no headache at the consultation, the person going about normal activities."

I clapped my hand against my mouth, muting my voice, worried I might draw attention to myself. The phrase "going about their normal activities" echoed through my head.

The cross-examination honed in on the issue of diagnosing a tension headache. "A tension headache has to have a physical cause. It's provoked by a disturbed nerve supply, the pain is due to an inflammation of a nerve, so I'd like to know where that nerve is and how it can be relieved," the witness stated.

Long hours later, Wayne, Ina and I headed to a café for lunch. My stomach revolted at the thought of oily Chinese food. I ordered a Greek salad. As I buttered my bread, I let my mind wander over the statements the witness had made that morning. The knife clattered to the plate.

"Did you two hear what the witness said this morning about being headache-free?" I exclaimed.

"Yeah, my ears pricked up at that," Wayne replied. "She said that to be called headache-free a patient has to not have taken any painkillers for at least twenty-four to forty-eight hours."

"And Lockwood told her to base her replies on the scenario that Mark had been headache-free at the consultation." Ina stirred her soup fiercely. "But Mark *had* taken painkillers beforehand." She picked up her serviette and wiped droplets of sweat off her eyebrows. "So much for having been headache-free."

We started to eat our lunch in silence, each lost in thought. After I finished my salad, I broke the quiet. "You know the psych who appeared as the second witness this morning testifying how Mark's death has affected me? I remember vividly going to see her."

Ina placed her hand on my arm.

"It was about two years after Mark died. I had trouble sleeping. All these images flooded my mind throughout the night." I swallowed. "Well, it seems so silly looking back now, but it wasn't until I read her report which diagnosed post-traumatic stress disorder that I understood what was going on with me." I shook my head.

"It's not silly at all, Katrin," Wayne replied. "You were under a lot of pressure. It was such an intense time."

"I googled post-traumatic stress disorder. And a list of all the symptoms showed up, and that's when a light bulb went on for me." I shuddered and put on my jacket. "It was only then that I realised that I have post-traumatic stress, and that this is different from grief."

We left the café and walked back to the district court. Ina slipped her hand through my arm. When the court session resumed after the lunch break, Dr. Hart was called to the witness stand. She rose from her chair, swift but not hurried, dressed in a knee-length business skirt and a white or beige blouse, and walked over to the witness stand, with an upright body posture as if she was at a yoga class. Her brown hair fell to her shoulders, framing her face.

"What happened at the beginning of the consultation?" Mr. Lockwood began the line of questioning.

"Mr. Den Elzen told me that he questioned a diagnosis of tension headaches – because he said he didn't have any stress in his life and so he wanted to know if that was right and he was still having those headaches." Dr. Hart stated that Mark did not have any history of headaches, and that he had told her that the headaches varied from mild to severe, and that he had had a headache that morning before the consultation. She did not look at me, but gazed straight ahead at her barrister.

I looked at her. This woman could have saved Mark's life. I swallowed hard, holding back the tears that threatened to spill down my face.

"And what did Mr. Den Elzen do when his headaches were severe?" Mr. Lockwood asked.

"He told me he'd go and lie down to rest." Dr. Hart sat erect. She did not bow her head but looked at the barrister or into the courtroom.

"Did you ask him about analgesia?"

"He said that he was taking pain medication regularly."

"When you were taking the history, what were you thinking?"

"I suppose ... well ... he looked ... I thought ... my index of suspicion was not as high because of the fact that he looked so well. He was well when he came to see me. He did not have a headache at the time of the consultation," she replied.

I glanced at Ina, barely moving my head, and saw the fire in her eyes.

Dr. Hart was still speaking. "You're always looking for anything urgent, you see, any Red Flag signs that notify you that something is serious. I felt reassured by the fact that he looked so well. So yes, I was concerned, but he looked well. It made me less worried about an urgent cause."

She was then questioned on what constitutes "urgent causes" and replied that that would be meningitis or raised intracranial pressure.

"What is the difference between an urgent and a serious cause?" Mr. Lockwood asked.

"The amount of time that you have to make the diagnosis. With a serious cause, you have a long time generally. For example, a brain tumour will present over many weeks or months." Her small frame and quiet voice belied the toughness of her words.

"So a brain tumour, is that an urgent or a serious cause?" her barrister inquired.

"It would be serious. As far as urgency of diagnosis, you probably have, you know, weeks to make that diagnosis."

I dug my fingernails into my palm.

"I told Mr. Den Elzen that I couldn't find any urgent or serious cause and that the pattern of his headaches was consistent with a tension type headache ... I didn't think he had a brain tumour."

Asked how he replied, she answered, "He mentioned again about the stress. He said, 'You know I mentioned to you that I didn't have any stress,' and I explained that the word tension is a misnomer, that people think that it is caused by stress, and although stress is often present, it isn't essential. The tension itself refers more to tension of the scalp muscles."

Then she told the court that, having seen about ten or eleven patients over the course of the morning, she drove home at about quarter to one and that she had thought about Mark in the car.

Asked why she did that, Dr. Hart replied, "Because I was concerned about him, that he's a person who ... you know headaches can be something more serious, and you just want to be ... mentally you try to make sure that there's nothing that you've missed. I reflected on him, I suppose, because of the fact that he was having headaches, that they had been severe over the weekend and hadn't got a clear cause for tension headache, so I was concerned. But having said that, he was well when I saw him and I felt that I hadn't found anything that would indicate an urgent problem."

My heart began to race as I heard her evidence, and I could not wait to discuss it with Ina and Wayne.

As soon as the court session finished that afternoon, Ina, Wayne and I headed straight for the lift. Outside, we walked along Hay Street towards the bus port. After crossing a side street, I stumbled to a halt. The others stopped, facing me.

"Oh my God," I said, "I couldn't believe it when she said that she'd thought about Mark on her way home. I mean, this shows, doesn't it, that her own intuition, her professional intuition, was working. It should have alerted her." The words tumbled out of my mouth. "She could've saved Mark's life then," I whispered.

Ina opened her handbag, pulled out a packet of tissues and offered me one.

"Katrin, I understand how emotional this must have been for you. I agree with you about her intuition working. At this point in time, she could have still picked up the phone and called Mark, at least offering him a CAT scan," Ina said.

Wayne put his hands on my shoulders and gently guided me to a bench a few metres away. "I wonder what the judge will make of that," he said.

"To me it means that deep down she knew something was not right about Mark's symptoms, and that she should have acted on her intuition." I wiped my nose.

"I was blown away by the fact that she only worked one morning a week, Tuesday mornings from 9 till 1." Ina looked across the road into the distance. "I mean, what are the chances that Mark happened to see her on that one morning?"

"Yeah, that's pretty bizarre," Wayne agreed.

~

The following morning, cross-examination began and my barrister questioned Dr. Hart about the presence of physical tension in tension headaches. He raised evidence given by a witness for the defence that the majority of patients with tension headaches have signs of musculature contraction and that this would need to be identified in order to reach a diagnosis of tension headaches.

"By the end of the examination you had no clinical findings of any abnormality of Mr. Den Elzen's neck," Mr. Dawson stated.

"That's correct."

"And you did not conduct an examination of his scalp?"

"No."

"I'm putting to you that you didn't examine his head to see if he had tension in any part of his head," Mr. Dawson continued.

"I believe that I would have done. I don't recall finding any abnormality, nothing to indicate any muscle tension."

Asked if she knew at the time that she saw Mark that a tension headache diagnosis should be one of exclusion, she replied yes. Then Mr. Dawson raised a series of questions relating to Red Flag Headache symptoms. "So someone of Mark's age presenting with a sudden onset headache should be seen as a Red Flag issue?"

"Yes." Her voice, though steady, had a barely discernible tremble.

"A history of someone waking at night with a headache should raise a Red Flag?"

"Yes. But I'm not saying that he woke with his headache at night. He did say he had them at night, but not that he was woken at night. If he had been woken by the headaches, that would concern me."

Later on Mr. Dawson revisited the issue of being woken at night from the headaches. "You knew that there had been some interference with his sleep?"

"No, I didn't say that it interfered with his sleep, well I suppose for him to have known that he had it at night he must have been aware of it …" Her voice trailed off.

"So?"

"Yes."

"If you had a patient who was not usually using analgesia but was using it for the best part of last week, that should also raise a Red Flag."

"Yes."

In response to Mr. Dawson's questions, Dr. Hart agreed that Mark did have a persisting headache for seven days with a sudden onset and that seven days would have to be the absolute outer limit for tension headaches. She also attested that she knew that there were times when the analgesia did not take effect, and that the headaches had been severe over the weekend.

"You knew at the time when you were assessing him that intracranial pressure could only be detected by a CAT scan?"

"Yes."

"You didn't discuss a CAT scan with him?"

"No, I didn't offer him a CAT scan or ask him if he wanted one."

The barrister then asked Dr. Hart if she should have used tension headache as her working diagnosis without having excluded more serious underlying pathology.

"At the time … with the clinical picture I had …"

She did not answer the question.

"You thought of him on your way home because you were worried that he might have a space-occupying lesion, and that you hadn't excluded it."

"I felt that I had excluded it," Dr. Hart replied. "I felt reassured that I wasn't dealing with a space-occupying lesion."

I heard Ina's sharp intake of breath. She drew a question mark on her notepad and tilted the page towards me.

Dr. Hart never met my eyes in the courtroom.

~

On the Friday scheduled as the last day of the trial, the defence produced a new report by their GP expert witness that claimed the "ultimate outcome" in relation to Mark's hydrocephalus would not have been any different even if a CAT scan had been taken. It asserted that Mark's death had been inevitable.

Wayne put his hand on mine as a lengthy discussion ensued, littered with laboured legal jargon that I did not understand, between the judge and the two barristers. In the end, the judge ruled that the defence could table the report, but deemed it to be new evidence. The trial was postponed.

My stomach tensed. No date was set for readjournment. The uncertainty made my hands shake. How much longer would I have to wait to get some resolution?

The judge instructed the defence legal team to send their expert witness who was waiting outside the courtroom away. As Ina and I sat stunned in our seats, not yet moving, a broad-shouldered man, salt-and-pepper thinning hair combed to the side, pushed past us and headed straight towards Dr. Hart in the front row. He leaned down over her small frame, placed both his hands on her shoulders and exclaimed, "This shouldn't be happening. You shouldn't be on trial."

The GP looked up at the man with wide eyes, silent.

Afterwards, outside, Ina and I walked over to a bench, but were both too pent-up to sit down.

"That was their expert witness, wasn't it? The one that couldn't be heard today because of this so-called fresh evidence." I looked at Ina. Small red blotches had appeared on her cheeks.

"Yeah, it was." She shook her head. "He made a beeline for Dr. Hart. He obviously knew her."

"What about impartiality, hey?" I said.

On the way home in the bus, I clenched my teeth until my jaw hurt.

At home, I took the stairs two at a time to phone my parents. I had been giving them a daily report about the trial. My dad would understand the legal jargon. He had a law degree and used to be a legal adviser for the German Ministry of the Interior. In fact, my dad had helped to draft the very first environmental bill ever to be passed in the German parliament.

My mum answered after just two rings.

"Mama, you won't believe what the defence did today."

"Uh, that doesn't sound good."

"No, I see this as a dirty trick." My fist hit the table. "They brought up the issue of causation. Apparently there're two points that have to be proven in a medical negligence case."

"Go on. Papa is standing right behind me. You're on loudspeaker. We can both hear you."

"So firstly, of course, there's the question of medical negligence. But then there's also the issue of causation. That's to say, even if malpractice has occurred, there's no court case if the 'ultimate outcome' wouldn't have been any different." My voice was thick. "In other words, if the patient would have died anyway."

"But that would need to be claimed at the outset of the trial." My father's calm baritone vibrated through the loudspeaker of the handset.

"Yeah, that's right. So what they did is, they did not note it as an issue on the pleadings."

"Ah, they didn't raise the issue of causation and now they've changed the plea," my dad said.

"You know, they tried to get their expert witness onto the stand there and then. To continue with the trial." I stood up and punched the air with my fists. In my mind I saw him walking into the courtroom and striding straight over to Dr. Hart.

"But the judge wouldn't have a bar of it. This causation thing the defence raised falls under fresh evidence, because normally it's raised before the start of the trial. And because it's newly introduced evidence, the trial got postponed. On the fifth day of the trial."

"What?" My mum's voice was high-pitched. "Until when?"

"I don't know. Indefinitely. No date has been set."

"I'm surprised that a medical negligence case is going on for so long," my mum said.

"Yes, I didn't know it'd be this long." I paced up and down the living room. "From what I can gather it's highly unusual for the defence to raise this as an issue this late in a trial instead of at the outset."

That night I lay on my sofa and tried to relax by watching *The Terminal*. Like Tom Hanks' character, I was caught up in politics, in my case, medico-legal politics. I couldn't keep my attention on the movie. With all that anger in my belly, I had barely touched my dinner that night. I turned off the TV and stared at the blank screen as I took stock of what had taken place so far. The judge had expressed his expectation that this case should settle at mediation. The GP had admitted that she knew that Mark had woken up from the pain at night despite having taken pain-killers, that his headaches had been severe at times. And yet, here I was, the trial postponed indefinitely on the grounds that even if a CAT scan had been ordered, it would have not saved Mark's life. Instead of settlement, the defence team had unlocked a new arsenal of weapons.

28

A hand wielding a needle and thread moves its instrument of terror directly towards my eye. My hands fly to my mouth, too late to stifle my shriek. I sink deeper into my seat, suck in my breath and avert my gaze away from the cinema screen. Wayne puts his hand on my arm and squeezes it.

Three years after Mark's death, I was watching the movie *The Diving Bell and the Butterfly*, which is based on a true story about French editor, Jean-Dominique Bauby, who was locked in his body in 1995 for eighteen months following a sudden and unexplained stroke. The parallels between Bauby's and Mark's experiences were astounding, given the extreme rarity of locked-in syndrome. They were practically the same age, forty-three and forty-two.

Despite dreading what I might discover, I went to see the movie because I had wondered over and over, haunted by the shadows of the silent, heavy nights, what it must have felt like for Mark to be imprisoned in his paralysed body. I desperately wanted to know how he might have coped mentally.

Here was the cinematic rollercoaster with all its graphic visual imagery, and it did give me insights into how it felt to be locked in. Profound scenes showed how Bauby used his imagination, drawing on memories and fantasies, to escape the reality of his locked-in syndrome. It offered him a degree of freedom. I hadn't heard about such flights into the imagination in the context of extreme illness, and wondered if Mark had also been able to draw on the power of his mind. At the same time, the movie vividly portrayed the suffering in the every-day life of being fully paralysed. It forced me to acknowledge, to feel the embodied reality of such monstrous torment. I did of course know, after all the months of visiting and watching Mark, but the graphic images verified my worst nightmares and intensified my knowing.

Some time after I had watched the movie, I sat down on my sofa at home and thought over what I'd seen. I had learned a great deal about the experience of being locked in from the movie. Because the camera lens acted as Bauby's one seeing eye, we experienced much of the film from his perspective. Contemplating it now, I am deeply moved by Bauby's almost superhuman ability to take flight for periods of time in his exquisite imagination. The movie showed the worlds Bauby's powerful mind entered, such as Paris' finest seafood restaurant. In his mind he could savour the food that his mouth was no longer able to taste. At other times, his imagination inhabited beautiful landscapes. Summoned up images of wild, roaring oceans. A tender brush of skin wielded, not by the electric impulse of nerve endings, but the power of imagination and memory.

In what feels to me like an unbelievable twist of fate, Mark had read a long article about Bauby's locked-in-syndrome in the weekend magazine of *The Australian.*

"Katrin, have you finished reading the article about the French guy who was completely paralysed?" Mark called out from the balcony into the living room. Earlier he had walked over to me and given me the magazine to read, already open on the article.

"Yes, I've just finished reading it." I stared at a picture of Baulby seated in a wheelchair at the hospital.

Mark put down the paper, walked inside and sat down next to me. Surprised, I looked up at him.

"What a shocking fate, don't you think? Cruel." Mark's brows furrowed and a muscle twitched in his cheek.

I nodded. "Absolutely unbelievable. I can't even begin to fathom what it must be like."

"And so young – he was so young. And just like that, it was all taken from him."

"Had you ever heard of this condition, locked-in syndrome, before?" I asked Mark.

"No." He shook his head.

Mark was to suffer the same fate as Bauby, at the same age. Also caused by strokes that affected the brain stem. This is the oldest area of our brain and is responsible for movement. It is the only area of the brain where brain damage can lead to locked-in-syndrome, whereby the patient is intelligently present yet completely paralysed. The first time I had corroboration that Mark was intelligently present was when tears rolled down his cheeks when I told the story of how we met in Egypt. And right up until Mark's death, there was sad confirmation: the nurse at the hospice told me that once the staff explained to Mark what they were doing, such as showering him, he responded by relaxing and stopped moaning. It was not until some time after Mark's death, though, that I researched locked-in syndrome on the internet. In one of my Google searches, I came across Bauby's book. The title evoked an immediate memory of the conversation I had had with Mark about the article. A vivid image of Mark repeatedly shaking his head in disbelief at the cruelty of the condition, his eyes wide, made me slide off the couch onto the floor. Mark's strong emotional reaction to the article was in stark contrast to his normally reserved demeanour. I did not have the strength to read the book.

Before watching the movie, I had not been able to grasp the power of the mind to take flight from the imprisoned body, entering a world of imagination sculpted out of visualising tactile and sensuous imagery that the body itself could no longer physically access. Providing the illusion of touch, smell and taste denied by the nerves of the flesh and taste buds of the tongue.

This reminded me of reports and memoirs I had read about the Western hostages in Lebanon in the late 1980s, who had been imprisoned for many years, often for years on end in solitary confinement, subjected to beatings and chained to the wall. What stuck in my memory from having read their accounts over a decade earlier was that they, like Bauby, took solace in their imaginations. I recall that one hostage, perhaps it was Terry Waite, had played chess in his mind against an imaginary partner, able to remember the positioning of both the black and white pieces of the chess set.

That night I lay awake, thinking: did Mark's sharp, witty mind take flight in imagination? And if so, how much solace had this offered him?

The movie showed how Bauby dictated his entire memoir to a transcriber. Every single word had to be painstakingly dictated with the blink of his only eye, letter by letter. I had never heard of an alphabet board before. The next day I googled them. Images of different boards appeared in front of me. They had been designed for stroke victims who were paralysed and could only blink. I stared at the screen. Why had Mark never been given the chance to use an alphabet board? Why? Why had he been denied that chance? This would have offered him the opportunity, however rudimentary, to communicate with the outside world. To prove to the doctors that he was not in a vegetative state. As it was, the entire time that

Mark lived locked into his body, he never got to communicate with the medical staff around him. He had been able to blink for me, answering my questions yes with one blink and no with two.

Almost a decade later, my daughter was to experience the same level of anger and devastation, and in her case, professional disbelief, that her father had been denied the chance of using an alphabet board. By this time, Rahel was a social worker on the rehabilitation ward of a hospital in Melbourne. In yet another ironic twist of fate, this ward mainly housed stroke patients. None as completely paralysed as her father had been, but paralysed to the point where some needed an alphabet board.

I was at home in Perth when she called me from Melbourne. In the context of her explaining to me what her work involved, I asked her professional opinion about alphabet boards for stroke victims.

"Mama, I can't believe they never offered Dad an alphabet board." Her anger streamed down the line. "It's such standard practice."

Afterwards I stared at the phone in my hand. My daughter, now an adult, was experiencing, with a time lapse of a decade, the same despair that I had felt. Her pain reignited mine. I froze. It took me a long time to put my phone down on the kitchen bench. Her hurt weighed down on me and cracked open old wounds.

The Diving Bell and the Butterfly allowed me to put my foot into the visceral world of being locked into the body. One of the things I took from the movie was Bauby's sense of humour. He told himself jokes, born out of his daily life at the hospital. Thinking about this, my shoulders tightened and my neck stiffened. Should I have appealed to Mark's strong sense of humour? Did I fail him in some way, not having been able to make jokes at the hospital? I remember one single incident where we laughed at the hospital whilst visiting Mark. My parents, the children and I were all in the room. Fluids regularly collected in Mark's tracheotomy, causing him to cough sharply. On this day, some of the mucus that his coughing loosened up was ejected into the room. My little boy, who was terrified of all bodily fluids, quickly jumped out of the way and hid behind a wall. This scene was so comical that we all burst out laughing. This was the only time I laughed in Mark's presence during his ordeal. I even recall having felt guilty afterwards for laughing. How ironic that I should now feel guilty for not laughing.

Humour was so far out of my reach at the time that joking with Mark was not possible for me. The reality of visiting him at the hospital had continued to be heartbreaking. But now, I admonished myself for not having thought of catering to his wit.

At home, Mark's playful smile looked straight at me from the enlarged picture mounted in an antique-looking, silvery, thick frame. I could almost see him move his head in that typical quick sideways tilt, accompanied by a wink. I've seen that tilt and wink a thousand times. Lately, writing down my story, I have wondered why I cannot put Mark's humour into words, why I cannot capture his quick wit and sharp mind with language. His gestures and intonation at the time of delivering his dry humour are inscribed onto my memory, readily available for recall. But his actual words cannot be seized, like a stream of water running through my fingers.

When I travelled to Melbourne, I asked two of Mark's oldest friends if they could remember an actual example of his humour. They both raised their gaze towards the ceiling. With a heavy sigh, they both shook their heads, a flash of sadness passing over their eyes, surprised as I was at their inability to characterise Mark's distinctive trait. Contemplating my ability to conjure up the emotions that were ignited in me by Mark's humour, but not the essence of the humour itself, I told a friend about my confusion.

Sitting on the sturdy grass that left its indents on my skin, I spoke to Helen on the phone. With her uncanny way of being fully present, I could feel her undivided attention. It put me immediately at ease, this refreshing presence.

"You know, it's so weird, how I just cannot put Mark's humour into words, even though it was so much who he was." Leaning against the rough bark of a marri tree, I stretched out my legs in front of me.

"Did he tell jokes?" Helen asked.

"He didn't tell jokes. No, he came up with these quick-as-a-flash remarks, observations really, in response to something being said." I uncrossed and recrossed my ankles. "The thing was, sometimes these short phrases, maybe just two words, were pretty close to the bone, and so I'd pull a face in response, and Mark often said to me, *you don't like my humour.*"

That wasn't true though, and I wished I could have explained better to him that I did like his humour, that I was in awe of his quick wit, his eye for the obscure. Sitting there on the lawn, I missed his ability to make me laugh.

"So, these clever remarks, they're like a lightning flash in the sky," Helen remarked.

"Yes," I exclaimed. "That's it. I like that image. Too quick to earth itself."

"Yeah, and because there's no earthing, the mind does not get the chance to carve the words, the experience, into its folds."

"There is no reference point for the mind to latch onto. Nothing that'll make it stick." I leant into the solidity of the tree. "That's why it feels like water trickling through my hands."

I smiled to myself, relieved. I had been sad for a long time at this inability to capture Mark's humour, yet another loss. It made me feel better to recognise that if even his oldest mates could not grasp his remarks, it was something about the nature of Mark's wisecracks, delivered at lightning speed, that stopped them from being repeated. But the true legacy of my memories was the essence it left behind, the echo of my belly laughs.

Joschka comes up with quick remarks, with the same lightning speed, and, my God, does that remind me of his father's humour. Too young to remember, it's not as if he has ingested his dad's brand of humour growing up. And yet, it's so alike.

29

With my head arched back, my gaze wandered upwards along the high-rise across the road. The sun above me was a honeycomb-yellow globe in the cloudless sky. I took a deep breath and braced myself for entering the District Court building. The change of season from winter to summer recorded the eight months that had passed between the two periods of court hearings. It was now February 2008.

As I crossed the road, Ina strode along the footpath towards the entrance door. We entered the building together. Walking into the courtroom, I saw Dr. Hart sitting in exactly the same chair as she had eight months ago, as if time had not marched on.

The time delay meant that many court cases had passed since, and the legal actors on this civilian court stage had to re-familiarise themselves with the evidence. The freshness of witness statements had wilted like lettuce leaves in the sun.

The defence GP witness who had written the medical expert report that was used on the last day of the initial trial to evoke the whole issue of causation was called to the stand. He gave evidence in relation to his report. Causation, I recalled, means that even if it is found that malpractice has occurred, there's no grounds for a court case if the "ultimate outcome" wouldn't have been any different. That is, if the patient *would have died anyway*.

The three days of court hearing that followed this evidence are blurred for me now. This is primarily due to the bombshell that this GP detonated. Sitting in the witness stand, his eyes darted erratically about the room as he informed the court that the report did not relate specifically to Mark. Rather, it was a generalised medical report applicable primarily to aged patients. He shuffled in his seat.

My attention was highjacked from thereon in.

But while events are blurred, my emotional memory is crisp, tangible and vivid.

At the break, I grabbed Ina's hand, pulled her out of the courtroom, along the pavement outside and dragged her into the next side street.

I shrieked at the sky. Passers-by swivelled their heads to look. I did not care. "There's no justice to be had. This is all a farce. Only power matters, not the truth."

I kicked the wall of the building.

"Their witness has basically just retracted his own report that claimed that Mark would have died anyway, even with a CAT scan, claiming that was a *generic* report that would more generally refer to a case of an old patient, I think he might have said an eighty-year-old patient, but did not apply to a *forty-two-year-old male*." My mouth stumbled over the word generic.

"Yes, the very report that has singlehandedly caused this lengthy delay of the trial." Ina clenched her right fist. "And now he's reversed his opinion, in actual fact stating the opposite, namely that it would have made a difference," she exclaimed. "But the damage to the impact of the initial witness statements is done now because so much time has passed. Did you notice, the judge did not seem to remember that he had pushed for mediation on the second day of the trial?"

I nodded. I pressed my hands into the rough surface of the textured concrete wall. My palms began to throb. I was startled by the town hall clock ringing twice.

"We must get back," Ina said.

Things worsened during cross examination. Under questioning from our barrister, the witness confirmed that he had not written the report himself, but had only signed it. It transpired that the defence legal team had written what was tabled as a medical expert report, and then obtained the signature from their expert witness. I expected a reprimand, or at least some response in this matter from the judge, but it never came. My trust in the legal system was wiped out, leaving bitterness in its wake.

The other part of the evidence this GP gave that has firmly entrenched itself into my memory was that he attested that tension headaches can only range from mild to medium pain levels, which means that severe pain precludes a diagnosis of tension headaches. However, he went on to state that the mere fact that a patient describes pain as severe should not be taken at face value and that in his opinion patients cannot be trusted with an accurate description of their pain.

That afternoon, Wayne, Ina and I stood on a street corner close to the court building at the end of the day. I turned to face both of them. "You know, what I don't understand is why my own barrister did not cross-examine the GP expert witness about the issue of him having merely signed and not written the report himself. And that the report did not refer to Mark himself at all, but rather to a hypothetical eighty-year-old? Wouldn't it be a legal requirement for an expert witness report firstly to be written by the expert himself and not the legal team, and secondly refer specifically to the deceased?"

"Were you able to speak to your barrister directly?" Ina asked.

"No." I shook my head. "I only get to speak to my lawyer, who communicates with the barrister. But I didn't get a chance to discuss this because it was all revealed in court during cross-examination of the expert witness."

I still don't understand why the issue of Red Flag Headaches or symptoms was raised but not addressed in more detail during the trial. The expert witnesses for my side emphasised the importance of history taking in order to judge the severity and effect of the headaches on the patient's wellbeing. Asking about what activities the patient had been able to do or had been unable to do was identified as of primary importance. However, Dr. Hart's medical notes barely mentioned any history taking. What I would have expected her to have to address was the fact that Mark never returned to work after the previous Friday morning following his first consultation, something I was cross-examined on in what to me was a hostile manner. There was consensus amongst witness statements from both sides that not being able to work, especially in the case of a self-employed man, precludes engaging in normal activities. But *going about normal activities* was what the defence barrister demanded our expert witnesses base their evidence on.

I don't recall what my barrister said in detail in his closing argument, but I don't understand why he did not seem to highlight the issue of Red Flag Headaches more that had been identified during the trial and confirmed by Dr. Hart during her cross examination, for example that Mark woke up from his headaches at night. As an objective marker of severe headaches, this would preclude a diagnosis of tension headaches. I had no input into the closing argument and during the court case, I had minimal chance to talk to my lawyer – we only briefly touched base. Then it was all about waiting for the ruling.

~

On 25 July 2008, the judge delivered his ruling in a written report. I scanned the front page.

Case dismissed.

The defendant was not negligent in not sending the deceased for a CT scan on Tuesday 27 January 2004.

In a twenty-eight-page report, he outlined his reasons for the judgement. In his findings, the judge addressed the issue of history taking. He quoted our expert witness as having said that the taking of history was generally acknowledged to be "ninety percent" of diagnosis. He found that although *the defendant's clinical note is brief, in relation to the history, she gave evidence of a more detailed conversation, and that must be considered.* He ruled that *the history taken by the defendant was not inadequate, but was rather consistent with her obligations as a reasonably competent and careful medical practitioner in medical practice.*

He wrote, *the deceased presented to the defendant with a history of headache which had improved over the previous two days, which was not then present.*

I gasped. My heart pounded against my rib cage, fast and furious. My body bent forward, both of my hands landing hard on the table. *Headache-free*, I thought, the metallic taste of injustice heavy in my mouth. Monday had been Mark's worst day. And on Tuesday morning, when the consultation had taken place, Mark had been on painkillers. The specialist expert witness for our side had highlighted that a patient cannot be considered to be pain free if they've taken painkillers.

Dr. Hart gave evidence that Mark told her that he had severe pain on the weekend. I have asked myself, given that he himself had told me on Monday that his pain had worsened and that he was scared, what would have been his motive for telling the GP in the consultation that his pain was only severe on Saturday and Sunday?

The judge turned in his judgment to the issue of credibility of the defendant and myself. Though he stated that, generally speaking, I was an *impressive witness*, he then criticised my credibility on the grounds that I did not voluntarily inform the psychiatrist for the defence that I had entered into a relationship. *It seems to me*, the judge wrote, *that the plaintiff, who is plainly an intelligent woman, must have appreciated that the information would be highly relevant to a psychiatrist... I consider her failure to inform Dr. [T] of it revealed a degree of partisanship, and that her excuse for not doing so was a lame one and not credible.*

I had been asked to see psychiatrists nominated by both sides in order to assess the psychological impact of Mark's illness and death on me. When I saw the expert witness psychiatrist appointed by my legal team, I had not yet been in a relationship. By the time I was questioned by the defence psychiatrist quite a while later, this had changed. My legal team was aware that I was seeing someone, and this was stated during the trial. I can only think it was in the context of the questioning of the psychiatrist expert witness for my side. I'm assuming this was the first time the defence psychiatrist was made aware of this. Anyway, why is seeing someone years after Mark's illness and traumatic death relevant to the impact Mark's suffering and death had on me at the time?

Images of my encounter with the psychiatrist for the defence flooded my mind. His honeyed voice echoed through my ears. Having driven around the streets in the city centre for fifteen minutes, I had to park my car several floors up in a multi-storey car park, and had been forced to take an elevator ride in a cranky old lift that had frayed my nerves.

I stumbled along the footpath, my hand-scribbled piece of paper with the address in hand, and found myself in front of a residential apartment building. I checked the house number several times. There were no medical offices, or offices of any kind. I rang the bell and was met by a diminutive man, dressed casually in a jumper and cuddling a fluffy dog in his arms.

This is the psych appointed by the opposition to interrogate me?

The elevator ride had set my heart racing and my hands perspired. I mentioned my discomfort to the man. His pasted-on smile did not alter. Entering the private apartment, I felt extremely uncomfortable to find that there were no other people present. No receptionist. No front desk.

"The receptionist is away today," he said.

I was asked to sit down in a sparsely furnished room. He shut the door and his lap dog curled up on the floor. The unprofessional nature of the setting, the voice that sounded unnatural to me, and the smile that never reached his eyes, his body language that was incongruent with the actual words spoken, concerned me.

The interview took a question-and-answer format. Initially, a couple of times, I had elaborated on my answer. He had brushed over my words, and with the smile still set like a plaster cast, had told me that I was only to answer his questions directly and not to drift into explanations. In the peculiar surroundings, I did as I was told.

All his questions were aimed at the present time, how I felt at this point of time in my life. No questions were directed at me that related to my experiences at the time of Mark's illness and death.

Afterwards, when I was driving home in my car, as if visited by a premonition, I had thought how odd it was that he had not asked me if I was seeing someone.

But that was not the end of it.

During the trial, the defence psychiatrist had claimed, under oath, that he had asked me if I was in a relationship and that I had answered that I was not. That he had written this in his notes. An "R" for relationship. I had gasped out aloud in the courtroom, which had earned me a rebuke from the judge, such emotional reactions being frowned upon in a court of law. It was only under cross-examination, after the psychiatrist had been asked to produce his notes from the interview, that he admitted that *perhaps* he might not have framed his question to me in such a way that I understood what he had actually meant.

In the courtroom, I had to swallow down my frustration because I was not called back to the witness stand to respond to these accusations. The assessment in the setting of a private apartment, bereft of witnesses, was used to denounce my credibility. With the ruling in front of me, anger thrummed through my veins. I clenched my fists. The worst of it was that even though the judge considered me an *impressive witness*, he used the interview with the psych to discredit me, when there was no relevance to the subject matter on trial: whether the failure by the GP to order a CAT scan and her diagnosis of tension headaches constituted medical negligence.

I felt betrayed by our legal institutions. First, the caseworker for the Office of Health Review had not informed me of the independent GP's recommendation that a CAT scan should have been ordered. My outrage was amplified because I was at a loss as to her motives. Thinking about how one of the GP expert witnesses for the defence personally knew Dr. Hart, I wondered if this too could have possibly been the case here. It seemed highly unlikely. Not being able to gauge the caseworker's motives reminded me of the actions by Mark's relative who had screwed up our life insurance policy. Here, too, I faced a painful lack of explanation, which had made that wrongdoing so much worse. And so much harder to let go of.

And now the judge had attacked my personal credibility for something that took place outside the courtroom and had nothing to do with the conduct of the GP during Mark's consultation. This injustice was even more intensified because there were no repercussions or reprimands for the psychiatrist expert witness, as had been the case with the GP expert witness who had simply signed the report written by the legal team. The wording used by the judge – *must have appreciated that the information would be highly relevant to a psychiatrist* – implied that he acknowledged that I hadn't been asked.

The brevity of the recorded history notwithstanding, the judge had written, and later on, *it is more rather than less likely that the defendant would have been concerned to obtain an adequate history.* This last statement was made in the context of her credibility.

I swallowed hard. The acid taste of bitterness settled into my throat.

How could I even begin to process all of this?

30

I woke up in the middle of the night. A storm raged, and the rain lashed onto the tin roof right outside my bedroom window. *Red Flag Headaches.* The phrase whipped through my mind, and I churned it over and over. Such an apt name, only it did not help Mark. His Red Flag symptoms had been waved in front of the GP's face like a blood red flag to a bull, screaming for attention: look at me! But instead of taking note of the warning of danger that was aching for attention like the rain pounding onto the roof, she cast her gaze onto Mark's tanned skin. *He looked so well.*

My heart pounded in my chest in tune with the lashing rain. It had taken me a while to grasp the full significance of what had transpired during the questioning of the GP about Mark's consultation. After the trial I had researched Red Flag Headache symptoms. A prolific number of webpages bearing medical information stared at me from the computer screen. I had studied the list of Red Flag Headache symptoms that are specifically collated to alert any doctor to the possibility of life-threatening causes of headaches. The mockery of that, I thought, my face wet in sync with the tin roof outside.

Out of the list of Red Flag symptoms, Mark presented with several to Dr. Hart during the consultation. There was the sudden onset of his headaches, probably the biggest flag of all. Secondly, headaches at night, which she attested to being aware of during the trial. And thirdly, the severity of the headaches. Tension headaches can only be classified as mild to moderate. Fourth, Mark's age put him in a higher risk factor. And lastly, tension headaches are said to last from thirty minutes to seven days. Whether Mark saw the GP on the seventh or the eighth day of his headache was an issue raised during the trial, but even if it was Day 7, this fact alone put it on the outermost limit of possibly being tension headaches. Also, at the trial the expert witness had stated that the need for analgesia would be a red flag in the assessment of pain.

And yet, though all Red Flag Headache symptoms explicitly fall outside the indicators for tension headaches and were raised by our barrister in cross-examination, one of the things that struck me was the stark absence of the term *Red Flag Headaches* in the entire twenty-eight-page ruling. If I could have asked the judge a question, I would have wanted to know why he did not address the presence of Red Flag Headaches, which Dr. Hart had attested to. Your Honour, if the presence of severe pain and other Red Flag Headache symptoms preclude a tension headache diagnosis, then doesn't that mean it's a misdiagnosis? And I would have liked to know, if muscle tension in the neck should corroborate the existence of tension headaches, why didn't Dr. Hart find such symptoms – why didn't she check his scalp?

But he looked so well. The GP had conceded during the trial that she gave a diagnosis of tension headaches. Reading through the webpages, I had discovered that it is actually not possible in medical terms to diagnose tension headaches. It is *only possible to arrive at a tension headache diagnosis after excluding sinister underlying causes.* Only the absence of other causes can be diagnosed. This, I learned, can only be achieved through diagnostic tools such as a CAT scan or MRI. What these texts highlighted to me was that a tension headache diagnosis made without the use of diagnostic procedures to exclude life threatening causes in the presence of Red Flag symptoms is viewed as a misdiagnosis.

The list of serious headache symptoms spun around in my head. Mark's headaches were too severe, too sudden, too long. There were no stress factors present, and no muscle tension on his neck so typical for tension headaches. *But he looked so well.* Doctor Hart had revealed that Mark came to her for a diagnosis, that he told her that he did not believe that he had tension headaches.

During the trial she divulged that she had reassured Mark that the name tension headache is a misnomer. That no tension or stress needs to be present to have tension headaches. And what are the causes of tension headaches if not tension, stress, I wondered? Professional literature about tension headaches certainly refers to stress as a cause. As did the print-out she had handed Mark during the consultation.

With this reassurance that tension headaches are a misnomer in mind, Mark's intuition, his inner suspicion that his headaches could be dangerous, diminished. In his fear-induced state, he clung to that assurance with all of the vulnerability of a drowning person.

~

On a sunny morning after returning home from a yoga class, still feeling calm from the relaxation at the end, I found a business letter in my mailbox. I turned over the envelope and saw that it was from my lawyer. The case had ended months ago – why would he write to me now?

All relaxation drained out of my body. I tore the envelope open and scanned the text. It was a letter from the medical insurance company demanding a large sum of money for recuperating their court costs. I stared at the figure. There was no invoice as such. In disbelief, I observed that there was no itemisation of costs, simply this figure, as if plucked out of thin air.

My heartbeat quickened its pace until it fluttered. And then I howled at the injustice of it all. I simply couldn't bear it, the weight of it. The shock. I fell to my knees onto the floor.

Through blurred eyes, I raised my head. I looked at my walls, the innocent acacias outside, remembered sitting at the dinner table with Mark and the kids. "Nooooooo." I worried that the unfairness of it all, of the costs having increased significantly because of the postponement of the trial based on the report that was not even written by the expert witness, would tip me over the edge. I dry-retched, thinking that this demand for costs included the fee for that very report. And the psych report.

What will I tell the kids when they come home? With my face red and blotched, they would know immediately that something was wrong. I cannot remember what happened when I saw them that afternoon. The shock lasted for hours, if not days.

A few days later Ina visited me. I opened the front door and we looked at each other, tears streaming down our faces. We sat down on the couch in my living-room, holding hands.

"This is too much." I shook my head, staring at the rug. "Just too much."

Ina squeezed my hand. She ran her hand over my hair.

"I could cope with losing the trial though it didn't bring us justice." My eyes remained unfocused. "I mean, I can't believe that the issue of Red Flag Headache symptoms was ignored in the judgement." I raised my head and looked at Ina. "But this …" I picked up the letter from the coffee table and stabbed it with my finger. The paper seemed to singe my hand as I handed it to Ina. "This is simply too much."

Ina read the letter.

"There's only a couple of sentences," she raised her voice. "How dare they send a demand without even providing an itemisation!" She placed it back on the table. "Didn't the health advisory service say to you that they've never chased a widow for court costs?" She looked out the window and then turned to face me. "Wouldn't that make you the first widow to have to pay the court costs for the medical insurance company arising from a medical negligence trial?"

I grunted. "It looks that way. I'm not sure."

"What are you going to do?" Ina asked.

I stared at the pattern of the Turkish rug. "I don't know." I sighed. "I don't know."

I knew I had to find a way to address this demand for court costs. With rage running through my body, nearly suffocating me, I sat down at my dinner table to contemplate my options. Initially, my lawyer had responded to the medical insurance company's demand asking for itemisation, which was met with a rebuttal and refusal. Still without itemisation, the demand for court costs was renewed. I decided to negotiate with the medical insurance company directly, or rather with their lawyers who had sent the demand for costs.

After some debating, we arrived at a settlement. I put this debt onto my mortgage. It meant that we could stay in our home, but put a further strain on my limited finances.

Anger and resentment at this final injustice festered, adding another thick, tightly-knotted layer to the long string of injustices.

31

The flourless orange poppy-seed cake is beckoning me from the tray behind the glass counter of my local café. Back at the table, I glide my fork through the moist texture of the pastry. I let it linger on my tongue and the sweetness explodes in my mouth.

"So, do you have any plans?" Meriel asked. I looked at her across the wrought iron table. I was drawn to the gentle features of my friend's face. It was her birthday, and her husband Brian had called me up the night before to invite me to the café.

"Well, nothing concrete. But the urge to tell my story is bubbling up more and more in me."

With one arm around Meriel, Brian leaned slightly forward.

"Why don't you do a PhD in creative writing? That'd be perfect for you."

My right hand, clasping the cake fork, hovered in mid-air. I looked back at him, wide-eyed.

"You know Meriel is doing a PhD in Welsh literature, and you love that, darling, don't you?" He faced his wife and stroked the side of her face with the back of his hand.

Meriel's eyes lit up and she nodded. I knew that she loved her studies. She placed her hand on my arm. "Brian is right. This might really be the right thing for you."

"But … I don't know if I can. I mean I do have an Honours degree, but it's not in English Lit." I looked at the poppy seeds on my plate. My heart began to race with the anticipation of possibilities.

"Do you really think this might be possible?"

"Yes." Brian's baritone and Meriel's soft voice replied in unison.

At home, I dialled the switchboard of Murdoch University. As I had studied there previously, this felt like a natural choice. I loved the small campus with its towering gum trees and abundance of black cockatoos and rainbow lorikeets. I closed my eyes and pictured myself walking across the lawn from the car park to the library.

The receiver quivered in my hand. I asked to be put through to the English department. I got the information I wanted to hear; they were offering a creative writing PhD and I was eligible to apply with my Honours degree in another humanities subject. Now I had to find a supervisor who would accept my proposed project. I squealed, returned the phone to its base and jumped up and down. This was what I wanted to do.

That night, excitement was still curled up in my stomach. I threw back the covers and turned the light back on. I worked out that it had been seventeen years since I had last studied. Jeez, I can't believe it's been that long. Will I be accepted? It took a long time for my exhilaration to unwind and abate.

The next morning, I was woken by the melodious chirping of birds outside my window at dawn. I got up before the kids and scanned the university's website. Within minutes, I found a supervisor I would approach.

I didn't know then how fortunate I was, not only to have found a supervisor straight away who accepted my project, but one who was incredibly good at her job as well as being a warm-hearted person. She was able to handle my difficult subject matter with compassion and professionalism, though her own area of expertise was fiction.

She had recommended that I start off with a Master's degree. Given that there was a large gap since I had last studied, I thought this was a good idea. And so, I began my postgraduate studies part-time.

The night before my studies officially started, I sat alone in my living room and turned off the ceiling lights. The room was now bathed in the gentle glow of a single upright lamp and the bright yellow walls were subdued. The atmosphere was peaceful. I drizzled a few drops of lemongrass essential oil into an oil-burner and lit the tea-light. Inhaling the soothing scent, I leaned back on the couch and let my mind wander over the last few years. Realising that it had been five years since Mark had fallen ill, I began to contemplate how I had spent those years on an inward journey. I had grappled with my grief, desperately tried to understand suffering and work towards acceptance of what had happened. I had spent so much time feeling my painful emotions, being floored by them, churning the events over and over in my head in search of some meaning, a snippet of sense. My innate tendency to read voraciously had been quietly put on the backburner. I had given up my casual job as tour-guide after Mark's death and focused instead on my children and on dealing with the emotional wounds I had sustained.

This inward-looking gaze did not take over my life. It was about my relationship with myself. Apart from spending a lot of time with my children, I socialised with my friends, forged new friendships, had entered a new, though difficult, relationship, travelled overseas, and lived through a trial with all that it entailed. I had not turned into a hermit, although I had spent vast amounts of time in my own company.

The decision to return to university was as if a switch had reset my internal barometer from an inward to an outward focus. My natural propensity to soak up knowledge, to throw myself into a project, was re-awoken from its long slumber. Only it wasn't a prince that had kissed me awake, but a wave of desire to tell my story.

I was ready for this project. It was a relief that I started part-time, because the children were still at school and I wanted to be around in the afternoon when they came home. Also, it was a steep learning curve after such a long break from university life. Library catalogues were now replaced with online catalogues, literally available at my fingertips as I sat at the computer in my study. The sheer flood of sources was overwhelming.

I developed a routine of sitting down at my computer after I had made breakfast and lunches for the kids and they had gone off to school. They were both at high school, located a short stroll from our house. A large olive green cup given to me as a birthday present sat by my side, the aroma of freshly brewed green tea wafting through the room.

After having spent the last five years without much of a routine other than revolving around school, I relished focusing on a project, especially one so important to me. But I was also daunted by the task of completing an entire degree by research, having to muster the daily discipline necessary to complete this degree without coursework and only the guidance of a supervisor. The research required to write my thesis spelled out an enormous amount of hard work.

I could not have foreseen then how fulfilling my studies would be and the degree of contentment I would experience. After some months of locating and printing a torrent of academic articles, I realised that the new research skill required was not to find the right texts in the library, but to learn to pay close attention to abstracts and to develop discernment as to what truly applied to my research topic. The internet had changed the landscape of academic research.

~

As part of my studies, I wanted to write an essay about the hospice where Mark had passed away. I rang the hospice and hoped that someone I knew was still working there. It turned out that the administrative staff the receptionist put me through to remembered me well and we made an appointment to meet up.

It was eerie driving along the road to the hospice that I remembered so clearly. It wove through a maze of car parks attached to the private St. John of God hospital. The public hospice was tucked away at the back of the hospital and nothing had changed, except that the native bushes out the front had grown.

My throat constricted as I walked down the main hallway, which was less familiar because it was devoid of the art exhibition that had made it explode with bright colours at the time Mark was there. Now its white walls looked stern.

As I entered the office of the administrator, not one, but two familiar faces greeted me with genuine, warm smiles. Linda stood up and welcomed me in a heartfelt embrace. She nodded towards the social worker, who I had met at the time, and I received a firm handshake and kiss on my cheek.

"Katrin, it is so nice to see you." Linda placed her hand on my arm and squeezed it lightly. "How've you been?"

Her intent gaze told me she really wanted to hear the answer. Her question was not just a courtesy.

"Oh, you know, I'm doing fine." I felt myself nodding, to emphasise my sentence.

"And the kids, how're they?

Both pairs of eyes were wide and expectant.

"They're good, thank you. Actually, they're doing really well. They're both at high school now."

"Oh my goodness, I remember them so well." Linda and her colleague exchanged knowing glances.

"Actually, we all remember you and the kids really well." A shadow briefly passed over her eyes.

"We talked about your family for a long time – you really struck a chord with us."

This acknowledgement reminded me of one of the hospice nurses who I accidentally ran into just a few weeks after Mark's death. I had just left the ANZ bank and strode along the sidewalk towards the shopping centre, my eyes on the paperwork I was tucking into my leather backpack.

"Katrin!"

Startled, I had looked up, not recognising the slim woman in front of me.

"I'm one of the nurses from the hospice." She had fixed the same intent gaze upon me as Linda had just now. "How are you?"

"Well, not that good. I'm trying to work through everything that's happened. It's all still a blur."

"I have to tell you, you and your family really touched the staff." Her eyes were soft with compassion. "It was really hard for us to see your husband dying, and the kids, and you, so young," she confessed. "We, I mean the nurses and doctors, found it very difficult to witness your loss."

I hugged her as a large four-wheel drive vehicle whizzed by.

At home, I had replayed that conversation in my mind. I was surprised at what the nurse had said, because I had thought the hospice staff might be able to "switch off", as they see people dying every day. That was obviously a naïve assumption. Her compassion had struck a deep chord in me. It revealed the human side and the dedication of the palliative care staff. I was glad that I had moved Mark from the rehab ward to the hospice; if the trained hospice staff found it so emotional, how much worse it would have been for the rehab staff? And it was a softer, quieter place for Mark's last days, with touching kindness.

I refocused on Linda sitting opposite me in the winter sunlight across her desk.

"I've recently gone back to uni. I'm doing a Master's degree and I'm writing my story."

"That's really good to hear. Your story needs to be told."

I nodded. "Well, I'm working on an essay at the moment, and I wanted to write about the hospice, maybe speak to some of the staff, what their work is like and so on." I straightened up my back. "I'm really grateful for the way you looked after Mark, and this hospice is very special. I'd really like people to know about it, to lose their fear of it."

The two women offered to put me in touch with some nurses and doctors.

A week later I received a phone call from Linda. She told me that Bill from the West Australian Palliative Care Association had approached them about the upcoming National Palliative Care week. He was looking for a spokesperson from a family who had used the service, to relay their personal experience both to the public and especially to the national organisation and stakeholders.

"We thought you're so articulate, and your story is so gripping, that perhaps you would consider meeting with Bill." Her request touched a chord in me. "He was very keen when we told him about you," she added.

I tried to digest her request. Becoming a public spokesperson. Sharing my story with palliative care people. Though this seemed daunting, I thought this could be an opportunity to contribute to some much needed change in access to palliative care.

"Yes," I replied, "I'll meet him."

I had no idea what was to come out of that meeting with Bill in the hospice.

As I entered through the support centre entrance, memories of the first few weeks following Mark's death, of the much needed, silent, understanding hugs by staff and volunteers, were ablaze.

A wiry young man with prominent large eyes that dominated his face greeted me. Linda was there to introduce Bill, and then she left us alone. As soon as he started to talk about the challenges his organisation faced in dealing with a rigid hospital system and medical staff in the hospital resistant to calling upon palliative care, I realised that Bill lived wholeheartedly for his job. His passionate way of speaking, underlining his sentences with intent eyes and strong hand gestures, made me want to support what he was pledging to do: to make palliative care more accessible to all people who needed it.

With a dry throat, I listened intently to his explanation that palliative care – end of life care – is not only there for people who are in the very last stages of their life. It is a misconception, he pointed out, that palliative care should only be called upon when the patient is in the process of dying. It is actually meant for people with a terminal, or life shortening, illness and they do not have to be dying right now – he emphasised this point by stabbing his index finger into the air – they could be quite a while, years even, away from dying. His frustration with medical staff refusing to call in the specialised care that well-trained palliative care professionals can offer was evident in his furrowed eyebrows and clenched jaw.

Then I told him my story, with a special emphasis on the lack of proper pain management Mark had received, and what I considered to have been inhumane suffering he had to endure as a result. I could see a vein pulsating on Bill's shaven head. He shook his head over and over, barely able to contain his rage.

"This is so unnecessary." His hands were clenched into tight fists. "Pain management has become so refined, there's such a large range of different pain medications on the market, but it requires a pain management specialist to attune the medication that will work for the patient, and this process can involve a bit of trial and error."

I stared at him. "So you reckon that a pain management specialist could have helped Mark, reduced his extreme pain down to perhaps mild pain?"

"Definitely, without question."

My head throbbed trying to take in this information.

"And your husband, in the condition he was in at the hospital, locked into his body, would have been eligible for a palliative care pain specialist. They would've just had to call palliative care."

After this conversation, I found it hard to focus on what else Bill had to say. I did, however, remember afterwards that Bill had asked me if I would consider being interviewed and giving a talk for the upcoming palliative care awareness week and that I had said I would. The details of what that would entail eluded me until Bill called me two days later, asking if I had given his request some thought. He then proceeded to explain that he would like me to speak at the palliative care convention to be held at the South of Perth Yacht club and to give a radio interview with a community radio station in Joondalup. I thought how Mark and I used to ride our bikes past the yacht club, just one suburb down from our own.

"A convention means a lot of well-dressed people talking policy, is that right?" I asked.

"Spot on." And after a pause, "So, will you do it?"

I took a deep breath. "Yes, I'm in."

I wanted to know what exactly he wanted me to talk about.

"Just tell your story like you told me. It speaks for itself."

I sat in front of the blank computer screen. It was as if the words for my talk wanted to tumble out all at once and at the same time remain muted.

As I began to describe Mark's level of pain, tears streamed down my face. It took me right back there, to the hallway where his moaning echoed, outside the High Dependency Unit. I prepared my talk, complete with a power point presentation, which I emailed to Bill.

On the day of the convention at the yacht club, I woke up tense and nervy. I was about to walk into foreign territory. How would a sea of suited policy makers react to my impassioned speech? And more importantly, would I be able to deliver my talk without crying? That seemed almost impossible. As I drew back the bed cover and slowly eased my legs onto the floor, I braced myself for a challenging and emotional morning.

Standing at the podium, clutching a remote control to operate the power point presentation in my right hand, I made eye contact with the audience, a mixture of administrators and policy makers, nurses and doctors. As I spotted Bill, he nodded encouragingly.

I began my talk, describing Mark's illness. When I got to recounting the level of pain he experienced and the hopelessly inadequate, minor pain medication he continued to receive, despite nurse after nurse documenting in their notes that *the patient was distressed and moaning,* my voice quivered. The entire room fell silent and no one even cleared their throat. I could feel my eyes filling with tears, but managed to hold back from crying during the talk.

When I finished, I could see a few moist eyes. Bill came up to me and looked at me knowingly, his lips squeezed together.

I did not know then that this was to be the beginning of a new role for me, spokesperson for palliative care, that I was to embrace for a lot longer than the duration of palliative care awareness week.

32

Looking out of the large bus window, I saw a cloudless sky painted an iridescent blue that seemed almost impossible, photo-shopped. I turned to look at Rahel, her long blond curls tied in a ponytail, sitting next to me.

"I'm so glad you're accompanying me, Rahel." I wiped my moist palms on my thighs clad in a cotton skirt. "I'm so nervous."

"Come on, Mama, that's understandable." She placed her warm hand on top of mine, squeezing it lightly. "You'll be great, I'm sure!"

Following the talk that I had given at the yacht club, Bill had told me that my words had touched people and approached me about speaking at the upcoming International Palliative Care conference, *Together!*, which happened to be held in Perth for the first time. He told me that it combined the Australian Palliative Care and the Asia Pacific Hospice conferences and stressed that this conference provided a rare opportunity for delegates from so many countries to get together and discuss Palliative Care from a broad international perspective.

"Well, how many delegates will this conference have, do you think?" I replied.

"I'd imagine about 1200 or so." His voice was steady, without much inflection.

"What? That's a lot." My knees went weak as I pictured myself addressing such a large crowd and I dropped onto a chair.

"Katrin, I've heard you speak. You'll be great. And your story is just what we need to show these delegates, the professionals, the other side of their work, the patients' perspective." He cleared his throat. "I'd really appreciate it if you would do this."

A pitch-black crow croaked outside my bedroom window the following morning. As I woke, I thought about Bill's request to speak at the international conference. I was disillusioned with a rigid system that had failed my husband. If sharing my story in front of an international audience could contribute to some much-needed change in the medical system in regard to pain management, then I would do it. I hoped I could help others to get appropriate pain management so that they would not have to endure what Mark had gone through.

The white, near-new Perth Convention Centre came into view as our bus looped down a road that stopped underground beside the building. Its semi-circular, elongated shape seemed to be hugging the skyline. The sheer size of the building intensified my nervousness and my heart was in my throat. Inside, at the conference desk, I was handed a black bag emblazoned with the impressionist conference picture of four black swans in flight, their necks stretched out toward a stylised sun.

"You're in the main theatre." The young volunteer smiled as she handed me the bag and name tag.

I twisted a strand of hair and tucked it behind my ear.

Rahel scanned through the conference programme. "Mama, look at this. There're delegates here from thirty-five countries." My gaze followed her index finger and the figure swam in front of my eyes.

We made our way to the entrance of the theatre. A session was in progress, so we sat down on a row of backless lounge-chairs overlooking the Swan River, bathed in bright sunshine. Looking at the yachts frolicking on the water reminded me of the similar view from the nearby hospital that I had over five years ago from the relatives' room after being told about Mark's brain damage.

At the podium, my speech written out word for word in front of me, the lights dimmed. I stood in the spotlight. As soon as I started to speak my nerves began to calm down. I lifted my head from the paper and let my eyes wander across the large auditorium. In the semi-darkness, I could only make out a sea of heads intently focused on me. My gaze settled on Rahel for a moment. Seated in the front row, the overhead lights shone on her and I could actually make out her face. I took in her encouraging expression and thumbs-up sign she made with her fists.

Somewhere at the back of my mind, as if observing myself from behind, I thought, is this really happening? Am I talking about this intimate experience with Mark in front of this large audience? I finished my speech with an impassioned call for the importance of ensuring easy access to pain management services and palliative care specialists. Thundering applause accompanied me as I stepped down from the stage.

The tension in my neck and shoulders eased off and my muscles relaxed. Relief that I had delivered my speech without stumbling over my words buoyed my spirit. When Bill called me that night, he said that the feedback from my talk had been astonishing. Delegates from poor countries who struggled with a minimum of sparse resources for a large number of patients simply could not believe that this could have happened in a resource-rich country like Australia.

Later, I thought about Bill's words. It made me realise how much the issue of pain management in Australia was about *access* to specialist services, for as Bill had assured me, a vast range of sophisticated pain medication existed.

~

This was a big month, September 2009. First, there was the fifth anniversary of Mark's death. And then the International Palliative Care conference. The day after I gave my talk, I left Perth to attend my first academic conference as part of my studies. It focused on the healing and ethical aspects of writing about personal experiences. This was right on the topic of my Master's thesis, and so I made the stretch to leave the kids and fly to Adelaide. This was the first time I had left them during school term. The first time I left them in Perth without me. Each summer school holiday I sent them across to Melbourne to spend time with their father's family. But this time I was the one leaving.

A colour chart outlining which parent would drive Joschka and Rahel to their after-school activities and where they would have a sleep-over clung to our fridge door. The logistics involved in leaving Perth for four days was reminiscent of a military boot camp. My friends were very supportive, and so I found myself on a plane to South Australia.

This was the beginning of a new chapter in my life. Listening to the engaging and thought-provoking presentations at the conference thrust me into my new role as life-writing researcher and allowed me to grow into this budding but welcome part of me. At uni, I had not met another memoir writer amongst my fellow students, and here, I found myself amongst peers for the first time. I was amazed at the personal nature of many of the presentations. In stark contrast to the deeply ingrained academic attitude that the personal should be kept out of research writing, here on an academic stage were incredibly inspiring and well-spoken people, – nearly all women – who presented highly personal experiences, such as raising a disabled child, facing a terminal illness, and undergoing a strained divorce. The dual approach of personal writing, aptly termed life-writing, and engaging theoretically with the practice of such writing, appealed strongly to both my intellectual and emotional sides.

I returned home daunted by how articulate and talented so many of the scholars I had listened to were, but also exhilarated that I had found my place in an academic field that was right for me in every way. I counted myself very fortunate to have stumbled into this field by a string of synchronistic circumstances.

The warm and satisfying feeling that I had found the right professional place fuelled my studies back home, and when the workload got overwhelming, I drew on the inspiration that still pulsed through my veins from having engaged with other life-writing researchers.

A month later, at the end of the first year of part-time studies, I applied for a scholarship at Murdoch University.

"Mama, guess what, I've been awarded the scholarship I applied for!"

"That's wonderful. Congratulations!" My mother's voice on the other end of the phone echoed my excitement. "I'm really proud of you, and so is Papa. He's right here and heard everything."

"Yeah, it hasn't really sunk in yet." My feet bounced up and down. "The only thing is, I'll have to study full-time – that's a requirement of the scholarship." My left hand fingered the luminous green pendant I wore.

"The kids are older now – they're at high school. I'm sure you'll work it out." I could hear the shuffling of newspaper. I pictured my mother sitting at home in Germany in her Tasmanian oak armchair in the living room, with her back to the enormous window which gave perfect light for reading. She must have been reading the paper when I rang. "If we were closer, we could help … but you will manage, Katrin. You always do."

Going full-time the following year was a significant and challenging change in my life. I would no longer be there when the children came home from school. An image of Joschka's anxious face back in the beginning in hospital flashed through my mind – his eyes wide, asking me if I would still pick him up from school. The memory of his fear then, written all over his little tense body, still echoed through me. He was a teenager now, with a testosterone-fuelled attitude, but I still felt bad about the thought of the kids coming home to an empty house.

Now, there were no more long morning walks along the river. No more occasional lunches at the *Juicy Beetroot* in Fremantle, a delicious vegetarian restaurant that was only open during the week. The workload involved in researching and writing the thesis was titanic. Not having any coursework, but being entirely self-paced, required considerable discipline. The first few weeks drained my energy like drops of water sucked up by thirsty, parched soil. In the evenings, I was exhausted, my eyelids heavy, even though I loved the research.

Sitting in my office at uni that I shared with two other students, serenaded by a chorus of black cockatoos perched in the towering ghost gumtree outside my window, I began to research contemporary bereavement literature. This was prompted by my thesis topic, which focused on published memoirs that narrated the loss of a loved one. One of the first texts I came across was Robert Neimeyer's ground-breaking book, *Meaning Reconstruction and the Experience of Loss*. I had no inkling then, as I looked at the title on my computer screen, that this book was to greatly influence the path of my own personal recovery. But I did anticipate from the title that this text that would play an important role in my research.

I raced along the short path from my office to the library and felt a rush of excitement when my hand grabbed the dark spine of the book and lifted it off the shelf. Back at my desk, I was immediately captivated by the revolutionary message of the book: it argued against the fixed stages of grief and against the old, rigid bereavement belief system.

A memory of small, pastel-coloured booklets thrust into my hands with a silent but emphatic nod of the head flashed through my mind. This had been the only literature I had ever been given on the topic of grief. All of these booklets presented Elisabeth Kübler-Ross's five stages of grief as an inevitable process. These stages – denial, anger, bargaining, depression and acceptance – have never proven helpful to me, and I had yearned for a more suitable guide to help me to understand my feelings.

Years later, I discovered that the research by Kübler-Ross had involved people who were dying, not bereaved people who survived their loved one. In 1996, Kübler-Ross wrote her influential book, *On Death and Dying,* based on her research with terminally ill people. Over time, the fact that her work was specific to people who were dying became masked, and what she herself had termed the stages of dying morphed into stages of grief. Psychologists, doctors and the general public wove this theory into its cultural tapestry without checking its validity, and thus the fiction of the five stages of grief had been given a perceived mantle of truth.

Neimeyer wrote in the introduction that there is no scientific evidence to support the stage-theory of grief, and that there is no obvious endpoint to grieving. No box to be ticked – yep, now I've "recovered".

Later on, Kübler-Ross herself publicly acknowledged in her 2005 book, *On Grief and Grieving*, that the five stages of grief were not meant to be interpreted as universal reactions to grief. She wrote in the very first paragraph: *the stages have been very misunderstood over the past three decades. They were never meant to help tuck messy emotions into neat packages.* Though she goes on to say that many people experience the emotional responses described in the five stages, she categorically states that *there is not a typical response to loss. Our grief is as individual as our lives. Not everyone goes through all of them or goes in a prescribed order.*

With *Meaning Reconstruction* in hand, a collection of contributions from a large number of bereavement scholars and clinicians, I realised that a new wave of grief theorists in the 1990s had begun to question the out-dated Freudian grief model and what constitutes "normal grief". I was captivated and threw myself into this research, reading for hours on end.

Generations of psychologists and therapists, it turned out, had been trained in grief counselling on the basis of a short book written by Sigmund Freud in 1917, entitled *Mourning and Melancholia*. The classical approach to grief claimed that the bereaved had to work through their emotions with the goal of detaching from the deceased loved one. The idea was to return to the way the person was prior to their loss, as if it had never happened. Continued thoughts about the loved one, especially the holding onto their clothes or belongings, and ongoing distress became labelled as *pathological*.

Instead of branding continuing thoughts about the loved one as problematic and pathological, these contemporary bereavement scholars developed alternative models to Freudian-influenced paradigms. One of the main concepts, in stark contrast to the classical model, was the idea of "continuing bonds" with the loved one. That is, a continued relationship with the deceased is not only normal, but even positive, playing an important role in integrating the loss.

Back at my desk, my attention honed in on the text like sunshine through a magnifying glass. The pages almost began to sizzle. Time disappeared. I entered "the zone" as I kept reading, too absorbed to stop for lunch. Even the loud screaming of the sulphur crested cockatoos outside my office did not distract me. The message of the book was that the central process in grieving was making sense of the loss we've experienced, especially in the case of loss that involves trauma. Such a loss, Neimeyer argued, usually leads to a loss of our sense of self, of who we are, and of the way we view the world around us. Thomas Attig's notion of having to "relearn the world" captured how I felt, spoke to my need to learn the texture, temperature and topology of this unknown landscape, both exterior and interior. I no longer knew either world.

As I read about the importance of finding meaning in my loss, I saw again the concrete barrier, like the Berlin Wall, rising steeply in front of me, stopping me from moving on. Finally, I understood. The absolute absence of meaning had forced me to remain stuck in the memories of incomprehensible suffering.

It was one of those "aha" moments that etch themselves into consciousness. I had been imprisoned by this unrelenting, sheer surface. Had belted it with my fists. Cursed it. Hated it. Pleaded with it. At uni, I looked out on the old gumtrees outside and the brown and white pieces of bark the wind had stripped from the trunks and scattered outside my window. Only now did I take my first baby step in freeing myself from the wall I had faced ever since Mark's death.

I had no idea how I would go about making sense of Mark's illness, hospital stay and death, or if this was even possible. Neimeyer shed new light for me on the process of finding meaning by offering a different perspective. Meaning did not have to be uncovered in the death itself, he wrote, but could be found in our own life following our loss.

I pondered this. In my quest to break free from the prison of meaninglessness, I could make sense of Mark's death in my own life, who I had become. Scaling the wall did not require me to find meaning in his suffering.

I knew instinctively that it would not be a fast, explosive blasting, but rather, a dismantling, brick by brick, scraping away the mortar with my fingernails.

33

I wondered if other people were as tortured as I was by this void of meaning. Again, bereavement studies held answers for me. Scanning Google, I found several studies that dealt with the loss of a loved one, a partner or child. I hadn't been able to meet other young widows in Perth, didn't know how other people reacted to their loss, so I was captivated by the findings of these studies. Reading through the articles, it became obvious that sudden death or loss at a young age creates a need for answers in the surviving relatives. According to these studies, the overwhelming majority of people begin to search for meaning and, what's more, will not find peace until they do.

I looked up from the screen. The humming of the computer drummed in my ears. Tears welled up and I felt strangely comforted as I realised that I was not alone in my aching quest for answers. Seeking to understand Mark's extreme torment had become like an additional layer of skin, ingrained in the fabric of who I was now.

I went for a walk in Wireless Hill Park. Lounging on a wooden bench amongst the wildflowers, my gaze settled on the large, luminous orange cone of the banksia in full flower. Mesmerised by the hundreds of little individual spikes that made up the larger cluster, I gently ran my hand over the cone, letting my fingertips linger on the soft yet firm texture of the buds.

I thought about how much my life had changed. Like the hundreds of little spikes of the banksia, my life had experienced regrowth in so many ways. I pondered how each one had contributed something to the larger cone. It felt to me as if I had transformed into another species of flower altogether. Raising my head, I looked out over the Swan River in the distance. I stretched my arms out in front of me, my hands grasping each other. I could almost see Mark's sun-kissed, freckled hand running over the length of my arm. Nearly all of my cells would have renewed by now, I thought. My skin was no longer the same skin that Mark had touched.

This movement of life, and of my physical body, ever-changing, renewing itself, was a move away from my connection with Mark. My sadness settled into its familiar folds in the depths of my stomach.

What remains? Thinking this question reminded me of the card I had at home, its front cover pasted in a similar orange to the banksia cone in front of me, just not as bright, more subdued. It posed this very question – what remains? And answered it: Love. This card had been sent to me from Germany, by the families I grew up with. They had all signed it individually. I had placed this card on the sideboard in my living room, in a prominent spot, catching my eye every time I walked from the kitchen to my bedroom. The card had become worn out from being held so often, its edges frayed. I reflected upon its message. It was not a platitude. Our love had remained, even if Mark's body had perished and mine had been renewed amongst the living. And this feeling of love nourished me. At the same time though, it did not diminish my yearning to be held by Mark, to look into his eyes, to have him make me laugh.

Some of the new spikes I had added to my cone were the times when I had shared my story and my message publicly: the need in the community to access appropriate pain management. I had emphasised that alleviating debilitating pain is the most important goal for palliative care.

After I had delivered my talk at the convention centre, a woman from the Cancer Council rang me up.

"Katrin, I heard you speak at the *Together!* conference. I'm a nurse educator at the Cancer Council." Her voice was soft, underscored with empathy.

"I think you have a very important message and I was wondering if you'd consider speaking at our palliative care nurses' training days."

I turned my car off, which I had pulled into a side-road and parked next to the curb when the phone rang.

"Ehm, this is very unexpected. I'd like to know what's involved." I ran my finger over the thick rubber of my steering wheel, firm yet malleable.

"Yes, sure, of course. How about you come and meet me in my office. We're in Shenton Park."

Shenton Park. The mere mention of the name sent goose bumps down my spine. Images of the closed ward, the long corridor and grey linoleum floor washed through my mind. I took the fact that the office was located in the same suburb as the rehab clinic as a sign that I was meant to do this.

On my way to meet the nurse educator a few days later, I pulled my car into Selby Street and slowly passed the driveway that leads up to the clinic. I had not been back along this road in five years, and the strong physical reaction of my body startled me. The fine hairs on my arms stood upright. My heartbeat increased and seemed to drown out the low humming of the motor. I wiped my eyes with my right palm while I kept steering with the left hand.

The Cancer Council was behind the various rehabilitation clinics spread out over a large area. Its proximity took my breath away.

Inside, the receptionist beckoned me to sit down in one of the upholstered chairs. I had barely walked across when Julie approached me in blue slacks and a white blouse sprinkled with tiny flowers. She had a firm handshake and I immediately took to the warmth she radiated. We sat down in her office.

"I know this is a big ask of you, but your message is so important." The blue of her eyes intensified and she looked straight at me. "I was deeply touched by your story. I'm so sorry for what you went through." She offered me a glass of water. "I'd like you to speak at our palliative nurse education days, to speak to the nurses that are being trained. They're a good bunch and will be a compassionate audience."

I took a moment to think this over.

"How often would that be?" I leaned into the back of my chair and sipped the water.

"Several times a year. If you can't make every one, that's okay of course. I'd be grateful no matter how often you can make it."

She gave me the details of the upcoming training day which was to be held in the same building, in just a couple of weeks. I drove home with a mixture of apprehension at retelling my story, but also inspired that I had the opportunity to impress the crucial topic of pain management on the palliative care nurses. I had heard too many anecdotal stories over the years since Mark died of patients suffering terrible pain. This had to stop. What angered me was the fact that we had the proper medications at our disposal in Australia. Why was it so difficult to provide patients with pain management?

On the appointed day, I drove past the rehab clinic again on route to the Cancer Council. It felt bizarre, that giving a talk about Mark was the reason I drove past the rehab clinic. As I got out of my car, I straightened my skirt as if I could just wipe away the fluttering in the pit of my stomach. My lower back hurt, and I rubbed it with my fingers in a vain attempt to loosen the taut muscles. I turned to look at the building towering over me. Dread at having to revisit my painful memories in detail in front of strangers closed in on me like fog. What if I have to cry? It seemed almost inevitable that this would happen. As if drawn by a magnet, my gaze wandered to the long driveway nestled in natural bushland. I longed to escape into the peace the shrubs and trees had to offer.

I took a deep breath and walked inside. The nurses were already seated although I was early. Julie waved at me. The chattering in the room died down and all eyes were on me.

I began to deliver my talk, clutching the remote control for my power point presentation. There were about twenty nurses in the room. The smaller audience, in such intimate proximity that I could see their faces and make eye contact, unsettled me. In a way, it was harder than the large, faceless audience at the Convention Centre.

"Although nurses wrote down in my husband's medical notes time and time again *the patient was moaning and distressed throughout the night,* no one ever called in a pain-management specialist." Tears burst forth and I could not hold them back. I ran my index finger across the cheekbone on the right side of my face and wiped away the moisture.

"Mark was in the High-Dependency Unit at the time. As nurses, you would know that this is one large room, with one bed next to the other." The heat from my tears burned my face. I knew what was coming next, and wasn't sure that I could continue.

"So, the other patients got so upset at witnessing another human being in such heart-wrenching pain that they moved Mark into the only single room in the High-Dependency Unit." I heard the nurses gasp in unison. I paused, before continuing. "And they shut the door on him to drown out his moaning, so the other patients wouldn't have to hear it."

As I looked up, my eyes met twenty pairs of moist eyes, some wide in disbelief. It was difficult to keep going. My voice was thick with emotion. I swallowed hard to stem the flow of tears.

Afterwards, some women came up to me to shake my hand and to thank me for sharing my story. Although it had been an emotionally intense, challenging experience, I was heartened – at least I had made some difference.

~

The talks continued over the next couple of years or so. Until I realised one day that I could not keep doing them, because they threw me into an emotional vortex that took a lot of energy to climb back out of. And they stopped me from moving on, from leaving the dark memories behind.

At the same time that I had this insight, so did Julie. She rang me the day after I had given another talk at the Cancer Council.

"Katrin, thank you so much for your time yesterday. I cannot put into words how much I appreciate it." She took a deep breath. "But I've been observing you, how painful it is for you to bring yourself right back there, again and again." A pregnant pause ensued, filled with a joint memory of my distress. "I don't think you should continue with the talks. It's too much for you."

"It's amazing that you're saying this, because I've just been thinking the same thing." I looked at Mark's photo on the side board.

"I wanted to ask you if you'd do it one more time, and then we'll film you. That way we can still keep showing it to the nurses and you don't have to keep re-living it." Julie's voice was determined.

"That's a great idea. Let's do that."

And thus, my active role as advocate for palliative care had reached its conclusion. Before Mark's death I could never have envisioned becoming a spokesperson for the Cancer Council. The irony was that palliative care had *not been* involved in Mark's care until the end, with such devastating consequences.

That night, lying awake in bed, with shadows dancing across my ceiling from a sliver of light that filtered through a small gap in my curtains, I thought back over my involvement as spokesperson and advocate for pain management. My public speaking engagements, I realised, had added texture to the fabric of my life, in particular, much-needed meaningfulness.

34

"Katrin, are you sitting down?" Through the phone, Wayne's voice was deep, with a hint of laughter.

Bemused, I wandered over to the couch and sat down. There was no urgency or alarming shakiness in his tone. Though I must have missed the slight tremble that denotes the departure from our comfort zone, barely tangible.

"Yes, I am," I replied with a chuckle. This was highly unusual and all of my attention was now focused like a laser beam on the black Nokia phone resting in my palm, metal against skin.

"Well, I wanted to let you know that my feelings for you have changed." He took a deep breath. "I wanted to tell you now, as I won't see you before you're flying to Melbourne."

I slowly let the air escape from my lungs. I knew Wayne. I knew precisely what he meant. I breathed in the possibility of romance ... love. As if I was observing myself from above, I became aware that it would be a good thing to take my time with my response, not to jump in straight away without thinking first, always so spontaneous and unbridled.

The line crackled with static. Not uncomfortable, but dense.

A flash of Wayne's smiling face settled in my inner mind, two eye-catching dimples framing his face, soft and gentle, in such contrast to his burly build.

"Thank you for letting me know." I leant back into the leather, cold against my skin. "This comes as a surprise, and I'd like to think about it, to feel into it. Is that okay?"

"Katrin, of course, I didn't expect you to say anything right away. But I had this strong urge to tell you, so you'd know, just so you'd know." A pregnant pause filled with possibilities lingered in the air. "Whatever happens from here, if we end up exploring whatever this is or not, is okay. You know that, you know me."

I looked outside. My hands were crossed over, resting, palms up, in my lap, still cradling the phone. Two pink and grey galahs had come to rest on the branch of the acacia right outside my window, gently touching it. They were so close, I could almost reach out to them. Their heads moved about busily. And then they turned to face each other and began to bill and coo with their beaks, in a gesture so touching that endorphins flooded my body, leaving a trail of serenity.

This is what I want, this closeness, the merging of two people where the borders between them becomes fluid. But how do I know if Wayne is the one?

Wayne, my Wayne. I shook my head at the twists and turns of life. Curiously, I thought, I had been thinking of him as *my Wayne* for ages now, years, though only in friendship. But our friendship, our close connection, the support that we had given one another and the dependable honesty that had developed over time, was as precious to me as my grandmother's wedding ring, stowed away in the homemade jewellery box in the top draw of my bedside table, worn thin over fifty years. Like that ring, Wayne and I had accrued many stories together over the years. He had even been there at the trial. As if we'd been building up to this all along, without even knowing it.

Still sitting on my couch, I breathed in the hot, dry summer air through the open window. I played Wayne's phone call over in my mind. Images of the last five years flashed by. Sitting on the plane next to Wayne on our way to the overseas workshop, chatting, feeling reassured by his solidity during unsettling turbulences. A plane trip that we had not booked together but happened to be on by coincidence. The way he had tucked me into bed in his hotel room, like a brother. We've always said we're like brother and sister, and both of us meant it, really meant it. Wayne didn't have a sister, grew up with three brothers, tough and barefoot in the country. There had been no room for female softness, nurturing. That day in his hotel room, he sat quietly on the balcony to let me sleep, not even boiling the kettle for fear of disturbing me.

I was confused about my own feelings. I didn't want to get this wrong. I didn't want to jeopardise our precious friendship.

Thinking about the times he had just been there for me, listening to my heartache without offering unsolicited advice, just being there for me, made me smile.

"You know, Wayne, I share everything with you that I would with my closest girlfriend," I had told him one day.

Wayne's dimples had deepened. His bright blue eyes glazed over with joy. "I've never experienced anything like this friendship before, Katrin. I'm just so glad to have that in my life." He had stared into the distance, nodding to himself.

It was this gentleness that I cherished in Wayne, the ability to feel deep emotion, so at odds with his rough upbringing. The combination of a big heart beating in an expansive chest deep enough to fit a baby lamb.

Outside my window, the canoodling galahs flew off, in unison. The branch was swinging from the force of their take-off. What was I going to do now? I decided to trust that time would tell, to give myself the time to find out for myself. Not to rush into things this time.

The next afternoon I was sitting with Ina in a coffee shop with exposed, recycled red brick walls of the old warehouse and stainless-steel counter tops – very inner city.

"I know that if I wanted things between Wayne and I to stay the same, they would." I gazed at the untouched moist lemon meringue on my plate. Picked up the small cake fork and bounced it on the white plate. I looked up at Ina. "But what really worries me is if I was to have sex with him and then find out that this isn't right for me. Then I'm buggered. He wouldn't hold it against me, and we'd still be friends, but it wouldn't be the same anymore. The innocence would be gone."

Ina reached across the table and rested her hand for a moment on my arm.

"Do you remember, when we were at the trial, and I said to you, why don't you get together with Wayne, you'd make a great couple?"

I dropped the fork. "No, I don't remember that." I shook my head. "What did I answer?"

"That you don't feel like that about Wayne." She picked up her coffee cup and raised it towards me, leant forward and slightly bowed her head in a salute, a cheeky smile settling into the corners of her mouth. "It was so obvious how well suited you are."

"Man, that's what … almost three years ago." I let my fork glide into the smooth texture of the cake. The tangy flavour lingered on my tongue. "I still don't know what to do."

Circumstances conspired to provide me with a two-week window of opportunity to contemplate. Wayne went on a fishing trip, out of mobile range, and then I flew to Melbourne and he was on night shift. We could not ring each other up.

The weekend before Wayne's unexpected phone call, Joschka and I had gone fishing with him. The sun had set over the estuary as Wayne's and Joschka's figures walked out through the shallow water, each holding one end of a fishing net, crabbing. When they returned, Joschka's face lit up with excitement. The net was full. Wayne fried some mullets on a stove on the back of his trailer. The salt encrusted sand cushioned our feet. Even Joschka ate a whole fish, bent over his plate under the gas lamp.

Later, he fingered my camera out of my rucksack and took photos of the bucket filled with fish. Then he told us to stand next to one another for a photo. Wayne, reeking of fish, a broad smile on his face, beaming, standing tall, put his arm around me.

A surge of warmth filled my body at the memory. It was then, in that moment, that something had changed between us. It wasn't chemistry yet, but I remembered clearly how much I would have liked to have snuggled into him, to nestle into those broad shoulders.

We'd only gone on this fishing trip because I had asked Wayne if he would be willing to be something of a mentor to Joschka. Once Joschka became a teenager, the absence of his father or any close adult male in his every-day life became more and more noticeable. Exhaustion had snaked its way into my bones. I was tired of his frequent arguing, the confrontations and the resultant tension.

On a Great Walk camping trip a couple of weeks earlier I had been chatting with Nicola, who had two teenage sons.

"You know, I just don't know what to do any more. I just want the arguing to stop. I've tried everything with Joschka, from coercing to reasoning. Not even switching off the internet to stop him from playing his computer games has yielded any results." I sighed. My shoulders ached. "I just don't know what to do." I wiped the tears off my face with my palms. A cool breeze blew across my moist skin. "At the same time, I'm so grateful that both he and Rahel did so amazingly well after their dad passed away. I just want him to talk to me more respectfully."

"Why don't you find a suitable male friend to mentor Joschka?" Nicola reached into her backpack for a tissue and handed it to me. "A friend of mine who's divorced and whose ex has moved away did that. It was really good. Her sons liked spending time with the friend she'd asked to mentor them and things improved at home."

A group of kangaroos leisurely grazed in the paddock next to the bush trail. One female pricked her ears, looked up, focused on locating the direction our voices came from. Her long dark eyelashes gave her a gentle expression.

"Mmm, it sounds like a good idea. Joschka doesn't really get to spend much time with adult men. My dad is overseas and there aren't any other male relatives either in Perth." The kangaroo bowed her head down to feast on the grass, reassured that the sounds posed no danger. "I can see how much Joschka craves male company. Here on the Great Walk, he's drawn to help the men set up our camp. Yesterday he even volunteered to dig up the fire pit."

"What about someone from the Great Walk? Miles for example, he's got a lot of experience with adolescents."

"Yeah, he'd be great. But he lives down south – that's too far away." I swiped away a persistent fly that had been whooshing around my head for the last five minutes. "I like the idea. I'll have a think about it, who might be suitable."

And so, when I had visited Wayne in Dwellingup a little while later and we had gone kayaking at Lane Poole Reserve for the day, I remembered my conversation with Nicola. Wayne mentored young Aboriginal men at his last job at a farm school, and we'd had a few conversations about it. Of course, I thought, Wayne would be great. Just the right male role model.

Wayne had agreed to be a mentor for Joschka, surprised, but very willing to take on this role. Doing boys' things together like fishing and learning how to use tools.

And thus, Wayne's invitation to the fishing trip was born. I only went along because there was no other way for Joschka to get to Wayne's house. Also, this was their first outing, and though Joschka knew Wayne, they hadn't really spent much time together apart from the couple of days at the fishing shack years earlier.

35

On a camping trip down south, we stopped at a tattered roadhouse, paint flakes peeling off the walls. I collected the key to the toilets. The miniature orange skittle that served as a key pendant weighed heavy in my hand. I stuck it into the lock and opened the door. It shut with a thump and I found myself in a windowless bathroom. The way the door clonked startled me and I turned to open it. Gripping the silver latch, I tried to twist it, but it wouldn't budge. Goose bumps crept down my bare arms and legs. I rattled the door and pushed one hand against the door frame to gain better leverage. Sweat slicked my palms and my left hand slipped down the door frame. I was locked in.

Wayne was walking past on the way back from the men's toilets, and heard my yelling. He shoved the men's key into the lock, twisted it and the door jerked open. I fell into his arms, panting, my legs shaking. Though I was freed in a short period of time, I was unhinged by how much this had shaken me, and how fast. My physical response was at odds with my self-image. Where had she gone, the intelligent woman who knew rationally that she was in no danger?

My first ever anxiety attack was four years earlier, on that Alm in Austria. Apart from these two incidences when I found myself locked in a toilet cubicle, I did not have another full anxiety attack. But these fear explosions were etched upon my body, and my anxiety in enclosed spaces continued over the years. Elevators in particular, and locking the door of windowless toilet cubicles, reduced me to internal quivering and a sudden surge of adrenaline that sent my heartbeat racing. I was fine in toilet cubicles if they weren't public and I didn't have to lock the door. Adding to my discomfort, I felt absurd for feeling tense about locked enclosed spaces in the first place. I did not know how to respond to the story my body was telling.

At first, I tried to avoid enclosed spaces. In my everyday life, I rarely encountered elevators, but during the trial I had to endure them several times a day. It always surprised me to notice that my internal havoc was invisible to the outside world, unless it was one of the few close people who knew.

Over time, I learned to manage entering enclosed spaces. Mind over matter worked to a degree. Deep breathing allowed me to ride in elevators, feeling uncomfortable at best, always tense. It took me several years to learn to accept my physical fear. Whenever possible, I continued to take the stairs instead of the lift.

The numerous personal development courses I had attended, as well as the meditation courses, practising deep breathing and mindfulness, reading scholarly bereavement literature and writing, had all played their role in allowing me to reach a level of recovery from grief and trauma that I had perceived as being out of reach in the early throes of my distressed state. These various tools helped me to work through my experiences and memories, to resolve the post-traumatic replaying of the most harrowing scenes in my mind, to the point where I regained my equilibrium, though it could always be disturbed by unexpected triggers.

By contrast, the reaction of my body, the dread of being locked into enclosed spaces, which began about a year after Mark's death, persisted. There was no kidding myself, I thought, my management strategies were band aids – they did not address the underlying cause. And thus, my quest was born to understand and heal the root cause of the claustrophobia.

My intention sent me on a path to discover and research the nature of trauma, in particular, the embodiment of trauma. Slowly the pieces of the puzzle began to form a picture. I began to understand that the trauma I had experienced was held in the body – *my body*. It was only after I began to write about my life after Mark's death that I became acutely aware of the difference between the grief and the trauma I had experienced. Although intertwined, I realised the two had distinct and separate paths to recovery.

It was only after meeting the psychologist nominated by my lawyer in the context of the trial about two years after my loss that I came to understand that *I* had suffered. This might seem strange, but my eyes had been firmly cast in Mark's direction and I had perceived my own pain as simply incomparable to Mark's. I had placed his suffering on the one hundred percentile marker, and I had not registered my own. It was as if he had inhabited a scale all of his own, shared only by the most severe torments experienced by humans, and I had no place on that scale, which seemed to exist in a different dimension.

This intuitive comparing of suffering did not serve me well, for it put me into denial for a long time about the severity of the trauma I had experienced. I would never compare it with what Mark experienced, but I recognised that suffering, like all experience, is subjective. Comparison has no place, no relevance.

I came to understand, a decade after Mark's death, that trauma is soaked up by the body. That my skin was like a sponge absorbing the pain bubbles it was immersed in. I realised that embodied trauma can only be released through the body and not by contemplating and thinking alone.

I have grown up in the western cultural belief system that privileges the rational mind, thinking over feeling, which has been summed up so succinctly in Descartes' notion, "I think, therefore I am". In my research, I came upon Antonio Damasio, a professor of neuroscience, who emphasises that emotions play a critical role in every aspect of our life. More than that, he says our emotions are what make us human. To underscore how passionately he feels about the role emotions play in our biological make-up, he has altered Descartes' famous statement to "I feel, therefore I am".

I was intrigued and began to study books written for nonprofessional readers on neuroscience and our emotions. I drew comfort about my fear response to enclosed spaces when I learned that we cannot switch our emotions off any more than we can consciously stop breathing.

My quest to understand the nature of trauma led me to Peter Levine's book *In an Unspoken Voice: How the Body Releases Trauma and Restores Goodness*. I read it on a holiday. Levine's book is based on the idea that trauma is neither a disease nor a disorder, but rather, an injury caused by loss and helplessness. An injury! And this *emotional wound* can be healed, as Levine's work with trauma victims had proven. Here was a scientist who had worked for NASA. Had been a member of numerous task groups that responded to large scale disasters. This experienced clinician defied the push by the medical establishment that presents post-traumatic stress as a mental disorder that can't be healed, but only managed with pills.

I was reading on the porch of an old fishing shack, my eyes glued to the text. One morning, I looked up from the pages to see a large school of dolphins, perhaps thirty of them, frolicking in the waves of the Southern

Ocean. I raced onto the rocks, scurried across rock pools and seaweed, and got within two metres of the creatures. The sun glistened on their wet backs. Some of the dolphins surfed right up to the shore, their bodies upright, balancing on their tails, the only part of them still submerged in the frothing waves. When one swam right past my rock, I saw several long, white scars on its back. This is what being in the moment feels like, I thought. Even after an injury, when we carry physical or emotional scars. I understood that swimming, being present with the ocean, is one way of allowing the body to release its story. Focusing on the body, like these dolphins who seemed to be having fun, without mind chatter, is healing.

One morning I was reading in my hammock, which had been tied to the metal rafts of the fishing shack, gently swinging. I dropped the book into my lap. A goanna ran across the concrete floor, its tail whooshing from side to side in swift movements, and I watched it linger under the kitchen bench. Then the black, elegant body covered in faint yellow stripes disappeared over the sand. I looked across the dunes onto the expanse of the seething, swollen ocean and breathed the wild air into my lungs. I could *feel* my body relaxing, how watching the goanna, observing the dolphins' surfing, inhaling the sea breeze, sensing the soft sand under my feet, helped my body to release her memories and to make inroads towards healing my emotional wounds. Perhaps it was the distance from the city, the solidity of the rocks, and the constant humming of the waves that gave me the space to reflect on my loss in the context of Levine's book. In this expanse of wide horizons and wind-tossed sea gulls, my fear of enclosed spaces seemed far removed.

36

Memory is a fickle thing. The photographic clarity with which I can remember the time Mark was locked into his body astounds me. Certainly, details of times and places fade, but what I can recall is my emotions, with all the specifics of their texture. The fallibility of memory is well known. But I assert the accuracy of my emotional memory, solid and tangible. This clarity of emotional memory also applies to the court case. Like a romantic portrait taken by a photographer that is blurred around the edges, details do fade into the background, but the anger, nerves, disbelief and disillusionment I felt at the trial remain in sharp focus.

My brain has always used emotions as the structure for its filing system: sadness, excitement, anger, joy, despair, and fear. It is these emotional memories that stick in my mind, not as a sticky-note that can be blown away by the first gust of wind, but pasted on with glue, superglue even.

But ask me for names of places we visited, and I cannot recall many of them. As if my brain simply refuses to employ a secondary filing system that does not utilise emotions as its marker. Mark was the encyclopaedia I relied upon for place names.

"What was that place called in Egypt, where we'd slept in a bed riddled with bedbugs?" I had asked him as we walked along a bush track.

"Ah, yes, Al Fayyum." The answer came, without missing a beat, his eyes alight with the joy of remembering our first few days together.

With Mark gone, my access to many shared memories was gone too. I could no longer reminisce with him about meeting in Egypt, the birth of Rahel on a beanbag with a hot shower slowly trickling over my back and legs, the first time Joschka wore his *Attadale Bombers* footy jersey. A lifetime store of joined memories, no longer merged, but mine alone. Now, the opportunity to reminisce together had been snatched from me, irreplaceable, never to be repeated. I could tell our stories to someone else or our children, but they are no longer shared memories, no longer relived together. The ache of that loss, of never being able to conjure up married memories with Mark, has left a dark void.

As a widow, I mourn the loss of countless details.

~

But one way to resurrect or preserve detail is in writing. Committing Mark's story to paper, seen through my eyes, is to make sure it does not get lost with the process of time. Writing makes it possible to bear witness for others, especially Rahel and Joschka, to offer the view of the adult to the memory of the child. It has also been instrumental for me in integrating my traumatic experiences. Narrating the past with sensory detail, remembering the smells, sights and sounds, evoking the emotions, is to relive it, unavoidably so. But it has also enabled me to release the memories from their imprisonment, not during the writing process, but afterwards. Redrafting provides the distance that entering the inner landscape during writing inherently lacks. Writing is equally cognitive and embodied, requiring both the body and the mind to divulge its story to the page.

I liken the process of writing to the way my visual perspective changes between short-sightedness and corrected vision. Being short-sighted hones my focus, like a laser beam, onto the close-up page, but with a lack of clarity in the distance and the periphery. The writing in front of me is hyper-crystallised. With the edges blurred, the wider world not only looks but feels different from the central, crisp surroundings in sharp focus. Both focal points offer different ways of viewing life. The laser beam-focused vision is much narrower, but brings with it a more intense distillation, undisturbed by the input of the bigger picture. It offers insight – a glimpse into the specifics of minute detail. When the gaze broadens and expands to take in the overall picture, the weave of the details becomes more blurred, less specific. They fade into the background.

Writing means to oscillate between the focus on the specifics, the sensuous detail, listening to the story of the body, and the broadening of the picture which puts these fragments in relationship with the larger world – the remembered past, the present and the imagined future – and in relationship with others, present and absent. Exploring these relational dynamics from the initial vantage point of the focused detail makes reflection and alternative discoveries possible. It is this interplay between delving into the close-up of experience and then including, bit by bit, the rest of existence that allows the fragmented picture to become whole again.

Traumatic experience had forced the haunting images to be played over and over in the involuntary cinema of my wounded mind. Like short-sightedness, it compelled my consciousness to focus on the experience, to relive it, again and again, this fragmented reality. Writing has played a pivotal role in the process of becoming whole again.

It has permitted me to break free from having to tick the box of the widow. And it has made it possible to remember my loss but not to be defined by it.

37

Wayne, the country boy, came from a background and upbringing utterly dissimilar to mine. I grew up in a high-rise in the most populated state in Germany. Wayne was one of four boys born within six years of each other in rural Western Australia, in the early years without running hot water. Sheep, cattle, repairing fences, bailing hay and driving tractors were interwoven into Wayne's memories and sinews. By contrast, my dad was the first in a family of tradesmen to get a tertiary degree. My upbringing was coloured by debates around the kitchen table rather than milking cows. And yet, Wayne and I made up a whole that worked. It did, however, require conscious input from both of us to make our two hemispheres fit. Wayne's mathematical and mechanical mind met my love for words. Shaping language was as strange to him as camshafts were to me. With maturity, we developed the tolerance and ability to embrace our differences. The cord that ran through our relationship was our shared belief system and values. Despite our different upbringings, they were surprisingly similar.

With Wayne living and working in the country, we have always maintained two households and never moved in together – intimacy interlaced with independence. Curiously, if someone had told me that the day would come when I would prefer to live in this way, I would not have believed it. I had loved being married, but death had changed my life course.

I do like the fact that living apart allows me to spend time with the children on my own. As Wayne regularly works weekends, I also relish the opportunity to catch up with my girlfriends. I have had endless conversations with my friends over a glass of Semillon, discussing the best way of combining a relationship with alone time. The most pressing question that always comes up is how to avoid losing oneself in a relationship. Separate households seem like the perfect answer for Wayne and me, a recipe that grants the best of both worlds, intimacy, love, not getting bogged down in the nitty gritty of domestic life – *can whites be washed with colours?* – and the opportunity to spend time alone, to pursue my writing and studies, to spend time with friends.

After the bitterness I had frequently encountered in divorced men after Mark's death, Wayne's gentleness, commitment, love and sincerity were refreshing and rejuvenating. He was even willing to fly to Melbourne one Christmas with us, as Rahel and Joschka wanted to spend the festive season with their relatives in Melbourne.

~

The emotional pain descended upon me every day for a long time. Slowly, very slowly, it began to skip a day every once in a while. It took a very long time before its wild storms became more dispersed. The spaces in between widened, but when it rose up, it was out of the blue. It is part of who I have become.

The unpredictable nature of grief, irrespective of where I was or what I was doing, was not only distressing but also terrifying. The unexpectedness of its onslaught meant I could not brace myself against it. It can still catch me today. Not long ago I went shopping at Woolworths and the words, "You are my number one, nuuuumber one," blared through the loudspeakers, the happy tune jingling in the sterile supermarket aisles. I was leaning over yoghurts and cold air brushed against the bare skin of my arms. Images of Rahel singing this song for her dad on Father's Day at the rehab clinic swam in front of my eyes as the cold crept under my T-shirt and spread across my back. Despite leaning over the fridge compartment, I could feel the heat stinging at the back of my eyes. Rahel's clear, high-pitched voice swirled around in my head. Goose bumps snaked across my arms and legs. I dropped the one kilo natural yoghurt container back into the shelf and fled the shop.

Can woundedness ever fully heal? Should it? I don't know the answer to that question. In medical terms, healing refers to a return to the state prior to the illness or wounding, ideally without scars, as if it had never happened. As if it were possible to erase the experience. But if healing is a return to the old self, then I don't want it. I don't want to be in denial of what has been. No, something new, more expansive has to be forged.

On a trip to Hawaii, I wandered across a large expanse of volcanic rock. As far as the eye could see there was grey, nothing but grey lava bordered by the rough ocean whipping its salty liquid against the barren surface. Suddenly I was struck by the sight of a single green shoot, a small stalk and a miniature palm leaf in vibrant lime tones that protruded from the unyielding stone. I stopped in my tracks in wonderment for this remaking. It was a moment of transformation.

I did not want my scars to be erased, obliterated with a magic skin potion. Like the ashen volcanic rock, they were the ground out of which my remaking had been shaped. Paradoxically, my new landscape, born out of disconnection and disempowerment, has allowed me to be more connected with myself than before Mark's death. I am more able to experience the full spectrum of emotion. It has taught me to give myself over to joy and bliss as much as to grief. Looking back, I realise I did not truly know compassion until I had suffered.

The absurdity is derived from having something positive moulded from the most terrible thing that has ever happened to me. To even think of it in terms of "positive" is counterintuitive. How could anything worthwhile come out of extreme torment? Is it even moral? Dishonouring of Mark? Initially, when I started to realise, many long years after Mark passed away, that I had become more connected to myself, my stomach twisted in repulsion. It felt so wrong. Only after lengthy discussions with my friends and repeatedly contemplating the situation in the quietude of my home did I become more at ease with it. Now I think of having regained a new sense of wholeness as a tribute to Mark, a legacy in his honour.

The other day, I let my mind wander over the last twelve years. My mellow mood was sparked by that particular atmosphere, home alone at night, with just a floor lamp bathing my living room in a soft light. I had watched a German romantic comedy filmed in Tuscany on *YouTube* and now sat in a peaceful, almost tender silence and contemplated how far I had travelled emotionally and psychologically from the time I was traumatised by Mark's suffering, locked into my inability to stop my visceral memories from haunting me. With surprise, I recognised that my trauma had changed shape, and I with it, so much so that I no longer considered myself traumatised. Those experiences have written themselves into my sense of who I am, though. I have given them a home but am no longer defined or imprisoned by them. Even the thought of my claustrophobia, this tangible, lasting signature, no longer scares me. I have turned its volume down and accept it.

It dawned on me that it all led back to one important moment in time. That night at home when Mark was still in the hospice and I had dared to make my decision that I would find happiness again one day. I realised that my decision back then had set my renewal in motion – more than that, made it possible. It was enormous willpower and determination that had seen me through. And my intuition, which guided me to whatever support and help I needed.

But this renewal is not a neat, clean wholeness – it is messy and jagged and it contains my vulnerabilities and fears. It is not fixed, but in flux, yet solid too. It is this feeling of solidity, missing so profoundly when I had been fragmented by loss, that is comforting. At the same time, the memory of the wounded self, of having been hurt beyond comprehension, having teetered on the edge of the abyss, brought to my knees, remains. Is it the memory of the wound or is it the wound itself? Who is to say?

This new, deeper connection lives within me now, but the emotional scar tissue and the lurking fear of another possible disintegration engendered by new loss lingers alongside my renewed self. Like conjoined twins, one exists with the other. My blood circulates between the two.

Epilogue

Completion is a powerful force. I remember standing at a particularly unrestrained stretch of coast, the roar of the waves in my ears, my body sprinkled with copious droplets from the swell, alive with the freshness of the salt-infused air in my lungs. My overarching sensation was awe of the incredible energy produced by this massive body of water, the surge to and fro that catapulted waves several meters high into the air. Its vitality uplifted me. Its visceral presence allowed me to tap into it. I feel like that now, over fifteen years after Mark's death. I am moving forward, invigorated by a powerful liveliness induced by two significant completions.

One is this book. While I was acutely aware of the transformative power of writing to facilitate wellbeing, I had not anticipated the surge of energy and peace that accompanied my memoir's conclusion. It mirrored an internal sense of completion. This is not a finite closure – grief: ticked off – but an invitation to new beginnings on the crest of a new set of waves able to reach me now. The memoir portrays chapters on the pages of my life, chapters that were experienced in capital letters, in bold and large font. Even so, this is not who I am. I am not my grief and trauma, though they are imprinted in my cells. I am much more than that. My book gave me the perfect lens to see that for myself. Like my short-sightedness that is corrected by contact lenses, the outline of my internal landscape has taken on a new quality, suffused with crisp sharpness. My desire for my children to grow up without being defined by the loss of their father has been fulfilled. And yet I imposed this very definition on myself for a long time. Perhaps to some degree knowingly. Largely subconsciously. What the completion of the book has given me is the freedom to move beyond my self-imposed boundaries and identification.

The second achievement is my doctorate. A year after I had completed my Master's, I enrolled in a PhD in creative writing at Curtin University. Though the degree required a lot of hard work, discipline and determination, I have felt all along a sense of fulfilment. The feeling of elation upon receiving my degree nevertheless took me by surprise. Although I have other degrees, this was the first time I attended the graduation ceremony. Garbed in academic attire, in a red velvet gown reminiscent of Harry Potter movies, I was part of the stage party, looking out onto the sea of faces of young graduates and their families for the duration of the two-hour ceremony, engulfed by a sense of the surreal. In a good way, though. Mark's illness had felt surreal for a long time, possibly years. Certainly for the whole period of his illness and death. It was a refreshing change to connect the surreal with joy and success. My family rejoiced with me. Rahel had flown from Melbourne to Perth to attend my graduation ceremony. Celebrating success was a new story we wrote together.

The reaction of others also took me by surprise. Family, friends and even strangers alike expressed their delight, and I could tell it was genuine. A flash of light in people's eyes and their animated body language underscored that this was sincere, not an act of politeness. The shared joy of completion and success became contagious, kindling a flame wherever sparks dropped. And one sentiment was repeated time and again: "You have turned tragedy into something that will help others. That's inspiring."

Together, these two significant events have merged and magnified my sense of meaningfulness and contentment. At the Western Australian town of Augusta, two oceans meet, the Southern Ocean and the Indian Ocean. If you stand in front of the lighthouse at the southwest tip of Australia, the two bodies of water meet, forming a visible line that extends out towards the horizon. It is not a pushing against each other, but a coming together. Merging and intermingling – not an antagonistic fight. Likewise, these two major closures of doctorate and memoir have come together and their joint energies have evoked a real transformation for me.

Synchronicity has imbued my post-PhD life with its gentle magic. The first significant synchronistic opportunity was connecting with the Grief Centre of Western Australia. It was the perfect place to hold my writing workshops to support grieving participants to move forward. The workshop that I designed was specifically aimed at people who were out of the all-encompassing rawness of initial bereavement, and now ready to process their grief and to transition into a renewed life, inclusive of the loss, but expanding its strangling boundaries.

Grief is like shallow breathing. Limiting – breath and life. A little while ago I had severe and persistent bronchitis. The intense coughing weakened my lungs, and I could not take a deep breath without forceful coughing. My lungs felt as though they had shrunk, only able to absorb shallow, small breaths. This went on for a few weeks. As my bronchitis slowly receded, and my lungs became stronger, they could expand a little more, bit by bit, allowing more and more air to be inhaled. There was still some mucus on the lungs, but this was no longer limiting the boundaries of my inhalation. Like grief, the cause remained, but it was no longer all there was.

I ran my six-week workshop on Thursday evenings. Several months after the first workshop ended, I ran into a participant at a function.

"Katrin!" She beamed at me. I asked her how she's been since the workshop. "I feel so much stronger as a result of the writing," she said. "Much more at ease with myself. I'm going well."

Her smile reached her eyes.

"Oh, and there's more. I've shared some of my writing from your course with my daughter, and it's healed our relationship. She's seeing me in a different light. We're in regular contact now." Joy danced along her words, reaching out and touching me.

Witnessing the unknotting and unravelling of pain into calmness or even peace in this participant and others uplifted me. The experience of offering participants various writing exercises and sharing fulfilled a deep desire for meaningfulness and purpose, for helping others to make grief more manageable. It was the culmination of everything I had experienced personally, carved out academically, and my training and participation in personal development courses. Everything converged on this focal point. Even before I submitted my PhD, the pathway to realise my passion had opened up.

The feedback and testimonials from the writing workshops were so positive that it strengthened my long-held vision to test and document the powerful benefits of Writing-for-wellbeing. During my Master's, I had researched the so-called Expressive Writing paradigm, developed by psychologist James Pennebaker, for people who had experienced a distressing or traumatic life event. Expressive Writing is based on a single writing-task instruction given to participants, who write for fifteen to twenty minutes usually for three consecutive days, always with the same writing instruction. So all in all about one hour of writing. Many Expressive

Writing studies showed the incredible emotional, psychological and physical health benefits that seemed to last for several weeks afterwards.

Over the years, I became increasingly convinced that if such a short set of writing sessions could bring about astounding health benefits, then it follows that more and longer-lasting benefits could be possible if the instructions were more varied and if the writing was undertaken over a longer period of time. I have designed a writing study over six weeks with twelve different writing prompts to test the effectiveness of more extensive writing in working through grief. It encompasses two-hour writing sessions, delivered once a week over six weeks and includes a range of creative writing instructions with a focus on emotion awareness and self-understanding. I have teamed up with a psychology professor from my university with a research interest in bereavement. And, in an act of soaring synchronicity, even Robert Neimeyer, whose work had played such a central role in my own grief processing, was supportive of this local study under the umbrella of the Grief Centre of Western Australia.

I had met Robert at a narrative psychology conference in Portugal where he was keynote speaker. One thing that struck me immediately was how down to earth he was, listening with palpable and full presence. In addition to telling Robert about my work with grief memoirs, I got to say thank you for his book on the importance of meaning making in grief, which was such a catalyst for me. This initial connection paved the way to collaborate with Robert on using writing to integrate grief. Synchronicity at its best.

My degree has not given me a clear access to a job in the way that is the case with, for example, scientists or doctors. It was always obvious that I would need to carve my own route forward. But my passion for writing as a medium for wellbeing, in particular for working through grief, has opened many doors to the realisation of it.

One of those doors was to go from designing the Writing-for-wellbeing research study to undertaking it with twenty participants in 2021, with the support of the Grief Centre and a Lotterywest grant. The research project evaluated and proved the feasibility and effectiveness of the six-week writing study in helping participants work through their grief and supporting them to facilitate adaptation, meaning-making and emotional wellbeing. This pilot study was well received, and participants reported that it was transformative, safe and personally valuable. As I had envisioned this study for many years, having realised my dream was one of the highlights of my life, much like the completion of my doctorate: meaningful, fulfilling and realising my goal of helping others through grief. It was also a way of honouring Mark.

This study had two groups, because grief occurs not only in relation to bereavement, but also as a response to other profound losses. One group had experienced the loss of a loved one, and the other group a range of other losses, including serious illness, disability, divorce and caring for a parent with dementia. As I ran the study in 2021, during the pandemic, it showed that writing helped people not only in relation to their existing losses, but also in relation to new ones, and it confirmed how deep and broad the benefits of personal writing can be.

Reflecting on Mark's illness and loss, I have moved forward in a way that I had dreamed about but never really fathomed to be achievable. Yet recovery from grief isn't black and white, clearly delineated, like a chess board. One thing I have come to learn is that opposite emotions, sadness and joy, can co-exist in surprisingly close proximity. The writing of my book and the sense of completion it brought has made it possible for me to experience inner peace. Its current, like the ocean, has caressed me to a welcome feeling of wholeness. I have broken free from being locked into my trauma. I have found peace.

Acknowledgements

My first heartfelt thank you goes to our children, Rahel and Joschka, for their love, and for their unconditional support for their dad during his illness. I am profoundly grateful for their tremendous courage in integrating their grief, and for the special, considerate, caring, and passionate people they have become. Thank you also for your support of my PhD and the writing of this book.

I want to thank Mark for his love, for all the wonderful experiences we shared over two decades, and especially for his heroic fight to stay alive for his family.

A very special thank you goes to my parents, Werner and Ingrid Obenhaus, in deep gratitude for their enormous ongoing support for all of us. My dad was my rock when I most needed him, and my parents' love helped me to find my way back to wellbeing.

I would like to give special recognition to my PhD supervisors from Curtin University, Rachel Robertson and Kara-Jane Lombard, for their exceptional support, expertise, and encouragement, and their professional yet compassionate guidance. I would also like to thank Rosemary Stevens for guiding the Curtin postgraduate writers' group, the Creative practice network, and all the participants of this group. The support, camaraderie, and feedback were a vital component in the writing of my memoir. A special thank you to my friend and fellow postgraduate student Carol Hoggart for her excellent and insightful feedback over the years and our rich discussions about the craft. And especially for the final copy-editing of this book.

Thank you, my dear colleague and friend Reinekke Lengelle, for our passionate and deep collaboration and reflections on grief and Writing for wellbeing. It is inspiring to have so many shared interests and experiences.

Thank you to my publisher, Ian Hooper, for his professionalism, passion, transparency, and availability and the team from Leschenault

Press. Thank you to Maria Hiske for her artwork on the front cover of this book.

A special appreciation for Robert Neimeyer for his moving, heartfelt foreword, and for his incredible dedication to helping others in grief, including myself, and his enormous expertise and professionalism combined with compassion.

I can't thank my dear friend Ina Iwanoff enough. You were always there for me, with tremendous support, both emotional and practical, loving care, kindness and strength. I also appreciate having been able to draw on our joint memories in writing this book.

I thank Mark's family for their support and the many flights to Perth during his illness to be here with us. Thank you to the many friends and acquaintances for supporting us in many different ways. I'd like to give a personal mention to Robert Kelderman, Yasmin McKenna, Uwe Klinge, Jonnine Kaiser, Anneka Pearton, and Vera Ross. Thank you to my friends' enthusiastic backing for this book.

Lastly, a heartfelt appreciation for my partner Wayne Smith, for having been a steadfast, loving anchor, for his support and insightful understanding of the writing process, and his tremendous encouragement for me and this book.

Milton Keynes UK
Ingram Content Group UK Ltd.
UKHW020318070624
443692UK00011B/209/J